KEEP YOUR HANDS OFF EIZOUKEN!

04

STORY AND ART BY

大童澄瞳

SUMITO OOWARA

CONTENTS

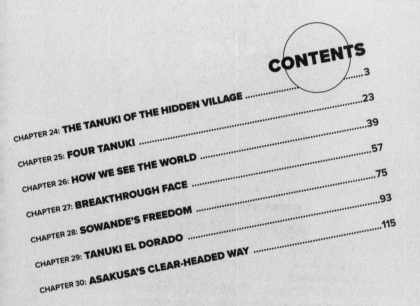

KEEP YOUR HANDS OFF EIZOUKEN! VOL. 4
TRANSLATED BY KUMAR SIVASUBRAMANIAN
SPECIAL THANKS FOR TRANSLATION ASSISTANCE: CHITOKU TESHIMA
LETTERING AND RETOUCH BY SUSIE LEE AND STUDIO CUTIE
EDITED BY CARL GUSTAV HORN

CHAPTER 24: THE TANUKI OF THE HIDDEN VILLAGE

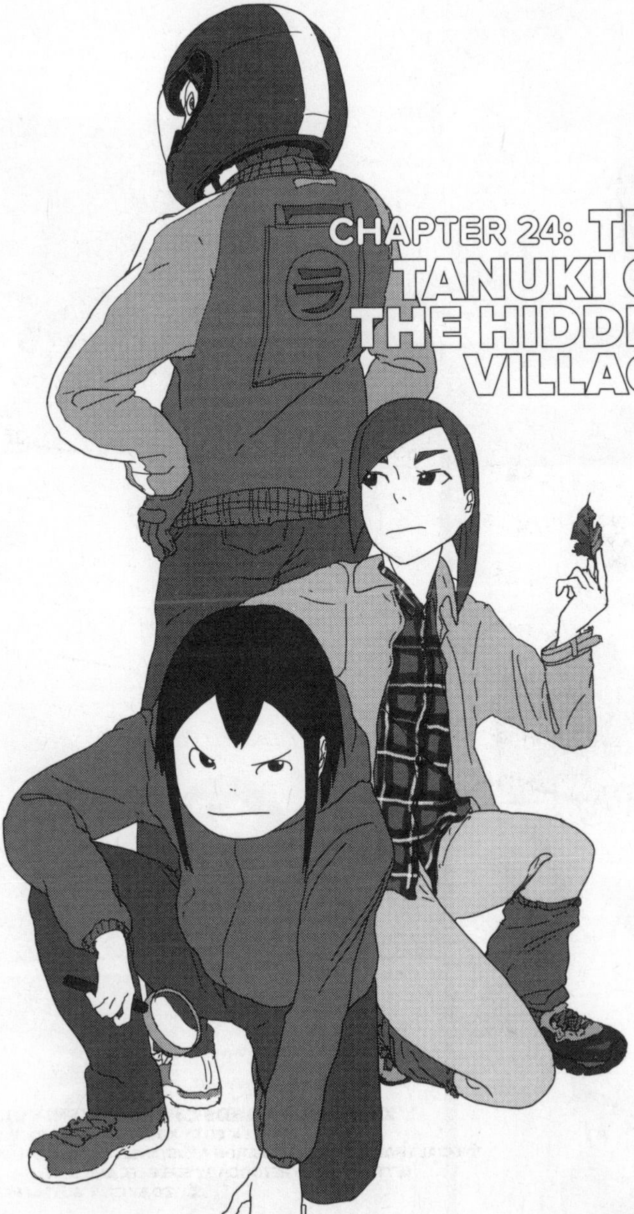

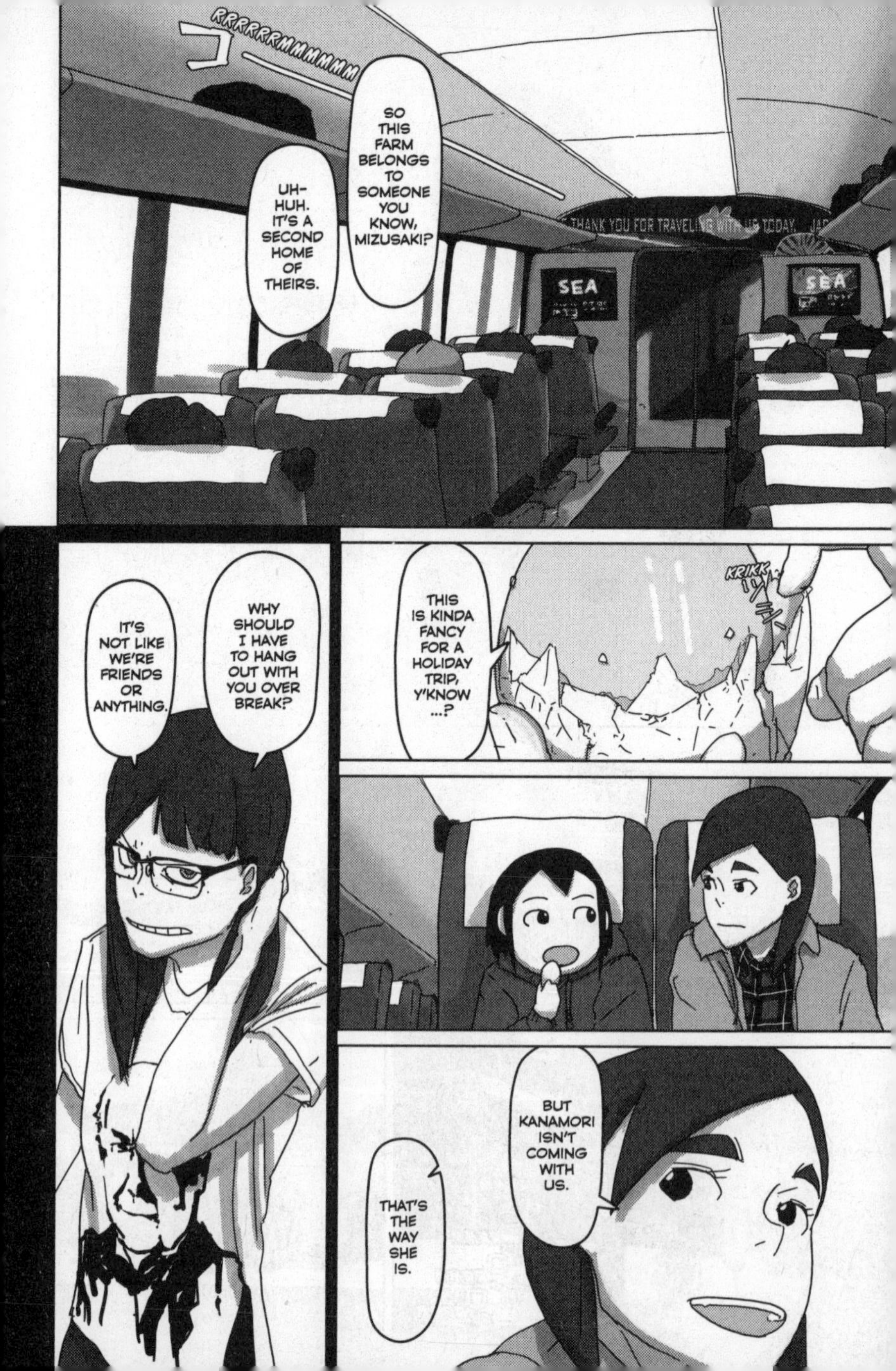

RRRRRRMMMMMMM
SO THIS FARM BELONGS TO SOMEONE YOU KNOW, MIZUSAKI?
UH-HUH. IT'S A SECOND HOME OF THEIRS.
SEA
SEA
KRIKK
THIS IS KINDA FANCY FOR A HOLIDAY TRIP, Y'KNOW ...?
BUT KANAMORI ISN'T COMING WITH US.
THAT'S THE WAY SHE IS.
WHY SHOULD I HAVE TO HANG OUT WITH YOU OVER BREAK?
IT'S NOT LIKE WE'RE FRIENDS OR ANYTHING.

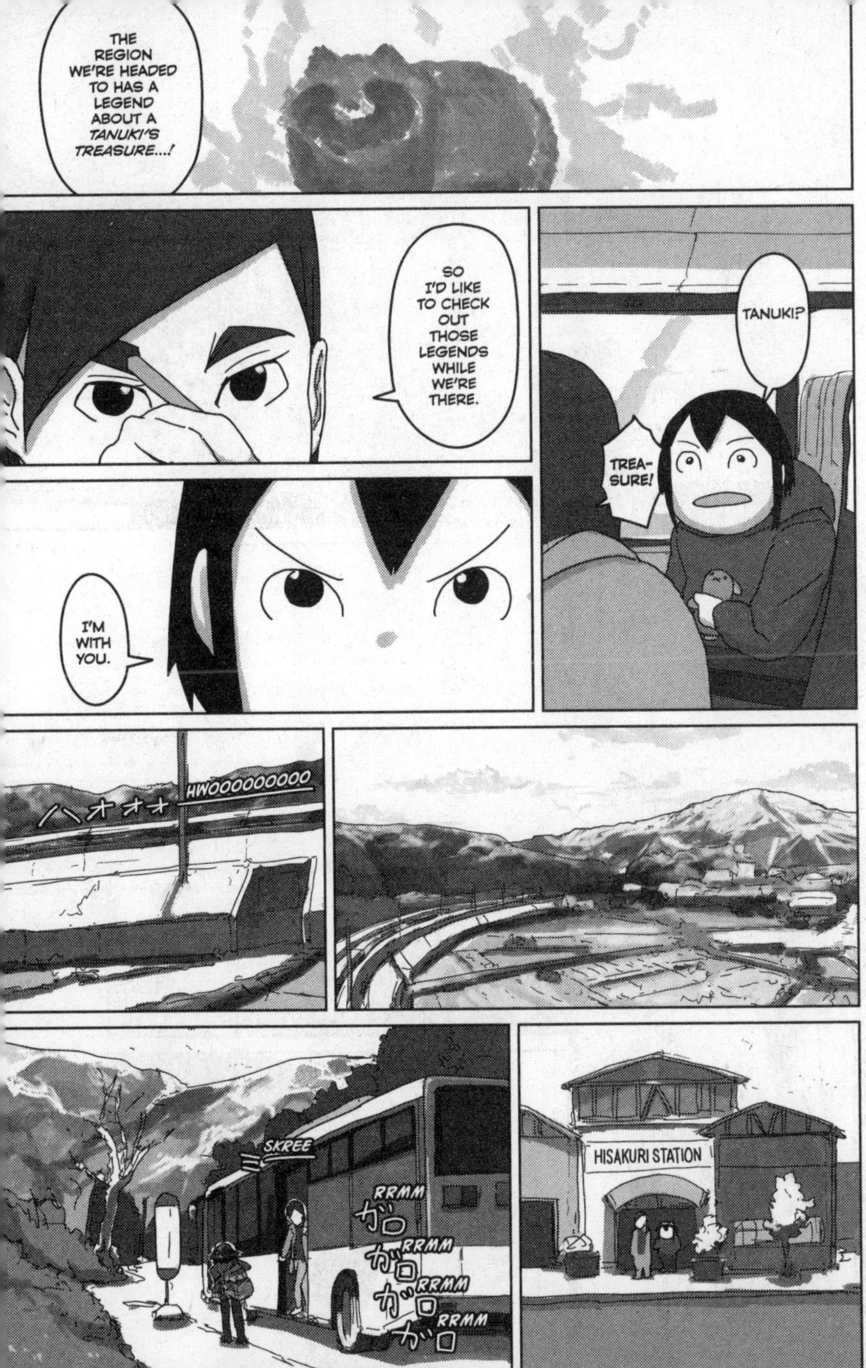
THE REGION WE'RE HEADED TO HAS A LEGEND ABOUT A *TANUKI'S TREASURE*...!
TANUKI?
TREA-SURE!
SO I'D LIKE TO CHECK OUT THOSE LEGENDS WHILE WE'RE THERE.
I'M WITH YOU.
HWOOOOOOOOO
ハオオオ
HISAKURI STATION
SKREE
RRMM
ガロ
RRMM
ガロ
RRMM
ガロ
RRMM
ガロ

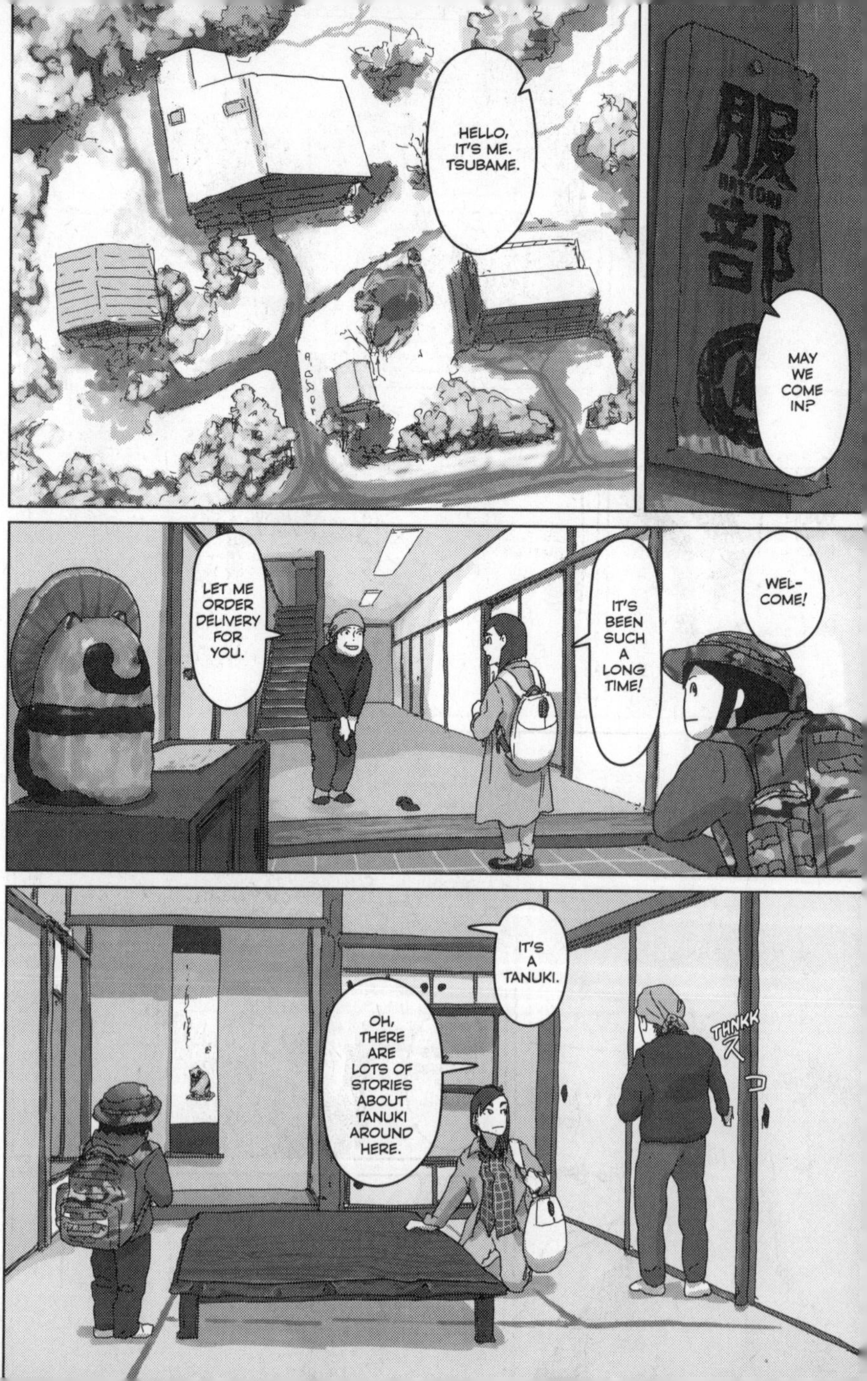
服部
HATTORI
MAY WE COME IN?
HELLO, IT'S ME. TSUBAME.
WEL-COME!
IT'S BEEN SUCH A LONG TIME!
LET ME ORDER DELIVERY FOR YOU.
IT'S A TANUKI.
OH, THERE ARE LOTS OF STORIES ABOUT TANUKI AROUND HERE.
THNKK
スコ

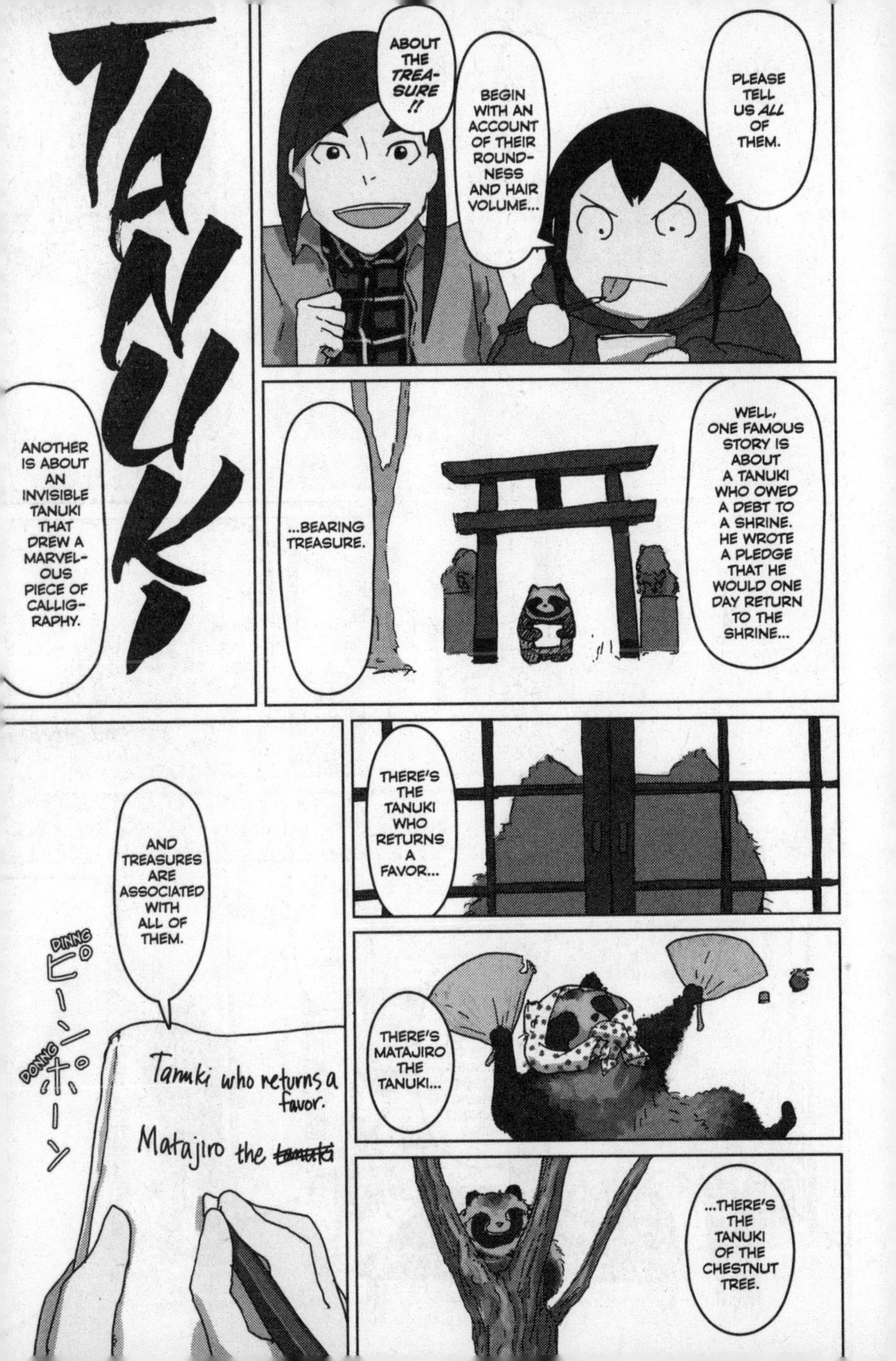
PLEASE TELL US ALL OF THEM.
BEGIN WITH AN ACCOUNT OF THEIR ROUNDNESS AND HAIR VOLUME...
ABOUT THE TREASURE!!
WELL, ONE FAMOUS STORY IS ABOUT A TANUKI WHO OWED A DEBT TO A SHRINE. HE WROTE A PLEDGE THAT HE WOULD ONE DAY RETURN TO THE SHRINE...
...BEARING TREASURE.
TANUKI
ANOTHER IS ABOUT AN INVISIBLE TANUKI THAT DREW A MARVELOUS PIECE OF CALLIGRAPHY.
THERE'S THE TANUKI WHO RETURNS A FAVOR...
THERE'S MATAJIRO THE TANUKI...
...THERE'S THE TANUKI OF THE CHESTNUT TREE.
AND TREASURES ARE ASSOCIATED WITH ALL OF THEM.
DINNG
ピーン
DONNG
ポーン
Tanuki who returns a favor.
Matajiro the tanuki

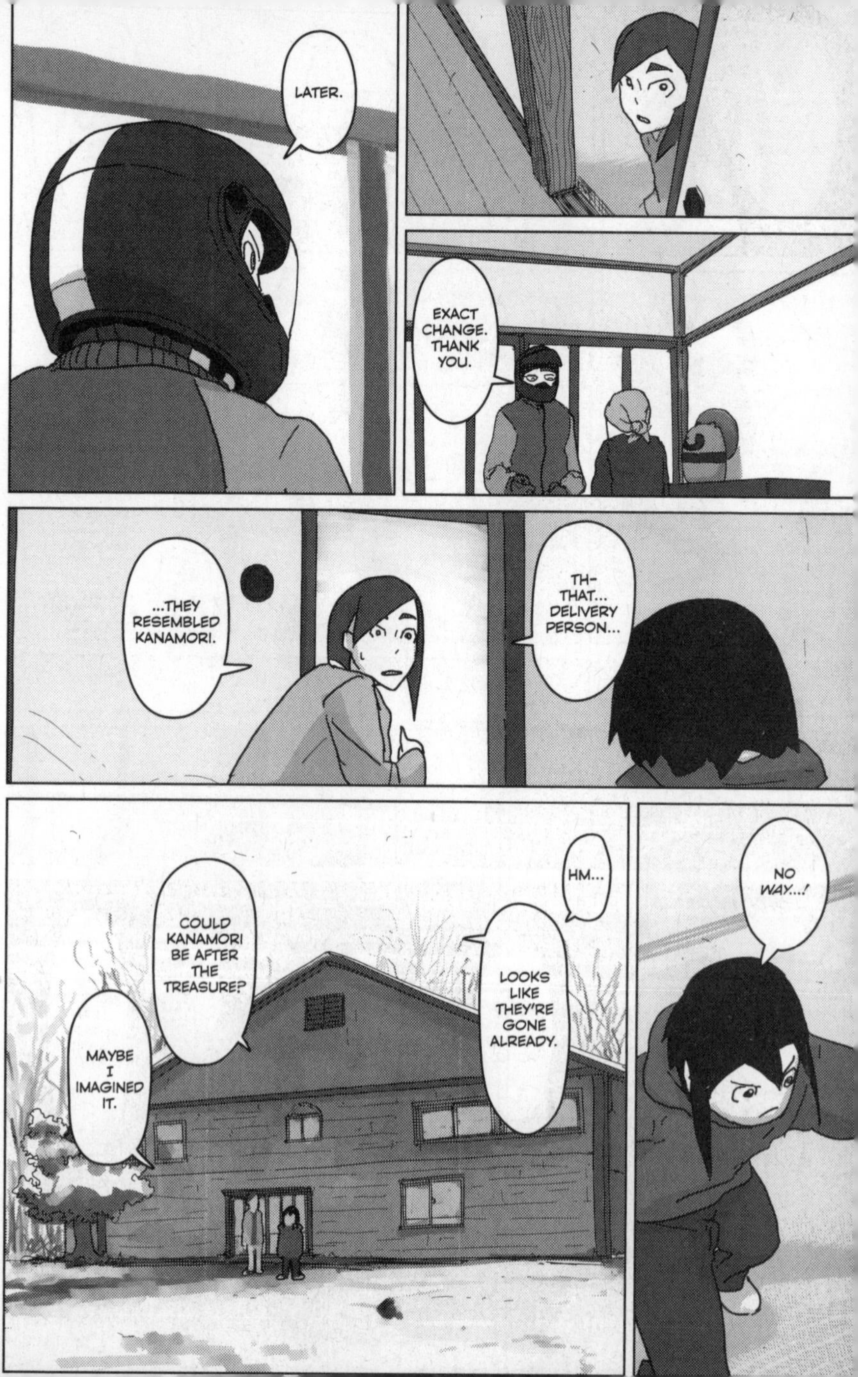
EXACT CHANGE. THANK YOU.
LATER.
TH- THAT... DELIVERY PERSON...
...THEY RESEMBLED KANAMORI.
NO WAY...!
HM...
LOOKS LIKE THEY'RE GONE ALREADY.
COULD KANAMORI BE AFTER THE TREASURE?
MAYBE I IMAGINED IT.

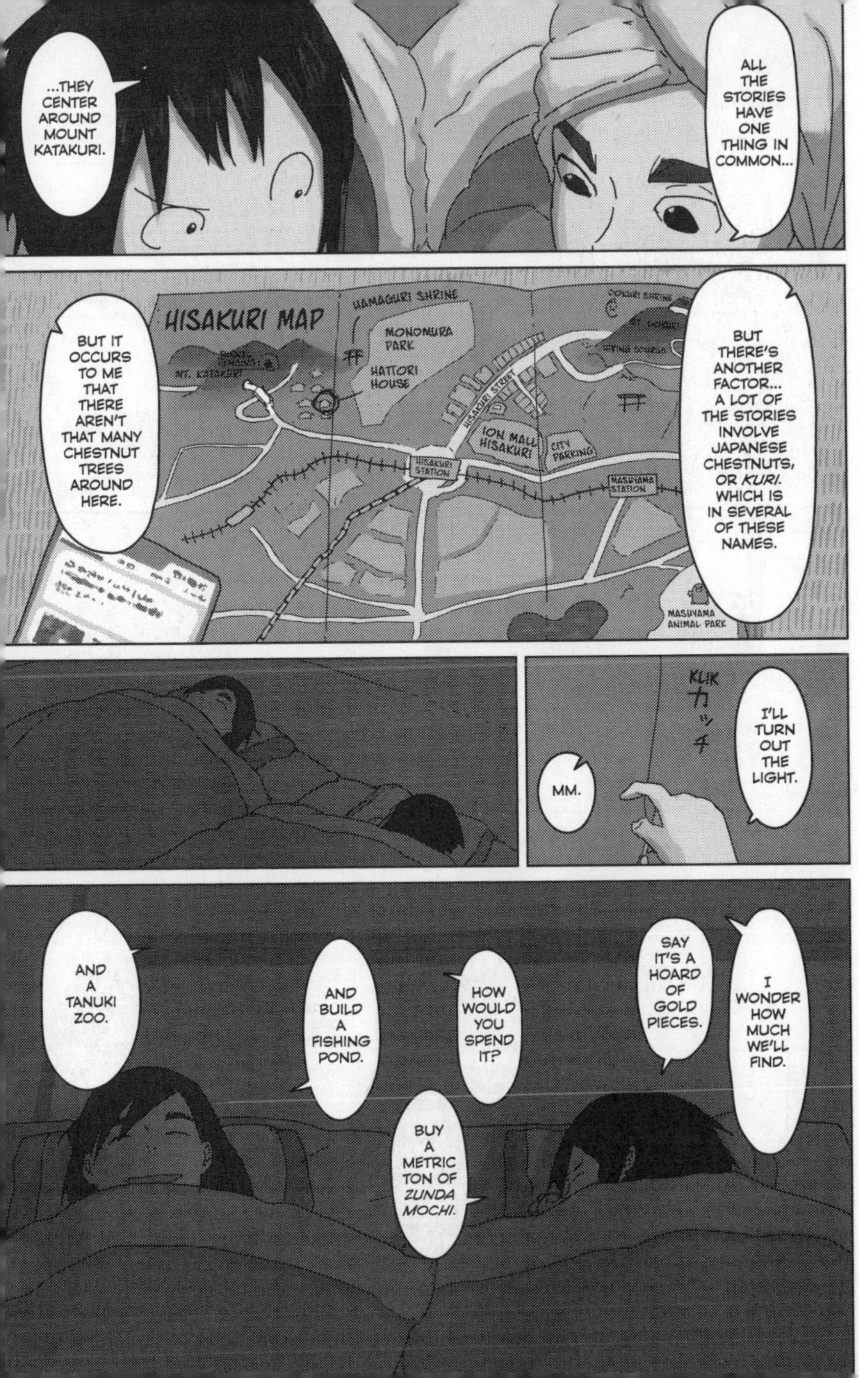
ALL THE STORIES HAVE ONE THING IN COMMON...
...THEY CENTER AROUND MOUNT KATAKURI.
BUT THERE'S ANOTHER FACTOR... A LOT OF THE STORIES INVOLVE JAPANESE CHESTNUTS, OR *KURI*. WHICH IS IN SEVERAL OF THESE NAMES.
HISAKURI MAP
HAMAGURI SHRINE
MONOMURA PARK
HATTORI HOUSE
MT. KATAKURI
HISAKURI STREET
ION MALL HISAKURI
CITY PARKING
HISAKURI STATION
MASUYAMA STATION
MASUYAMA ANIMAL PARK
BUT IT OCCURS TO ME THAT THERE AREN'T THAT MANY CHESTNUT TREES AROUND HERE.
KLIK
カッチ
I'LL TURN OUT THE LIGHT.
MM.
I WONDER HOW MUCH WE'LL FIND.
SAY IT'S A HOARD OF GOLD PIECES.
HOW WOULD YOU SPEND IT?
BUY A METRIC TON OF *ZUNDA MOCHI*.
AND BUILD A FISHING POND.
AND A TANUKI ZOO.

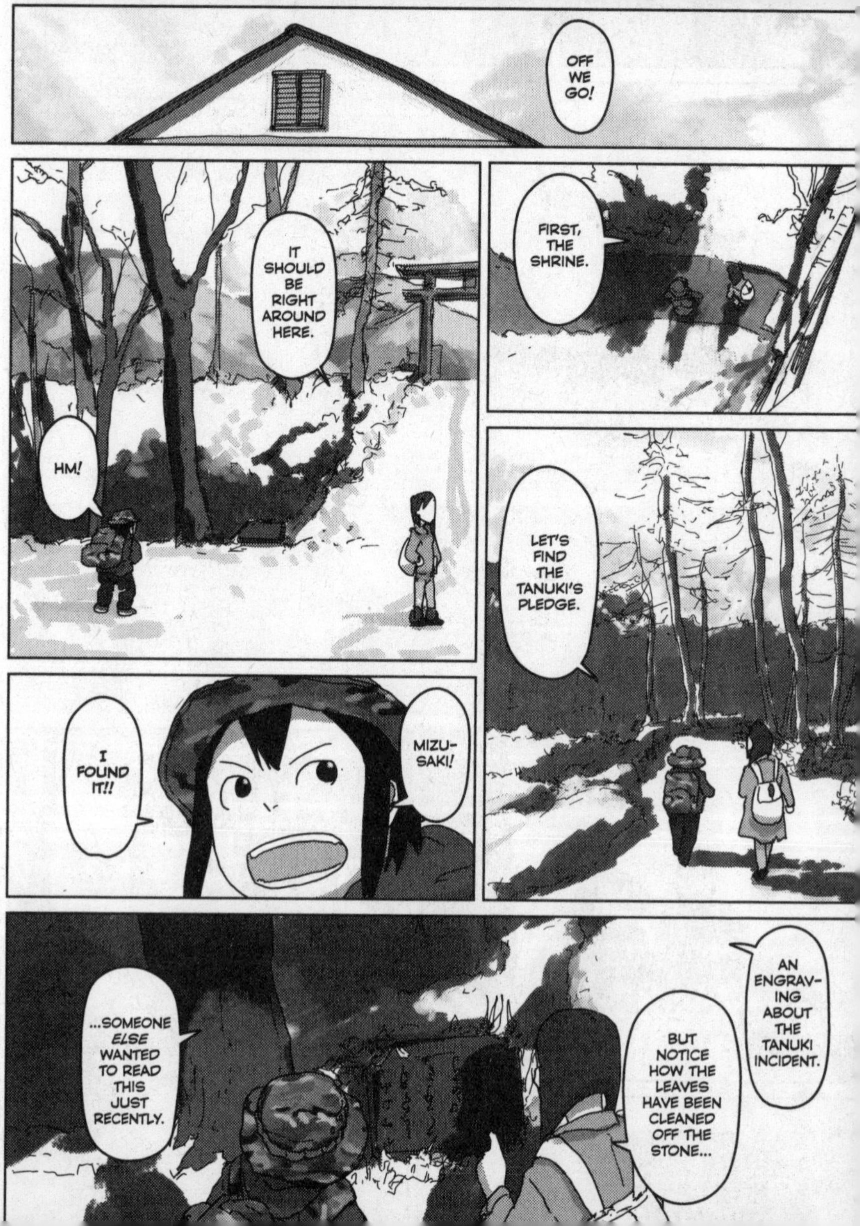
OFF WE GO!
FIRST, THE SHRINE.
LET'S FIND THE TANUKI'S PLEDGE.
IT SHOULD BE RIGHT AROUND HERE.
HM!
MIZU-SAKI!
I FOUND IT!!
AN ENGRAV-ING ABOUT THE TANUKI INCIDENT.
BUT NOTICE HOW THE LEAVES HAVE BEEN CLEANED OFF THE STONE...
...SOMEONE *ELSE* WANTED TO READ THIS JUST RECENTLY.

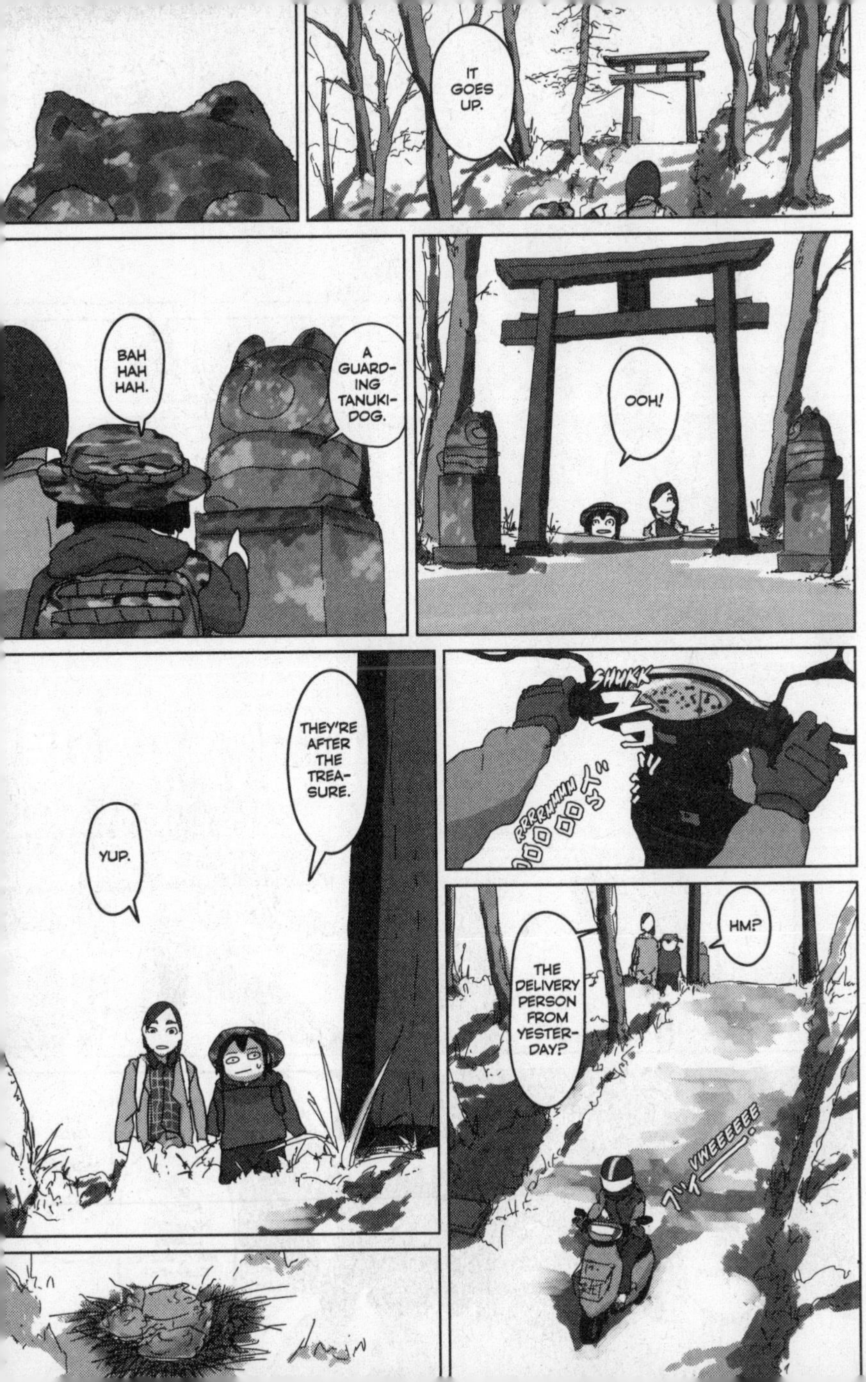
IT GOES UP.
OOH!
A GUARDING TANUKI-DOG.
BAH HAH HAH.
SHUKK
RRRRHMMM
HM?
THE DELIVERY PERSON FROM YESTERDAY?
VWEEEEEEE
THEY'RE AFTER THE TREASURE.
YUP.

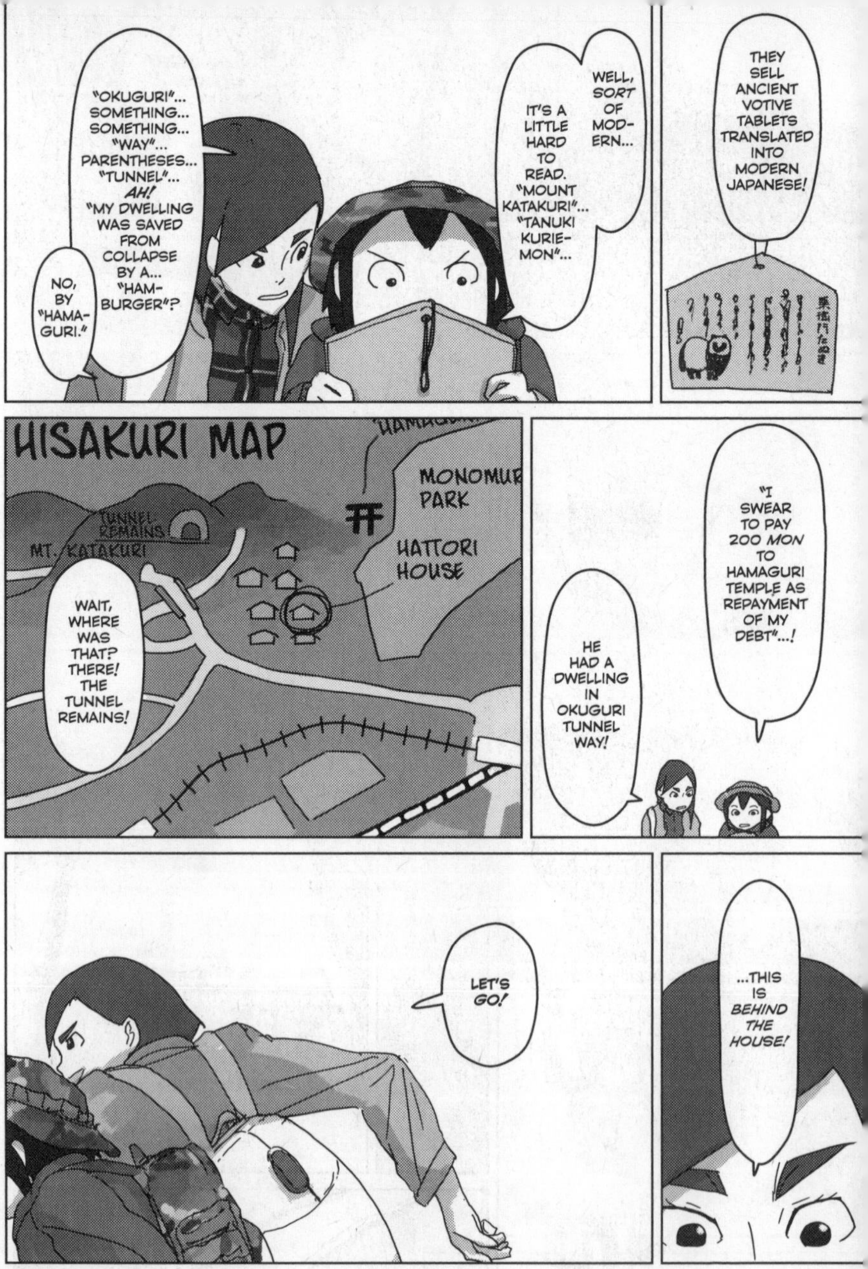
THEY SELL ANCIENT VOTIVE TABLETS TRANSLATED INTO MODERN JAPANESE!
WELL, *SORT* OF MODERN...
IT'S A LITTLE HARD TO READ. "MOUNT KATAKURI"... "TANUKI KURIEMON"...
"OKUGURI"... SOMETHING... SOMETHING... "WAY"... PARENTHESES... "TUNNEL"... *AH!* "MY DWELLING WAS SAVED FROM COLLAPSE BY A... "HAMBURGER"?
NO, BY "HAMAGURI."
"I SWEAR TO PAY 200 *MON* TO HAMAGURI TEMPLE AS REPAYMENT OF MY DEBT"...!
HE HAD A DWELLING IN OKUGURI TUNNEL WAY!
HISAKURI MAP
MONOMUR
PARK
TUNNEL REMAINS
MT. KATAKURI
HATTORI HOUSE
WAIT, WHERE WAS THAT? THERE! THE TUNNEL REMAINS!
...THIS IS *BEHIND THE HOUSE!*
LET'S *GO!*

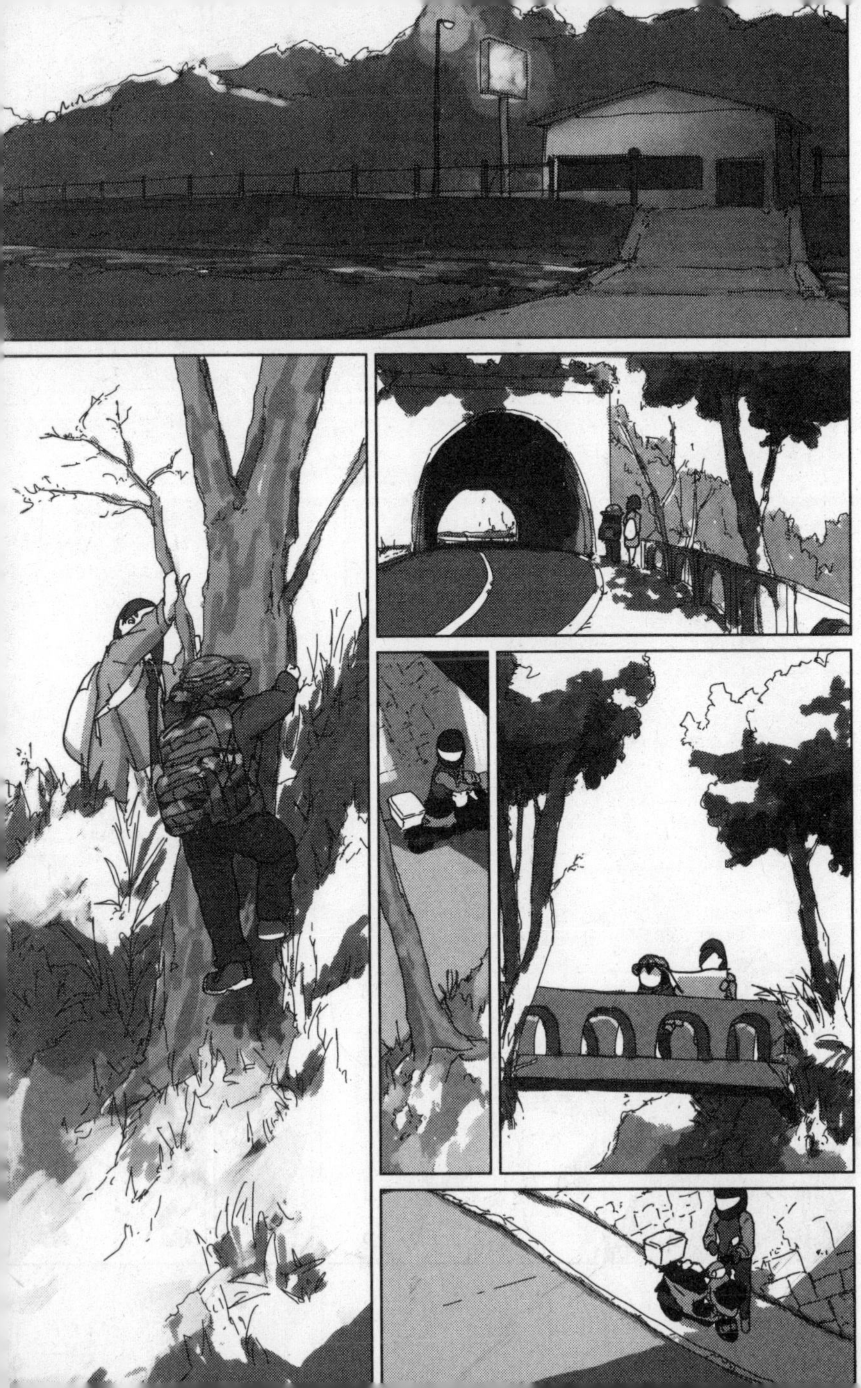

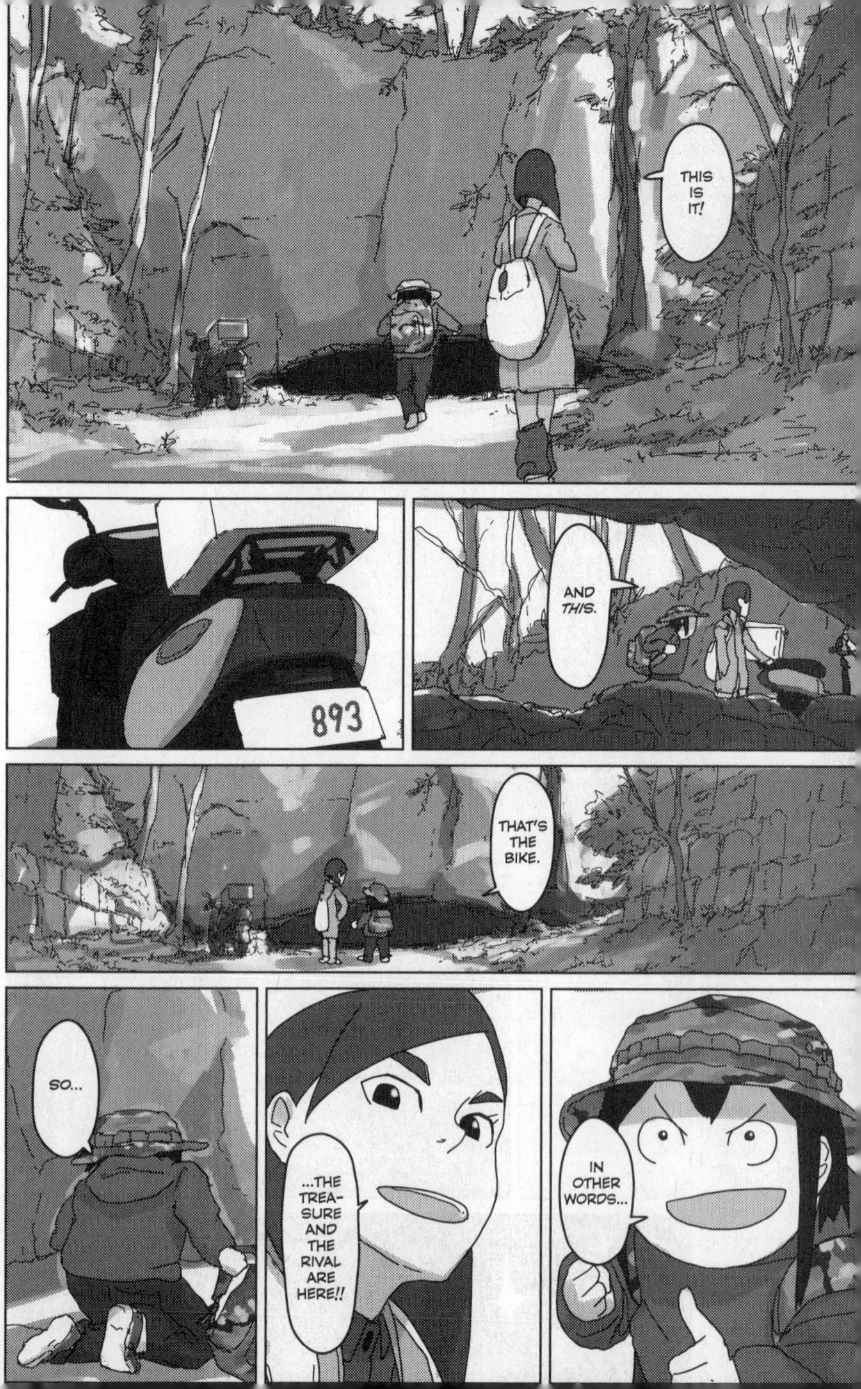
THIS IS IT!
AND *THIS*.
893
THAT'S THE BIKE.
IN OTHER WORDS...
...THE TREA-SURE AND THE RIVAL ARE HERE!!
SO...

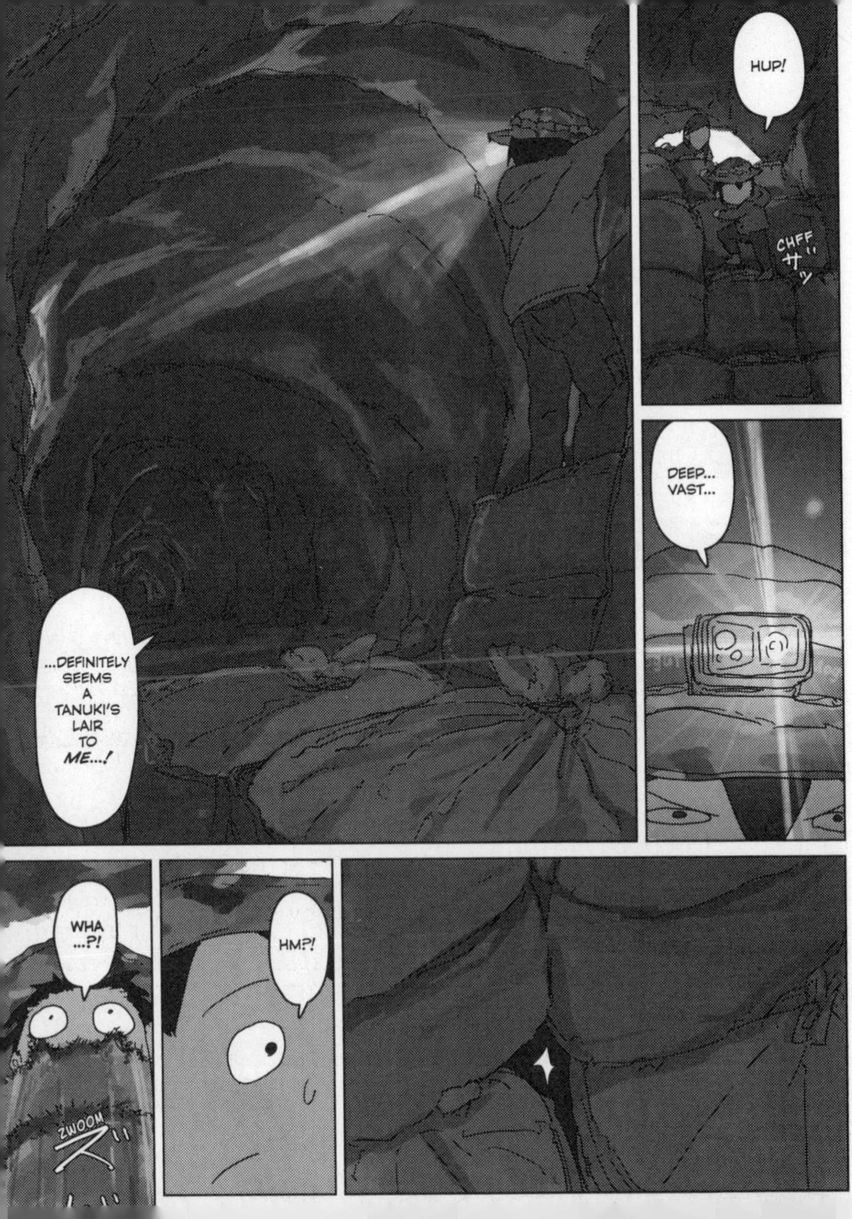
HUP!
CHFF
サッ
DEEP... VAST...
...DEFINITELY SEEMS A TANUKI'S LAIR TO *ME*...!
HM?!
WHA ...?!
ZWOOM

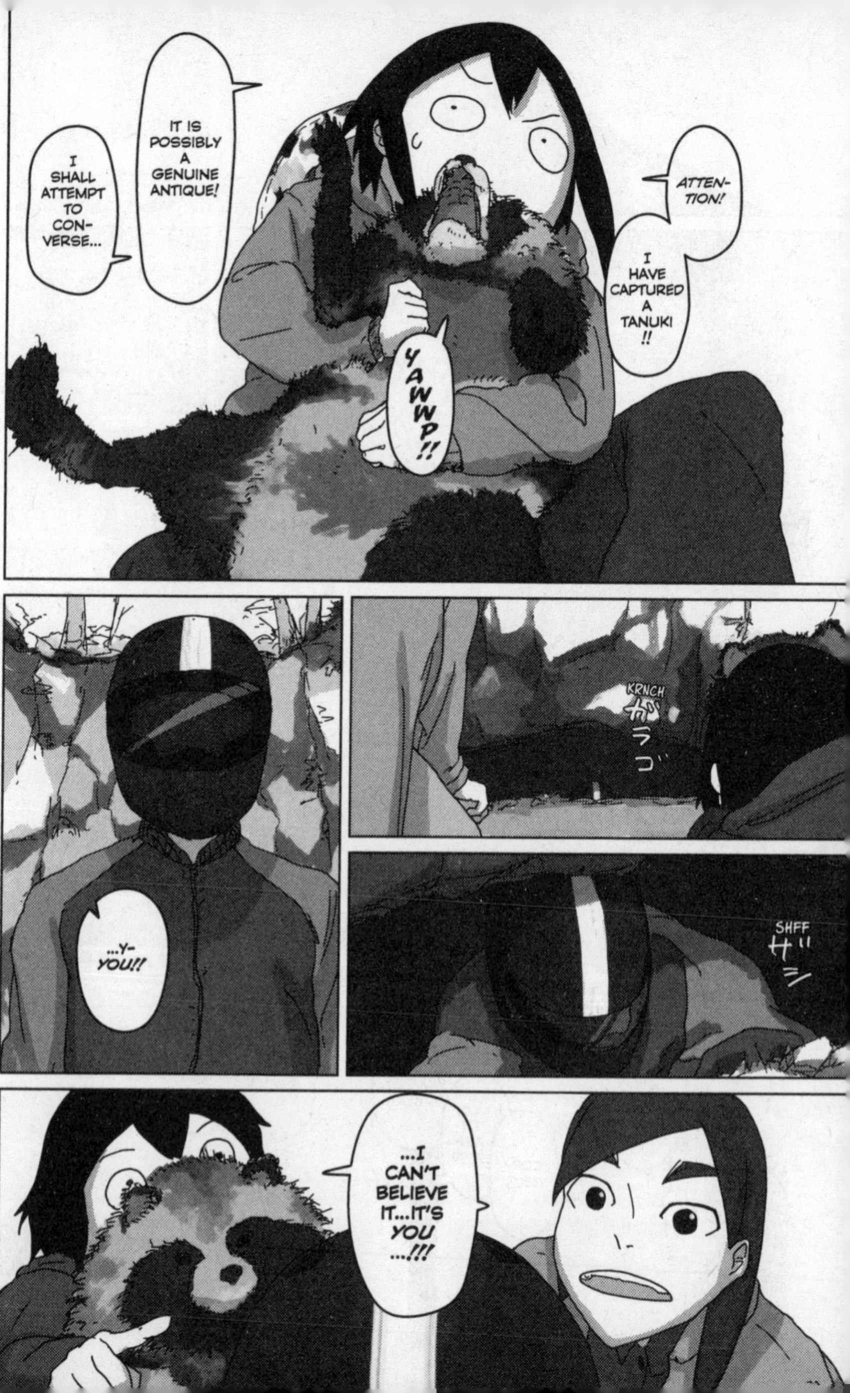
ATTEN-TION!
I HAVE CAPTURED A TANUKI!!
YAWWP!!
IT IS POSSIBLY A GENUINE ANTIQUE!
I SHALL ATTEMPT TO CON-VERSE...
KRNCH
SHFF
...Y-YOU!!
...I CAN'T BELIEVE IT...IT'S YOU ...!!!

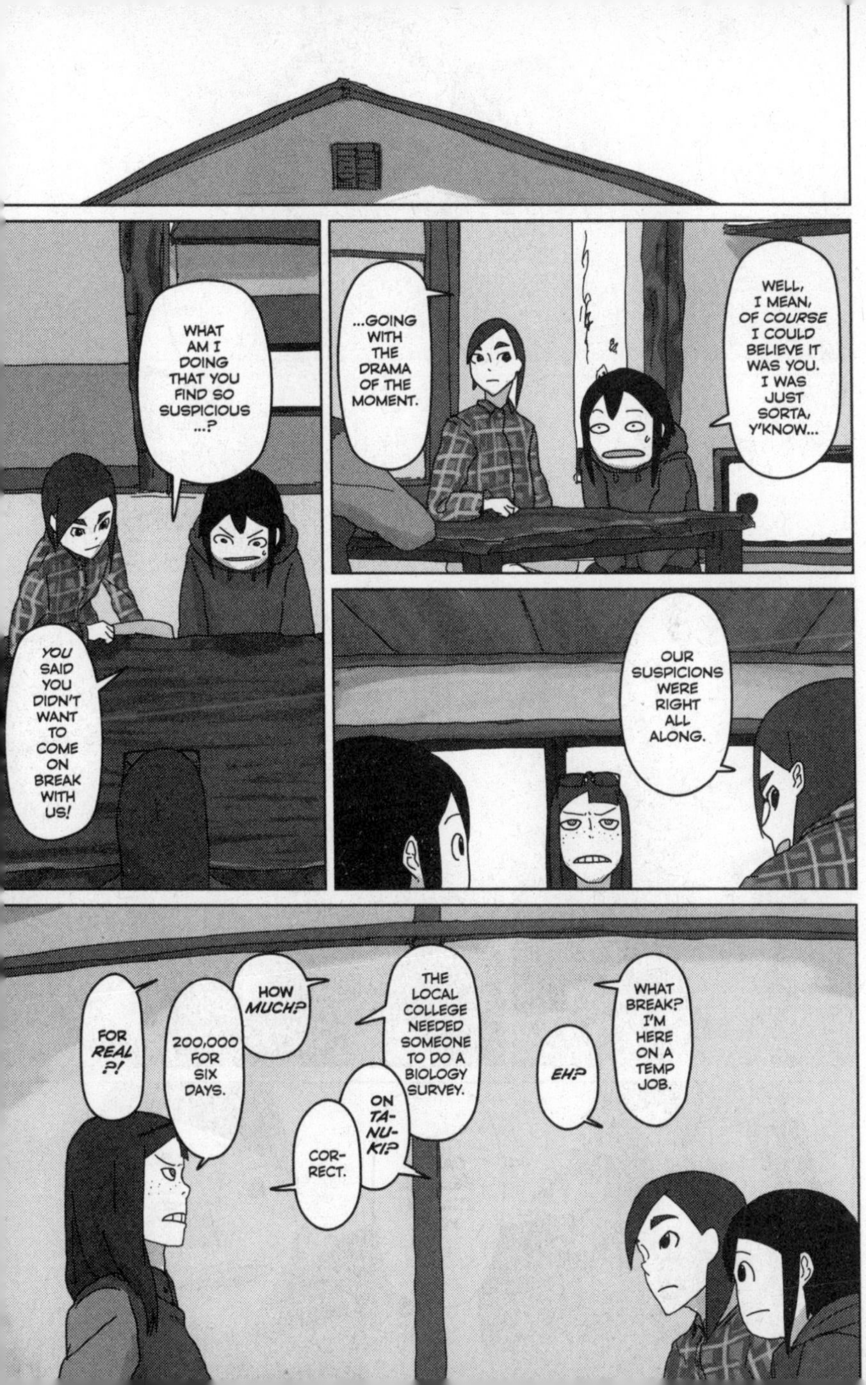
WELL, I MEAN, OF COURSE I COULD BELIEVE IT WAS YOU. I WAS JUST SORTA, Y'KNOW...
...GOING WITH THE DRAMA OF THE MOMENT.
OUR SUSPICIONS WERE RIGHT ALL ALONG.
WHAT AM I DOING THAT YOU FIND SO SUSPICIOUS ...?
YOU SAID YOU DIDN'T WANT TO COME ON BREAK WITH US!
WHAT BREAK? I'M HERE ON A TEMP JOB.
EH?
THE LOCAL COLLEGE NEEDED SOMEONE TO DO A BIOLOGY SURVEY.
ON TA-NU-KI?
COR-RECT.
HOW MUCH?
200,000 FOR SIX DAYS.
FOR REAL?!

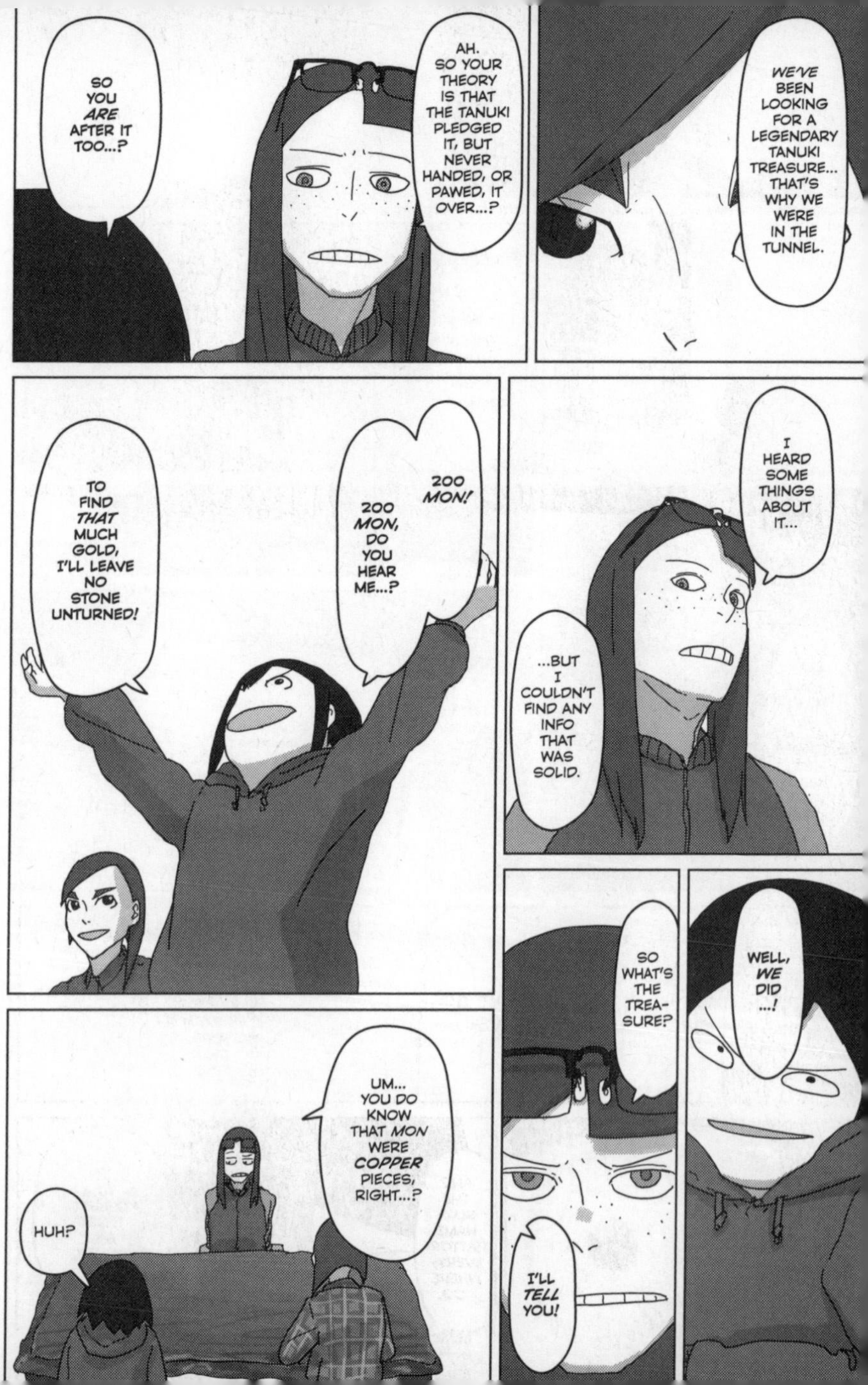
WE'VE BEEN LOOKING FOR A LEGENDARY TANUKI TREASURE... THAT'S WHY WE WERE IN THE TUNNEL.
AH. SO YOUR THEORY IS THAT THE TANUKI PLEDGED IT, BUT NEVER HANDED, OR PAWED, IT OVER...?
SO YOU ARE AFTER IT TOO...?
I HEARD SOME THINGS ABOUT IT...
...BUT I COULDN'T FIND ANY INFO THAT WAS SOLID.
200 MON!
200 MON, DO YOU HEAR ME...?
TO FIND THAT MUCH GOLD, I'LL LEAVE NO STONE UNTURNED!
WELL, WE DID ...!
SO WHAT'S THE TREASURE?
I'LL TELL YOU!
UM... YOU DO KNOW THAT MON WERE COPPER PIECES, RIGHT...?
HUH?

SEE, YOU NEED TO RESEARCH THESE THINGS.
NORTH TANUKI
EAST TANUKI
SOUTH TANUKI
HATTORI TANUKI KURIHARA
HAMAGURI
2.5km
500m
DEBT OF TANUKI
200 MON!
HOUSE
HATTORI HOUSE
HATTORI VILLAGE
A LOT OF HATTORI (AND TANUKI) LIVE AROUND HERE, I DO RECKON.
WEST TANUKI
FLUFFY AND ROUND
TANUKI UDON
OKUGURI TUNNEL WAY
TANUKI NEST!!
DISCOVERED
700m
TANUKI REPAYMENT OF DEBT, SAJIRO HATTORI'S HOUSE
DANJIRO TANUKI
TANUKI OF THE CHESTNUT TREE, ICHIROJI HATTORI'S HOUSE
SO YOU NOTICED... "KURI" AND "GURI".
AND THE SUR-NAME HATTORI EVERY-WHERE TOO.

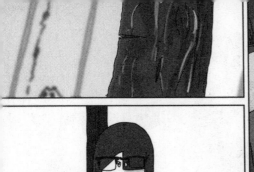

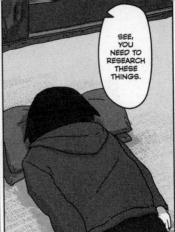

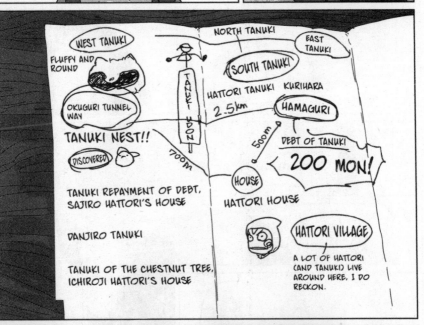

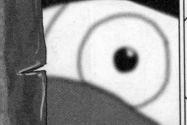

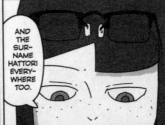

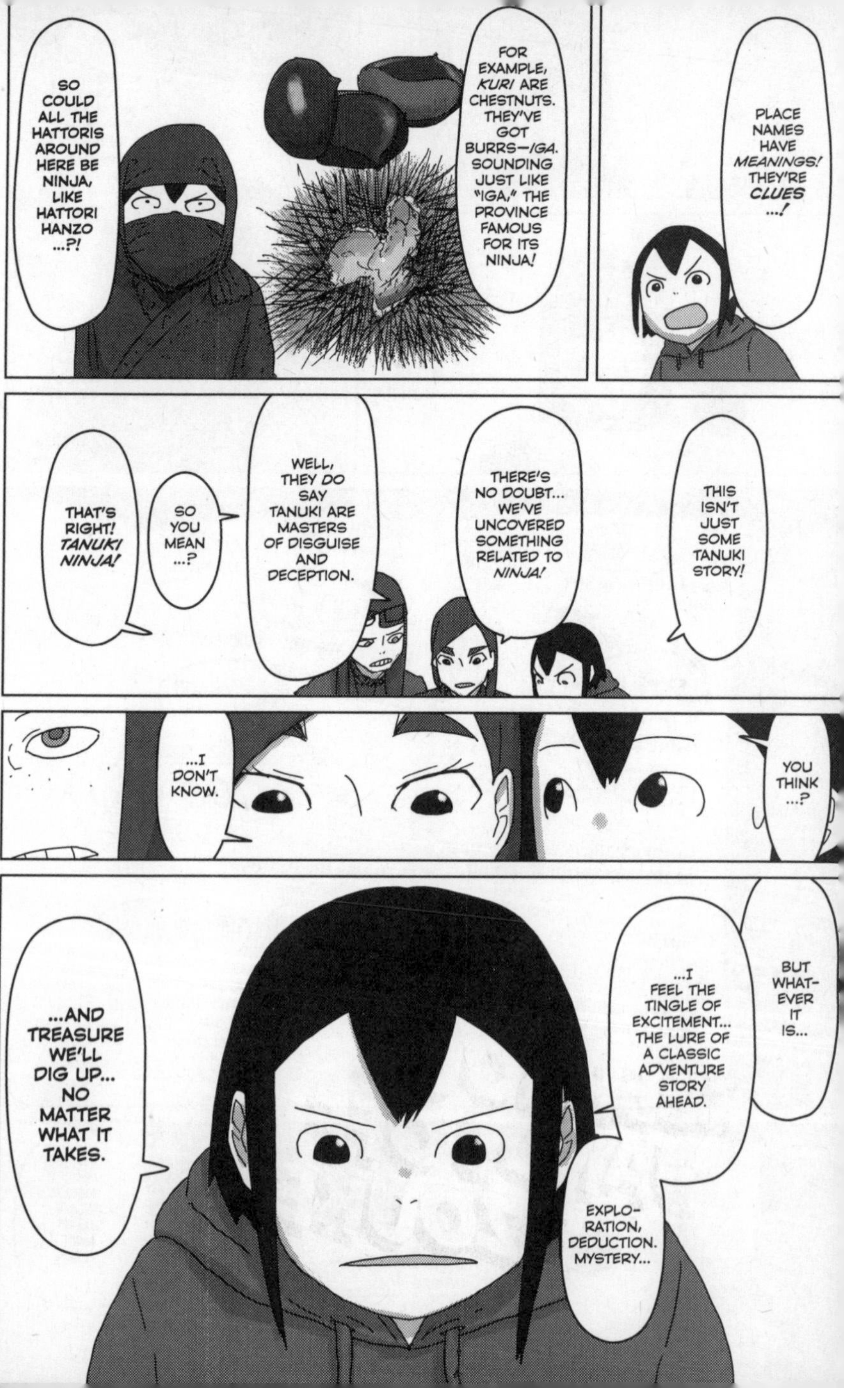
PLACE NAMES HAVE MEANINGS! THEY'RE CLUES ...!
FOR EXAMPLE, KURI ARE CHESTNUTS. THEY'VE GOT BURRS—IGA. SOUNDING JUST LIKE "IGA," THE PROVINCE FAMOUS FOR ITS NINJA!
SO COULD ALL THE HATTORIS AROUND HERE BE NINJA, LIKE HATTORI HANZO ...?!
THIS ISN'T JUST SOME TANUKI STORY!
THERE'S NO DOUBT... WE'VE UNCOVERED SOMETHING RELATED TO NINJA!
WELL, THEY DO SAY TANUKI ARE MASTERS OF DISGUISE AND DECEPTION.
SO YOU MEAN ...?
THAT'S RIGHT! TANUKI NINJA!
YOU THINK ...?
...I DON'T KNOW.
BUT WHAT-EVER IT IS...
...I FEEL THE TINGLE OF EXCITEMENT... THE LURE OF A CLASSIC ADVENTURE STORY AHEAD.
EXPLO-RATION, DEDUCTION. MYSTERY...
...AND TREASURE WE'LL DIG UP... NO MATTER WHAT IT TAKES.

KEEP YOUR
HANDS OFF
EIZOUKEN!

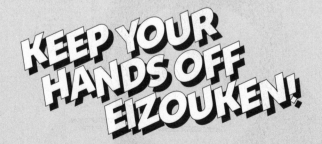

Memo from Mr. Oowara:

Don't go indiscriminately into holes and burrows. Avoid excessive touching of wild animals; otherwise, you might get sick!

CHAPTER 25:
FOUR TANUKI

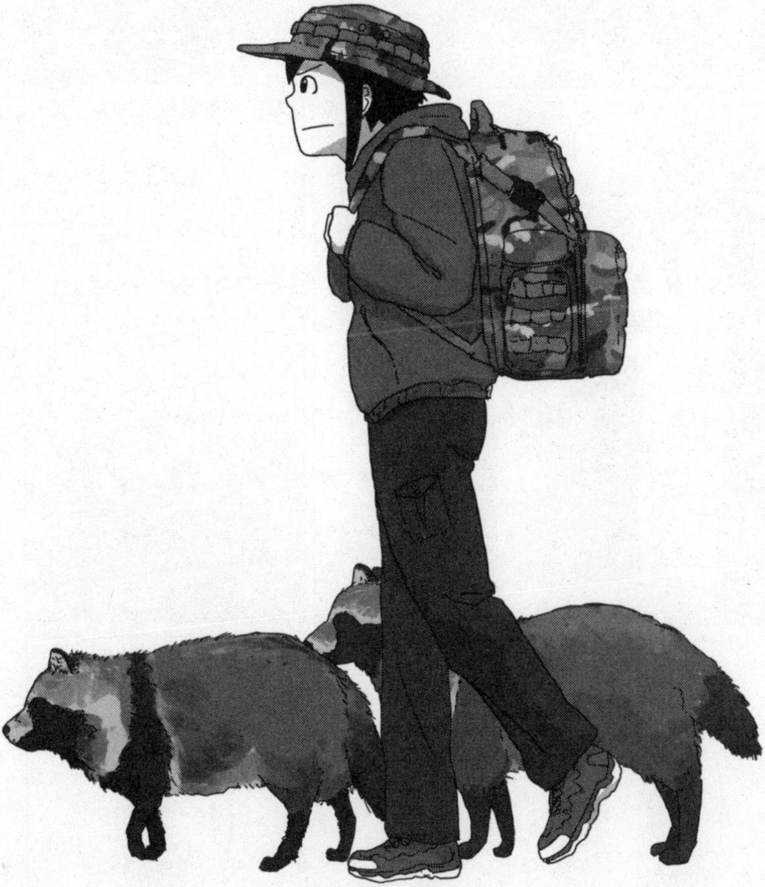

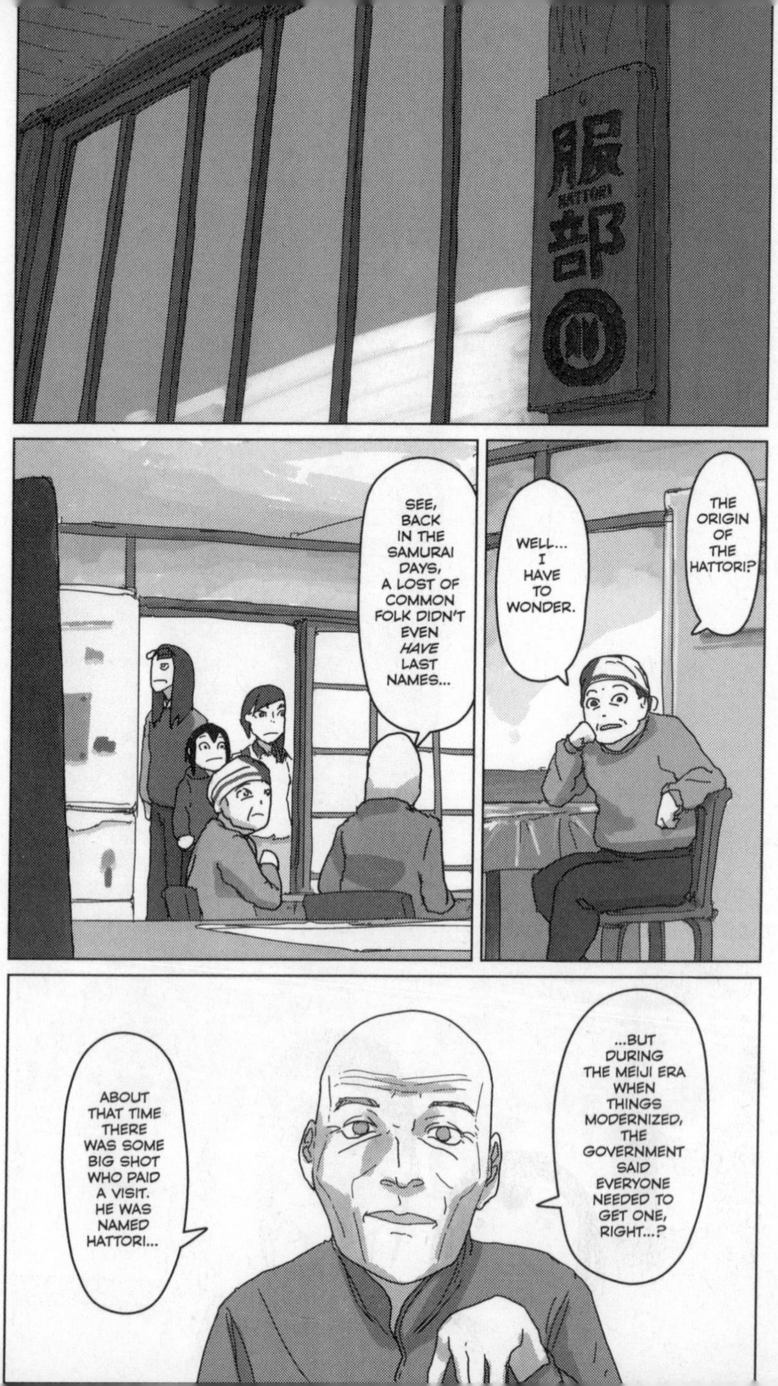
服部
HATTORI
THE ORIGIN OF THE HATTORI?
WELL... I HAVE TO WONDER.
SEE, BACK IN THE SAMURAI DAYS, A LOST OF COMMON FOLK DIDN'T EVEN *HAVE* LAST NAMES...
...BUT DURING THE MEIJI ERA WHEN THINGS MODERNIZED, THE GOVERNMENT SAID EVERYONE NEEDED TO GET ONE, RIGHT...?
ABOUT THAT TIME THERE WAS SOME BIG SHOT WHO PAID A VISIT. HE WAS NAMED HATTORI...

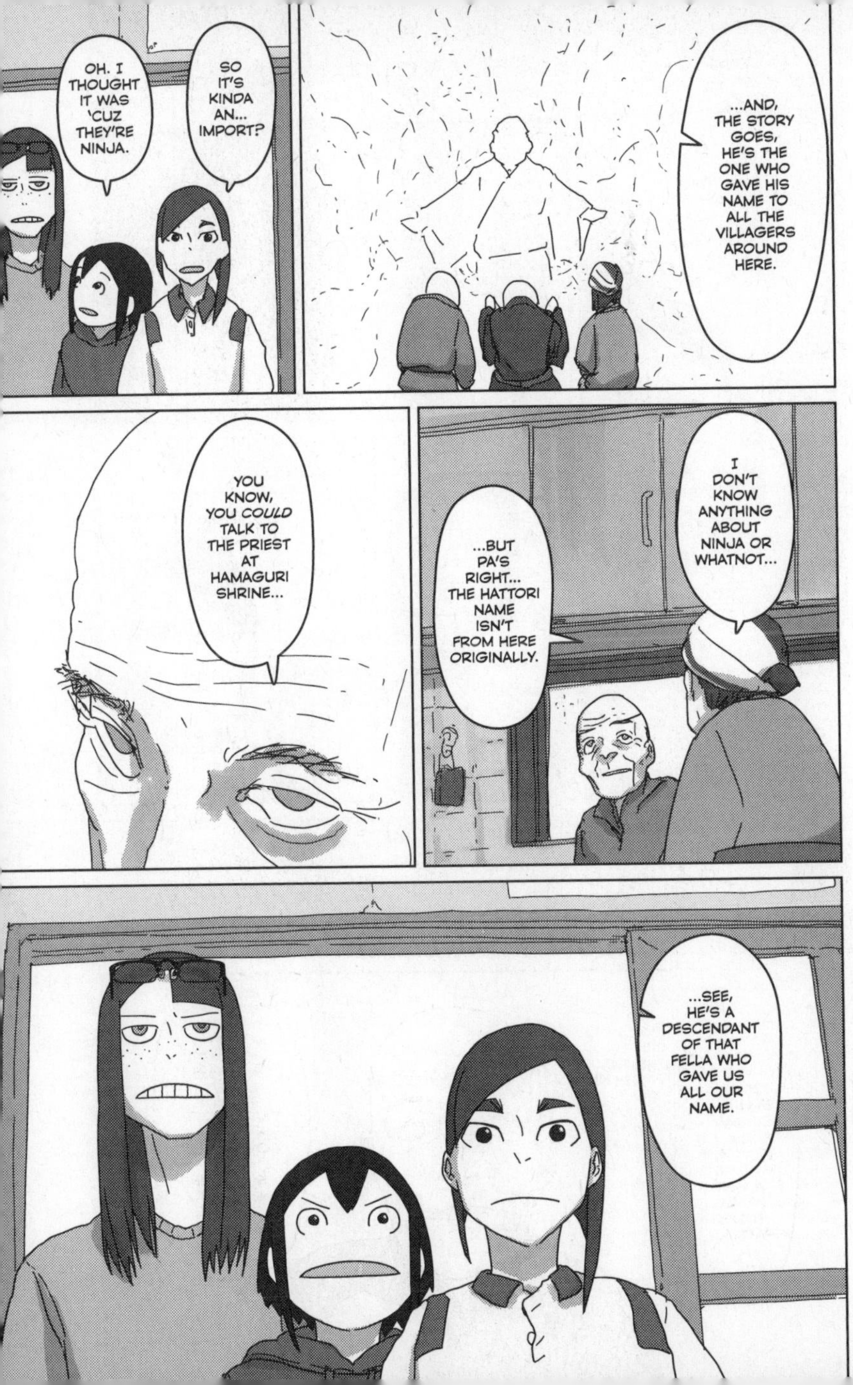

...AND, THE STORY GOES, HE'S THE ONE WHO GAVE HIS NAME TO ALL THE VILLAGERS AROUND HERE.
SO IT'S KINDA AN... IMPORT?
OH. I THOUGHT IT WAS 'CUZ THEY'RE NINJA.
I DON'T KNOW ANYTHING ABOUT NINJA OR WHATNOT...
...BUT PA'S RIGHT... THE HATTORI NAME ISN'T FROM HERE ORIGINALLY.
YOU KNOW, YOU *COULD* TALK TO THE PRIEST AT HAMAGURI SHRINE...
...SEE, HE'S A DESCENDANT OF THAT FELLA WHO GAVE US ALL OUR NAME.

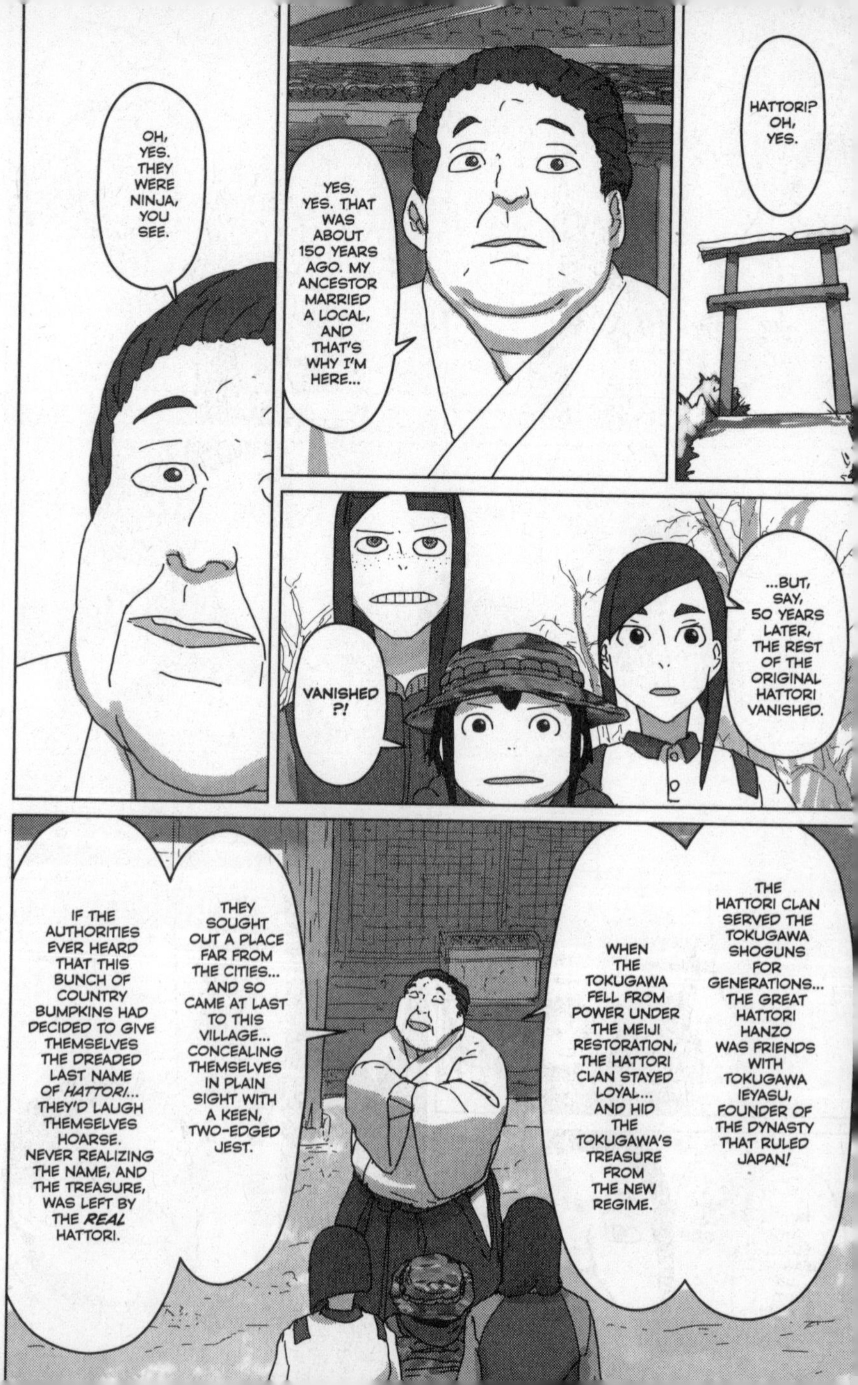
HATTORI? OH, YES.
YES, YES. THAT WAS ABOUT 150 YEARS AGO. MY ANCESTOR MARRIED A LOCAL, AND THAT'S WHY I'M HERE...
...BUT, SAY, 50 YEARS LATER, THE REST OF THE ORIGINAL HATTORI VANISHED.
VANISHED ?!
OH, YES. THEY WERE NINJA, YOU SEE.
THE HATTORI CLAN SERVED THE TOKUGAWA SHOGUNS FOR GENERATIONS... THE GREAT HATTORI HANZO WAS FRIENDS WITH TOKUGAWA IEYASU, FOUNDER OF THE DYNASTY THAT RULED JAPAN!
WHEN THE TOKUGAWA FELL FROM POWER UNDER THE MEIJI RESTORATION, THE HATTORI CLAN STAYED LOYAL... AND HID THE TOKUGAWA'S TREASURE FROM THE NEW REGIME.
THEY SOUGHT OUT A PLACE FAR FROM THE CITIES... AND SO CAME AT LAST TO THIS VILLAGE... CONCEALING THEMSELVES IN PLAIN SIGHT WITH A KEEN, TWO-EDGED JEST.
IF THE AUTHORITIES EVER HEARD THAT THIS BUNCH OF COUNTRY BUMPKINS HAD DECIDED TO GIVE THEMSELVES THE DREADED LAST NAME OF *HATTORI*... THEY'D LAUGH THEMSELVES HOARSE. NEVER REALIZING THE NAME, AND THE TREASURE, WAS LEFT BY THE ***REAL*** HATTORI.

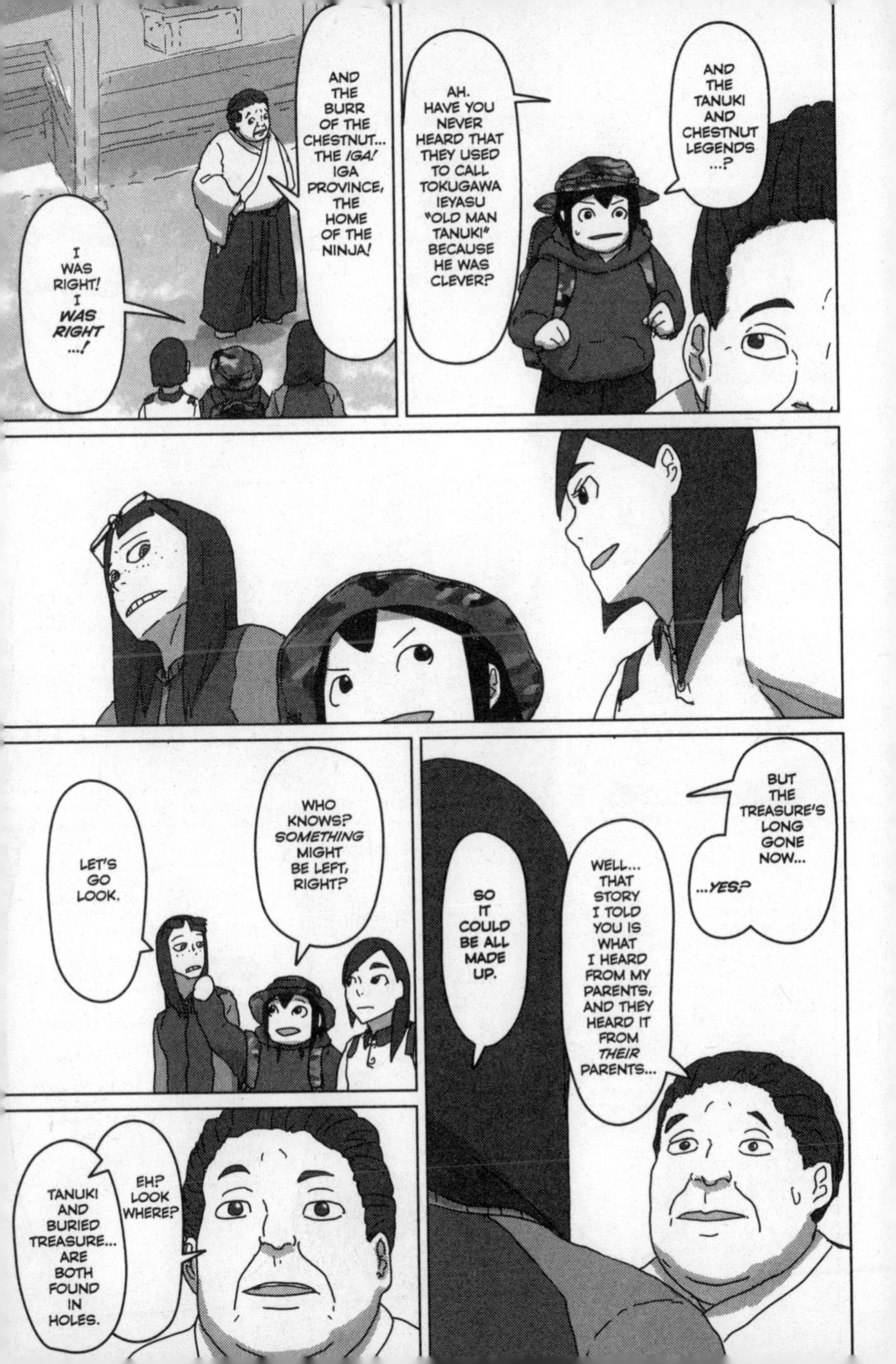
AND THE TANUKI AND CHESTNUT LEGENDS ...?
AH. HAVE YOU NEVER HEARD THAT THEY USED TO CALL TOKUGAWA IEYASU "OLD MAN TANUKI" BECAUSE HE WAS CLEVER?
AND THE BURR OF THE CHESTNUT... THE *IGA!* IGA PROVINCE, THE HOME OF THE NINJA!
I WAS RIGHT! I ***WAS RIGHT*** ...!
BUT THE TREASURE'S LONG GONE NOW...
...***YES?***
WELL... THAT STORY I TOLD YOU IS WHAT I HEARD FROM MY PARENTS, AND THEY HEARD IT FROM *THEIR* PARENTS...
SO IT COULD BE ALL MADE UP.
WHO KNOWS? *SOMETHING* MIGHT BE LEFT, RIGHT?
LET'S GO LOOK.
EH? LOOK WHERE?
TANUKI AND BURIED TREASURE... ARE BOTH FOUND IN HOLES.

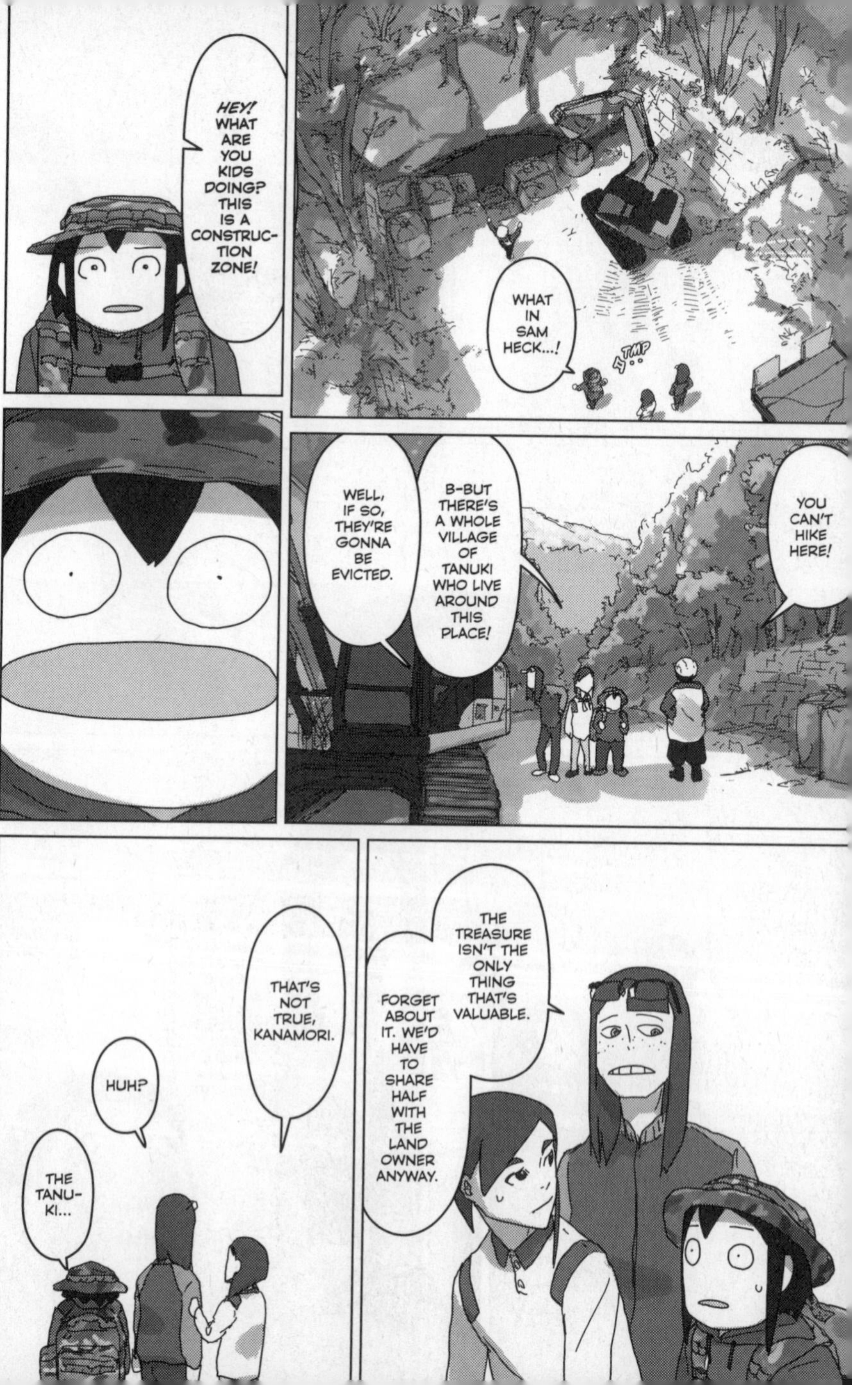
WHAT IN SAM HECK...!
TMP
HEY! WHAT ARE YOU KIDS DOING? THIS IS A CONSTRUCTION ZONE!
YOU CAN'T HIKE HERE!
B-BUT THERE'S A WHOLE VILLAGE OF TANUKI WHO LIVE AROUND THIS PLACE!
WELL, IF SO, THEY'RE GONNA BE EVICTED.
THE TREASURE ISN'T THE ONLY THING THAT'S VALUABLE.
FORGET ABOUT IT. WE'D HAVE TO SHARE HALF WITH THE LAND OWNER ANYWAY.
THAT'S NOT TRUE, KANAMORI.
HUH?
THE TANU-KI...

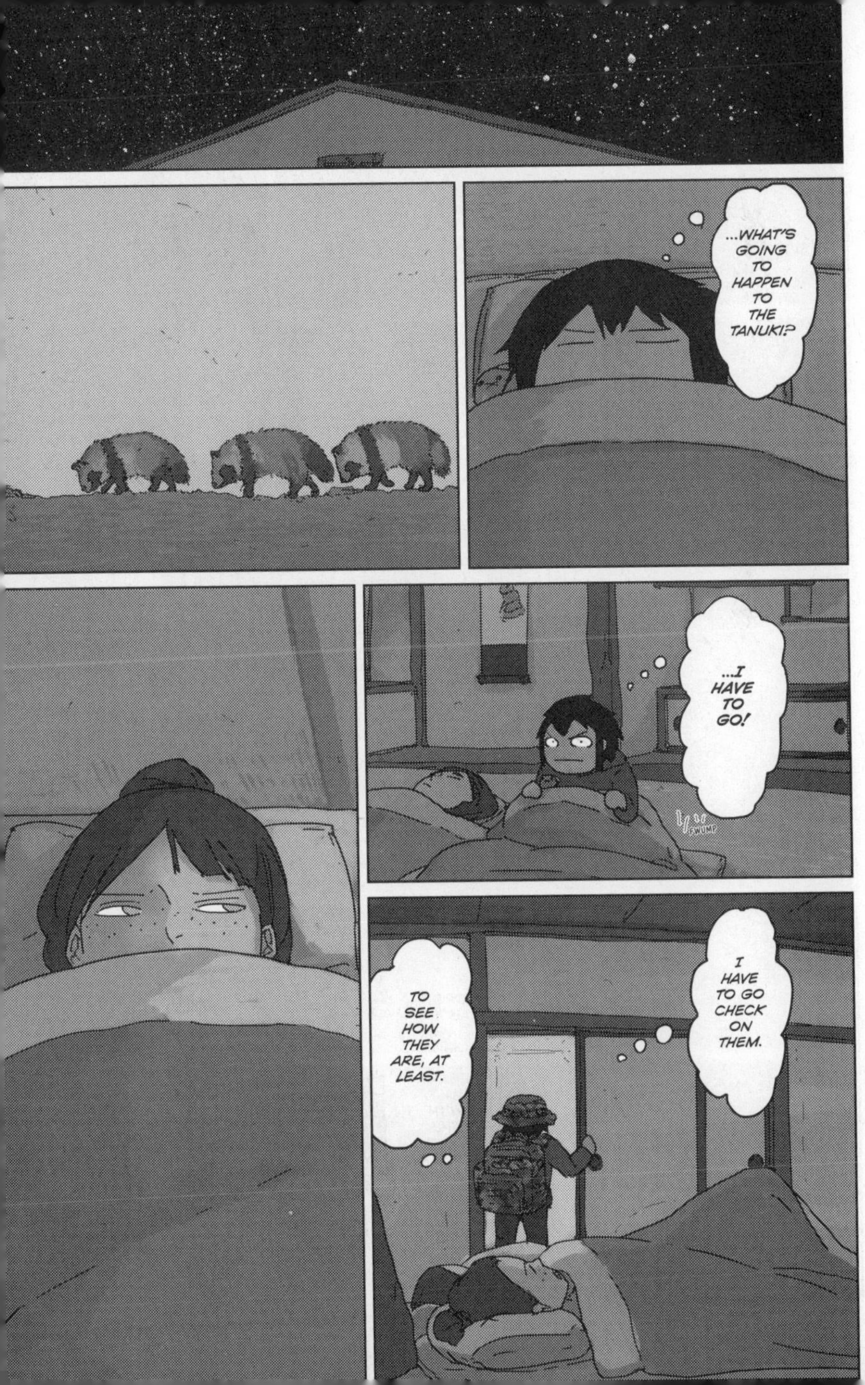
...WHAT'S GOING TO HAPPEN TO THE TANUKI?
...I HAVE TO GO!
FWUMP
I HAVE TO GO CHECK ON THEM.
TO SEE HOW THEY ARE, AT LEAST.

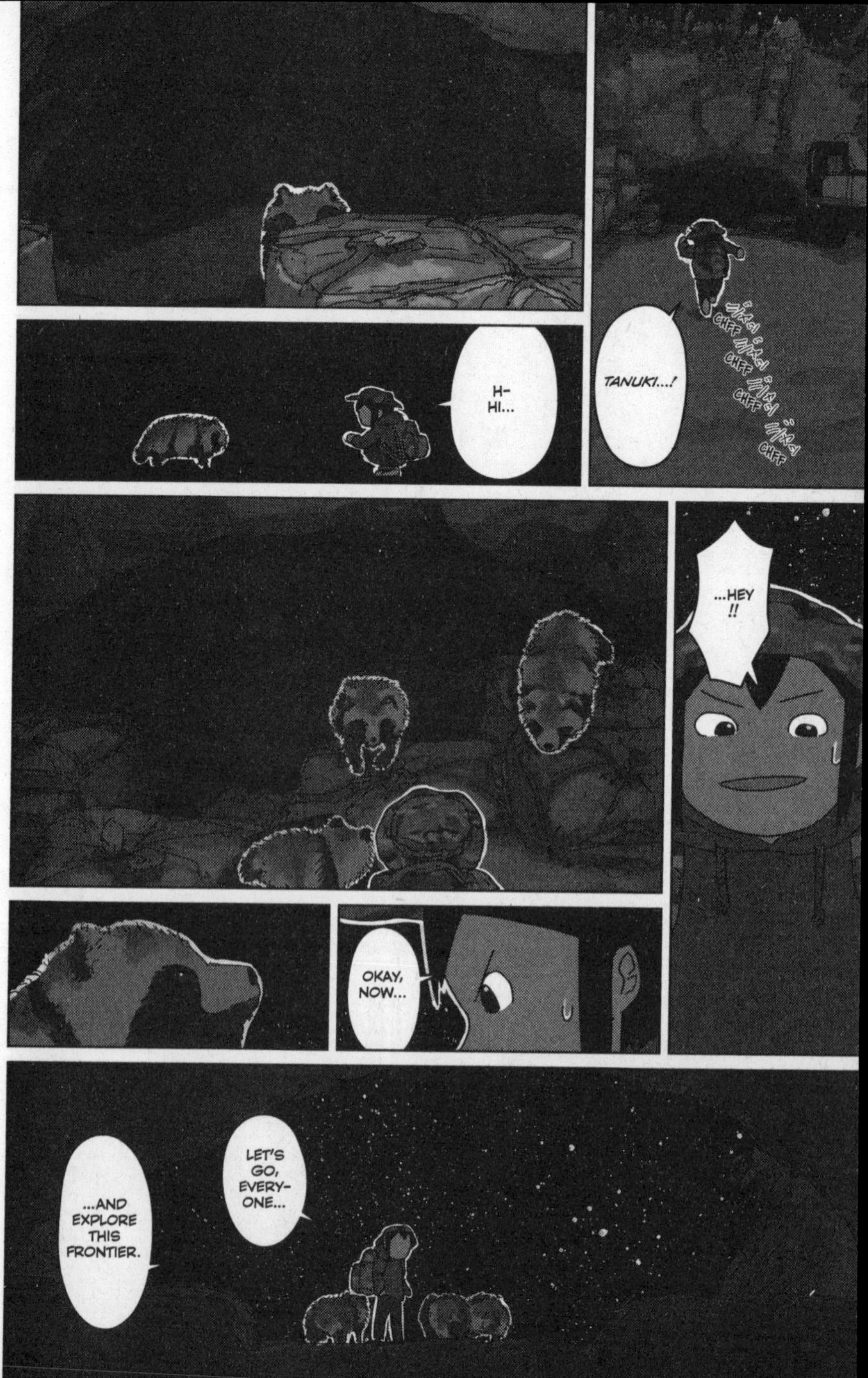
TANUKI...!
CHFF
CHFF
CHFF
CHFF
H-
HI...
...HEY
!!
OKAY,
NOW...
LET'S
GO,
EVERY-
ONE...
...AND
EXPLORE
THIS
FRONTIER.

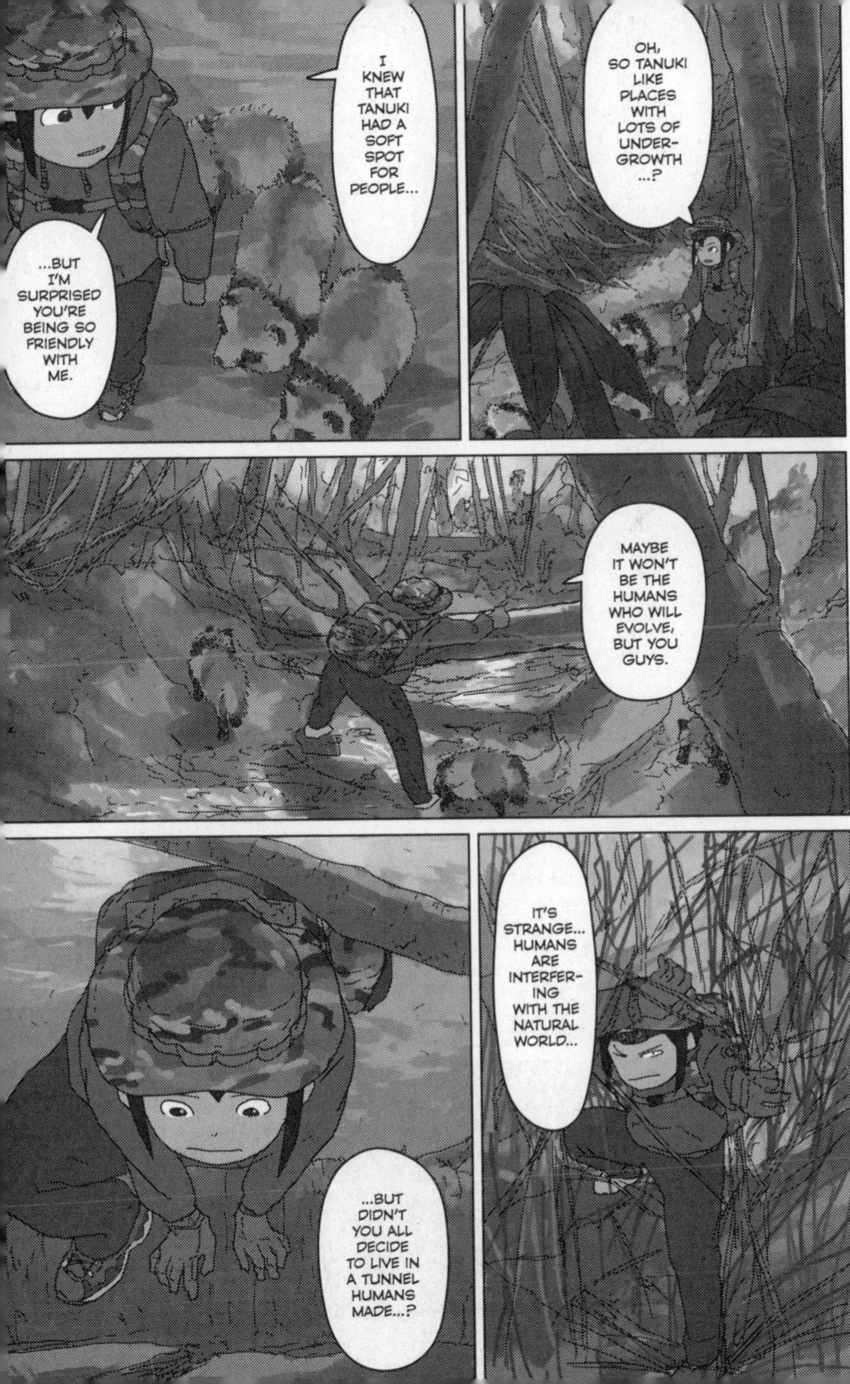
OH, SO TANUKI LIKE PLACES WITH LOTS OF UNDER-GROWTH ...?
I KNEW THAT TANUKI HAD A SOFT SPOT FOR PEOPLE...
...BUT I'M SURPRISED YOU'RE BEING SO FRIENDLY WITH ME.
MAYBE IT WON'T BE THE HUMANS WHO WILL EVOLVE, BUT YOU GUYS.
IT'S STRANGE... HUMANS ARE INTERFER-ING WITH THE NATURAL WORLD...
...BUT DIDN'T YOU ALL DECIDE TO LIVE IN A TUNNEL HUMANS MADE...?

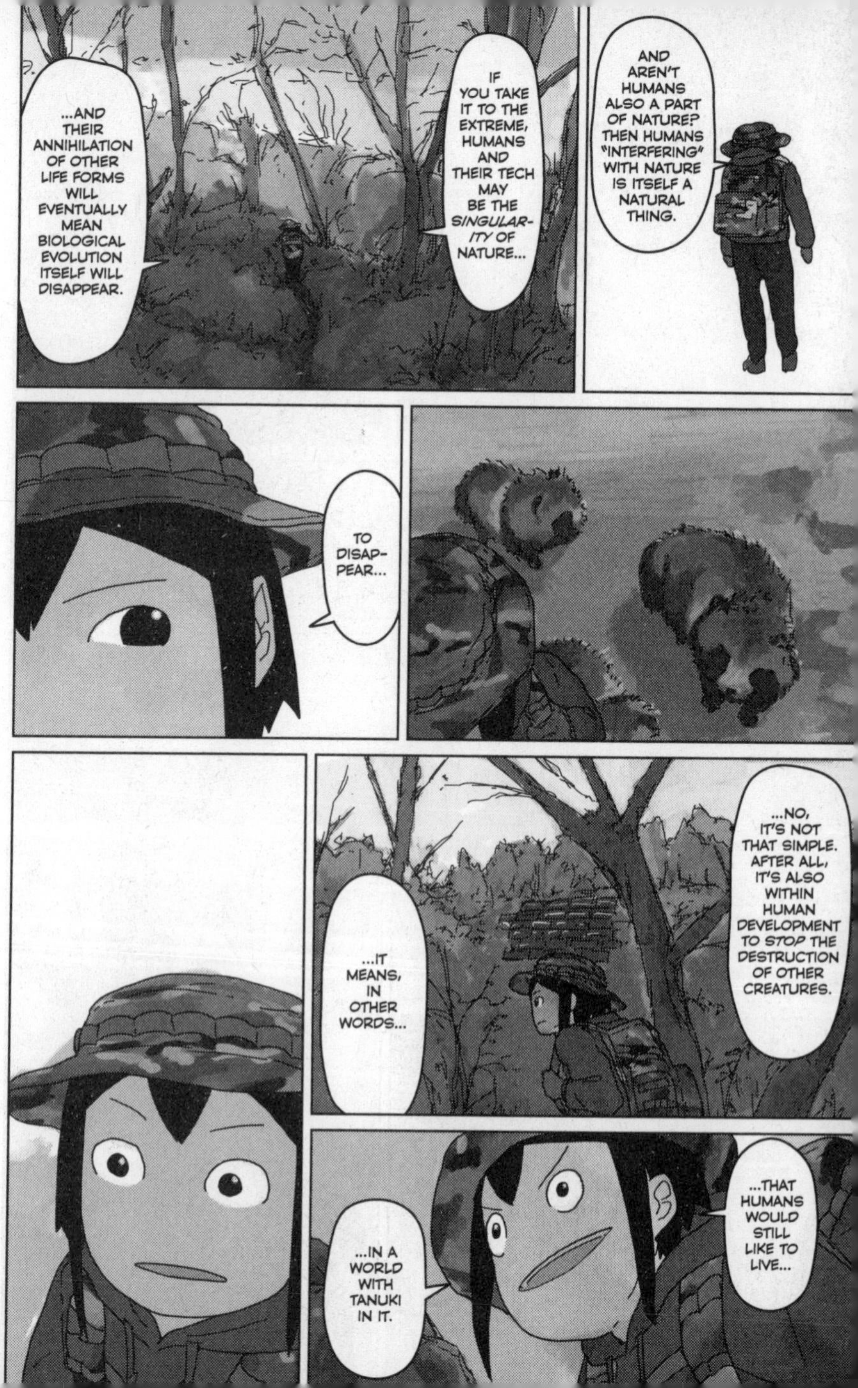
AND AREN'T HUMANS ALSO A PART OF NATURE? THEN HUMANS "INTERFERING" WITH NATURE IS ITSELF A NATURAL THING.
IF YOU TAKE IT TO THE EXTREME, HUMANS AND THEIR TECH MAY BE THE *SINGULARITY* OF NATURE...
...AND THEIR ANNIHILATION OF OTHER LIFE FORMS WILL EVENTUALLY MEAN BIOLOGICAL EVOLUTION ITSELF WILL DISAPPEAR.
TO DISAPPEAR...
...NO, IT'S NOT THAT SIMPLE. AFTER ALL, IT'S ALSO WITHIN HUMAN DEVELOPMENT TO *STOP* THE DESTRUCTION OF OTHER CREATURES.
...IT MEANS, IN OTHER WORDS...
...THAT HUMANS WOULD STILL LIKE TO LIVE...
...IN A WORLD WITH TANUKI IN IT.

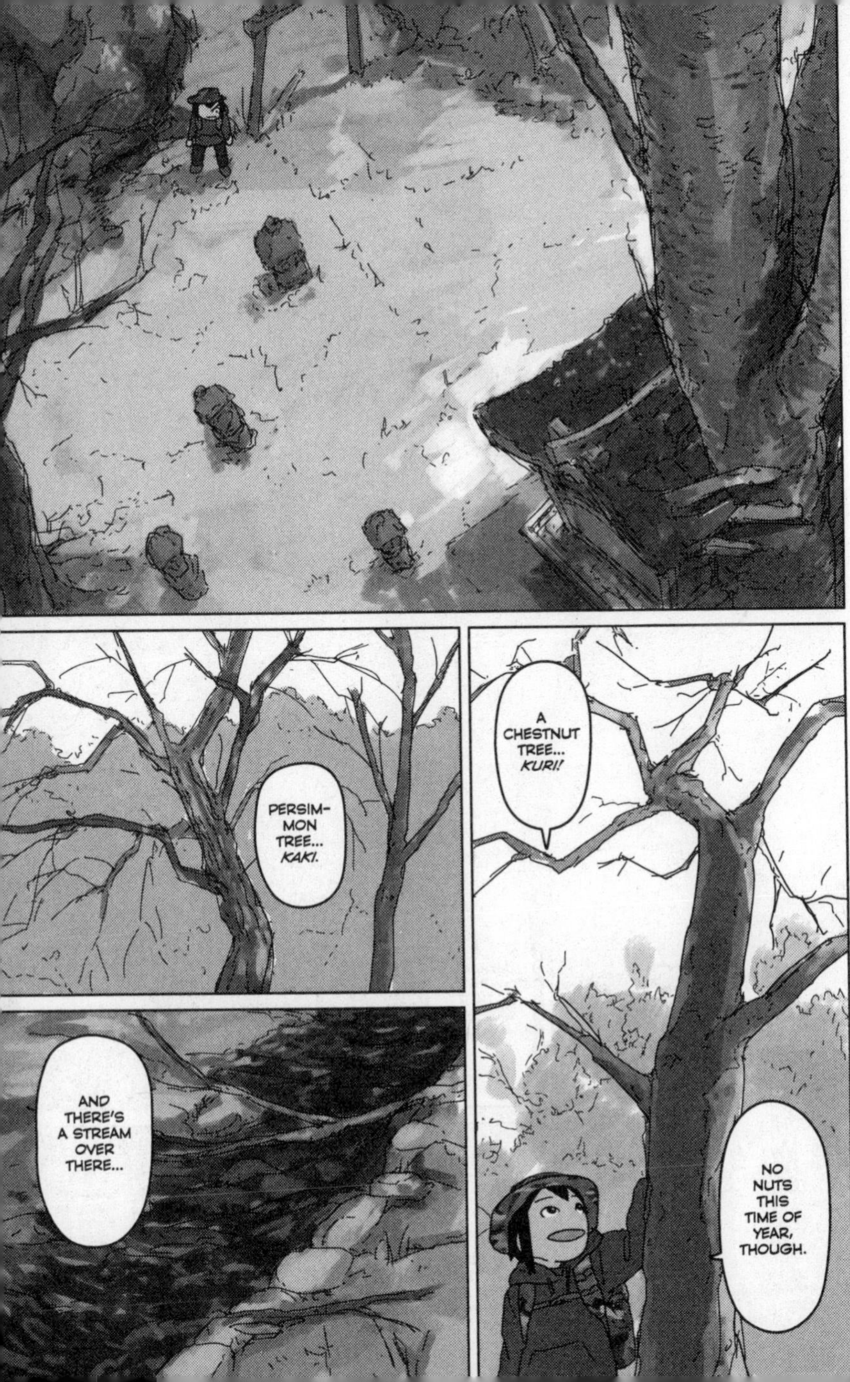
A CHESTNUT TREE... *KURI!*
NO NUTS THIS TIME OF YEAR, THOUGH.
PERSIM-MON TREE... *KAKI.*
AND THERE'S A STREAM OVER THERE...

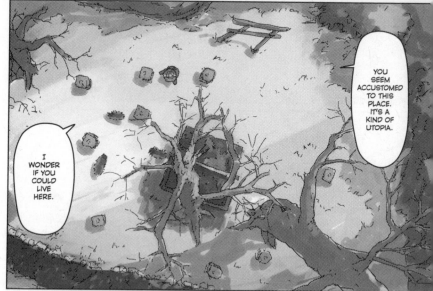

YOU SEEM ACCUSTOMED TO THIS PLACE. IT'S A KIND OF UTOPIA.

I WONDER IF YOU COULD LIVE HERE.

WHY ARE THERE SO MANY STONE LANTERNS HERE...?

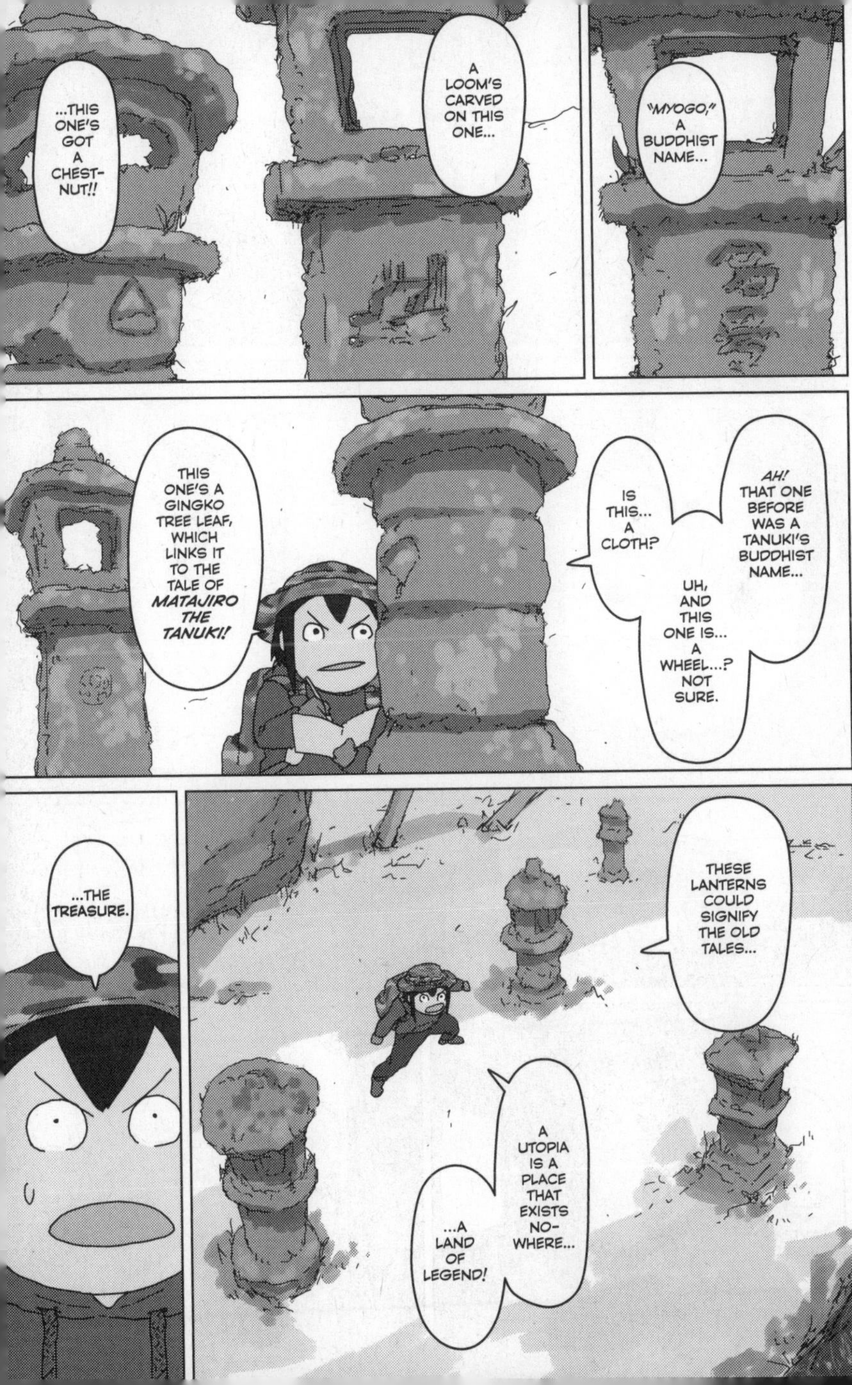
"MYOGO," A BUDDHIST NAME...
A LOOM'S CARVED ON THIS ONE...
...THIS ONE'S GOT A CHEST-NUT!!
AH! THAT ONE BEFORE WAS A TANUKI'S BUDDHIST NAME...
IS THIS... A CLOTH?
UH, AND THIS ONE IS... A WHEEL...? NOT SURE.
THIS ONE'S A GINGKO TREE LEAF, WHICH LINKS IT TO THE TALE OF MATAJIRO THE TANUKI!
THESE LANTERNS COULD SIGNIFY THE OLD TALES...
A UTOPIA IS A PLACE THAT EXISTS NO-WHERE...
...A LAND OF LEGEND!
...THE TREASURE.

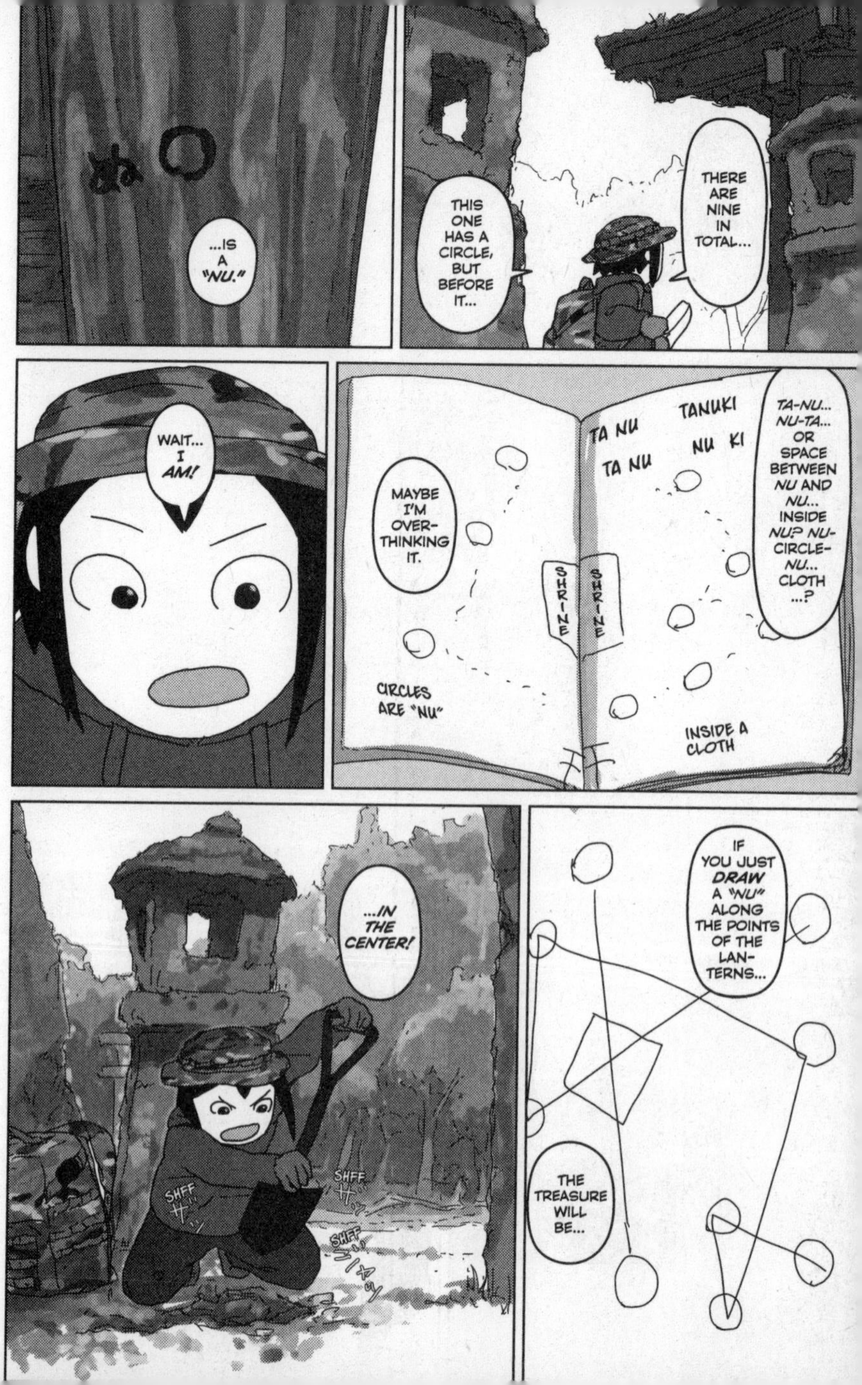
THERE ARE NINE IN TOTAL...
THIS ONE HAS A CIRCLE, BUT BEFORE IT...
ぬ
...IS A "NU."
TA-NU... NU-TA... OR SPACE BETWEEN NU AND NU... INSIDE NU? NU-CIRCLE-NU... CLOTH ...?
TANUKI
TA NU
NU KI
TA NU
MAYBE I'M OVER-THINKING IT.
SHRINE
SHRINE
CIRCLES ARE "NU"
INSIDE A CLOTH
WAIT... I AM!
IF YOU JUST DRAW A "NU" ALONG THE POINTS OF THE LAN-TERNS...
THE TREASURE WILL BE...
...IN THE CENTER!
SHFF
SHFF
SHFF

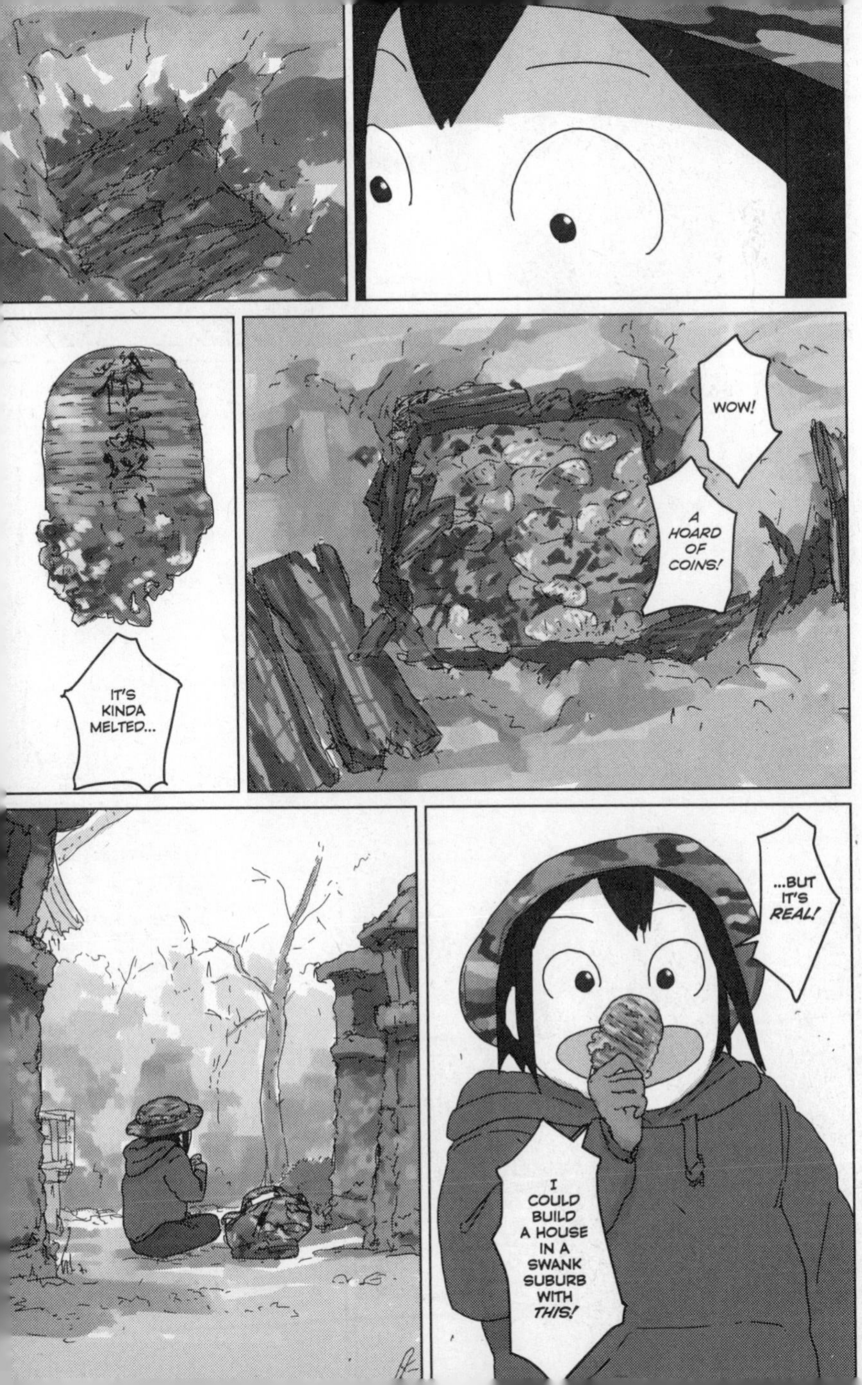
WOW!
A HOARD OF COINS!
IT'S KINDA MELTED...
...BUT IT'S *REAL!*
I COULD BUILD A HOUSE IN A SWANK SUBURB WITH *THIS!*

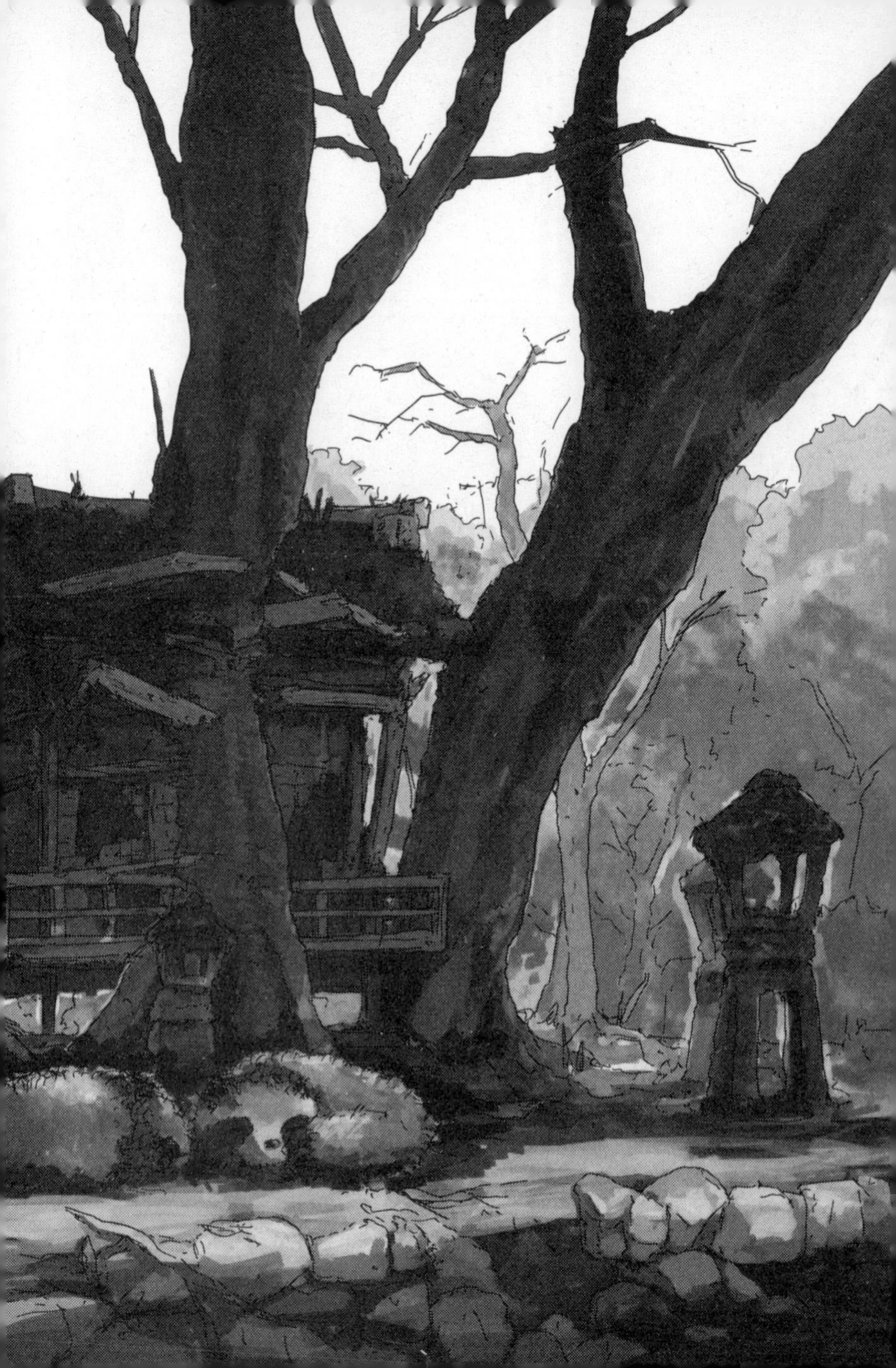

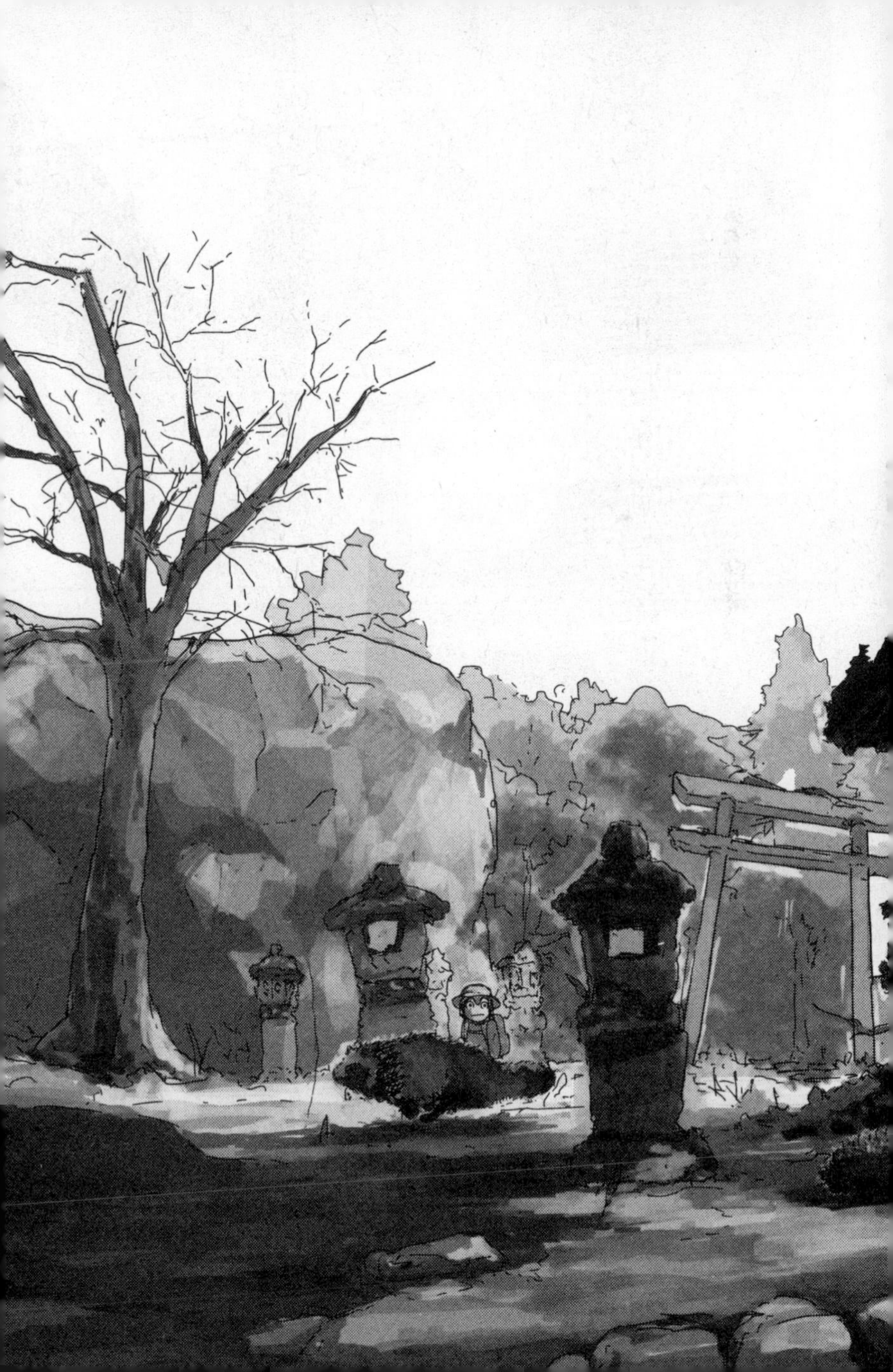

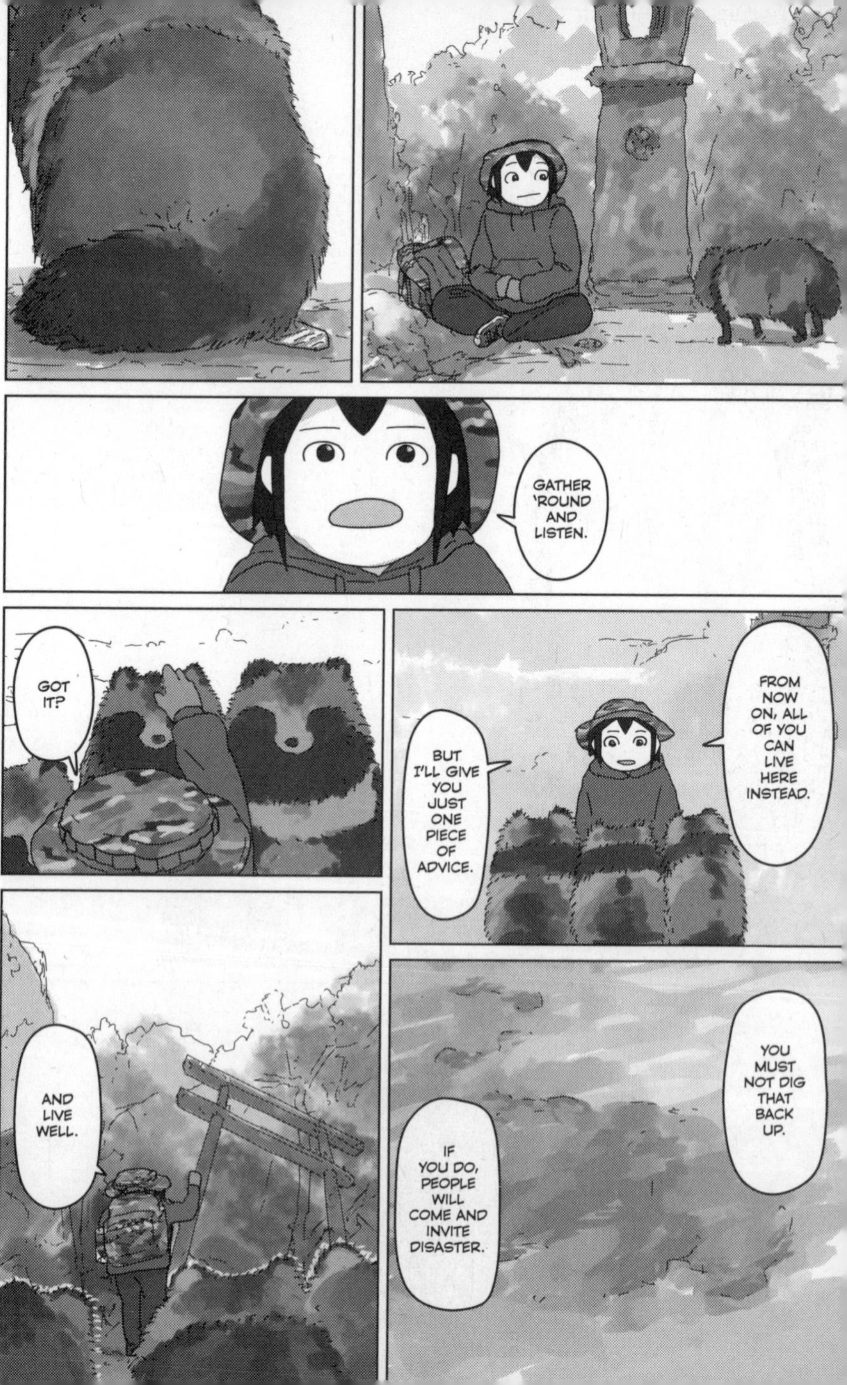
GATHER 'ROUND AND LISTEN.
FROM NOW ON, ALL OF YOU CAN LIVE HERE INSTEAD.
BUT I'LL GIVE YOU JUST ONE PIECE OF ADVICE.
YOU MUST NOT DIG THAT BACK UP.
IF YOU DO, PEOPLE WILL COME AND INVITE DISASTER.
GOT IT?
AND LIVE WELL.

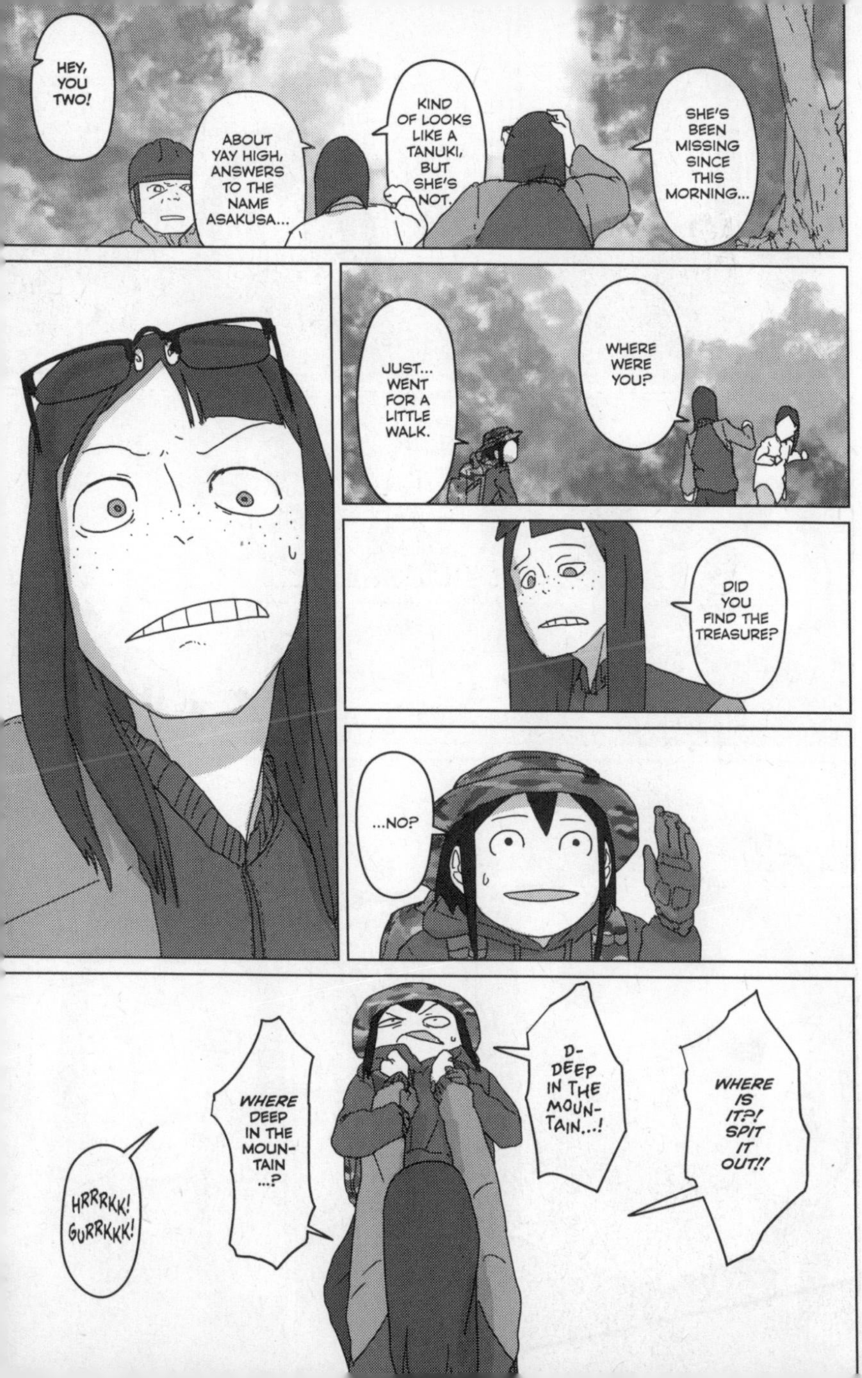
SHE'S BEEN MISSING SINCE THIS MORNING...
KIND OF LOOKS LIKE A TANUKI, BUT SHE'S NOT.
ABOUT YAY HIGH, ANSWERS TO THE NAME ASAKUSA...
HEY, YOU TWO!
WHERE WERE YOU?
JUST... WENT FOR A LITTLE WALK.
DID YOU FIND THE TREASURE?
...NO?
WHERE IS IT?! SPIT IT OUT!!
D-DEEP IN THE MOUN-TAIN...!
WHERE DEEP IN THE MOUN-TAIN...?
HRRRKK! GURRKKK!

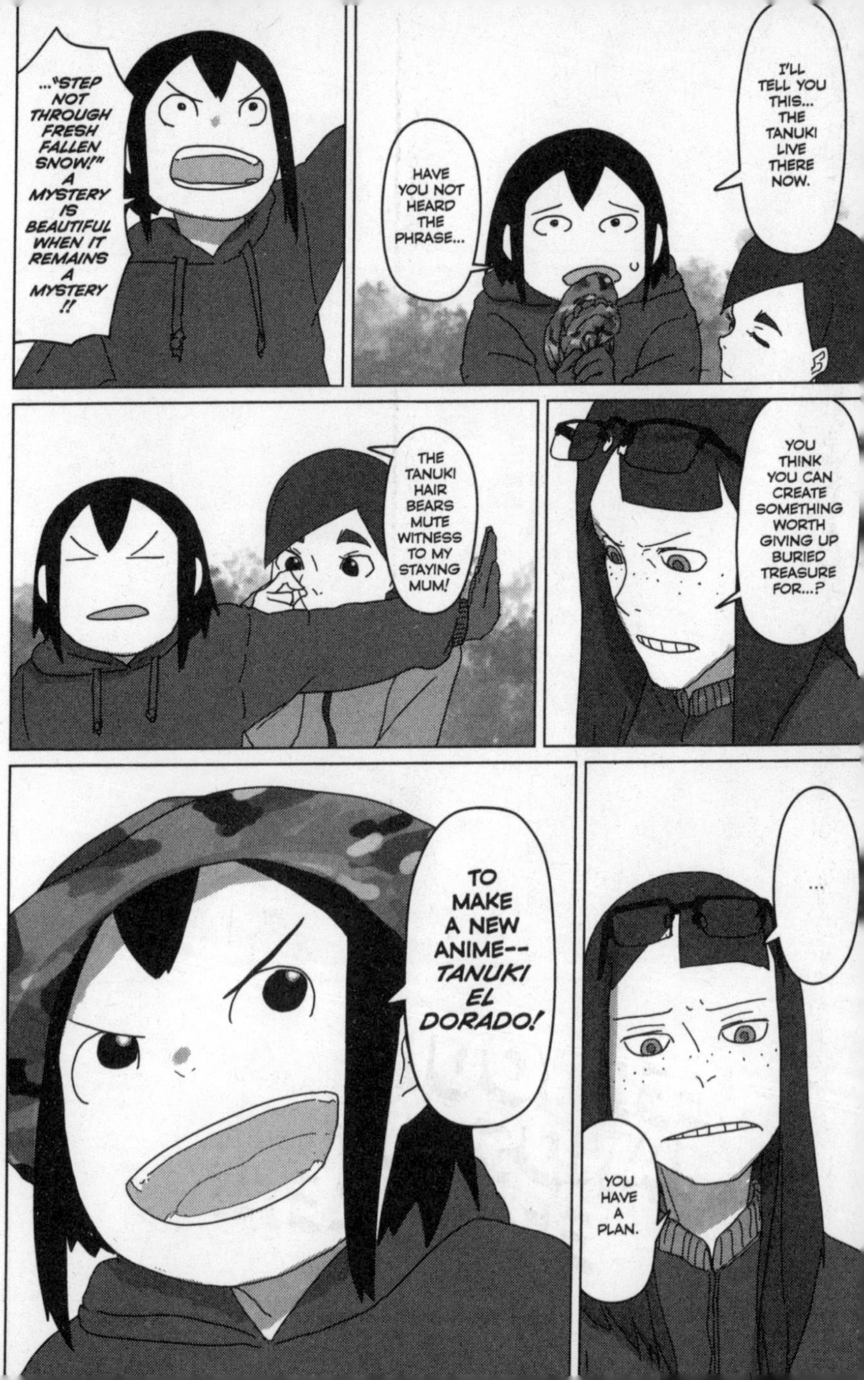
I'LL TELL YOU THIS... THE TANUKI LIVE THERE NOW.
HAVE YOU NOT HEARD THE PHRASE...
..."STEP NOT THROUGH FRESH FALLEN SNOW!" A MYSTERY IS BEAUTIFUL WHEN IT REMAINS A MYSTERY!!
YOU THINK YOU CAN CREATE SOMETHING WORTH GIVING UP BURIED TREASURE FOR...?
THE TANUKI HAIR BEARS MUTE WITNESS TO MY STAYING MUM!
...
YOU HAVE A PLAN.
TO MAKE A NEW ANIME-- *TANUKI EL DORADO!*

KEEP YOUR HANDS OFF EIZOUKEN!

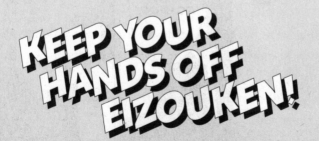

Memo from Mr. Oowara:

There are countless legends about tanuki raccoon dogs. If you're not a person well-versed in folk tales and legends, the number would probably surprise you.

It is said the big three legends about tanuki are that of the Matsuyama Disturbance and the Eight Hundred and Eight Tanuki, the account of the tanuki drumming at the Shojo Temple, and the tale of the lucky Bunbuku tea kettle.

When it comes to individual tanuki in legend, Japan's three most famous names might be Tasaburo Tanuki of Yashima, Danzaburo Tanuki of Sado Island, and Shibaemon Tanuki of Awaji Island.

The aforementioned are especially famous, but if you start investigating legends beyond these, there's really no end to them.

They live further away than rats and crows, but tanuki habitats are also sometimes relatively close to human settlements, and perhaps there could have been a fair amount of interaction there.

Stories that have been passed down orally become quite distorted, but there may be some truth to be found in them.

I wonder how much of those stories are based on something that actually happened.

CHAPTER 26:
HOW WE SEE THE WORLD

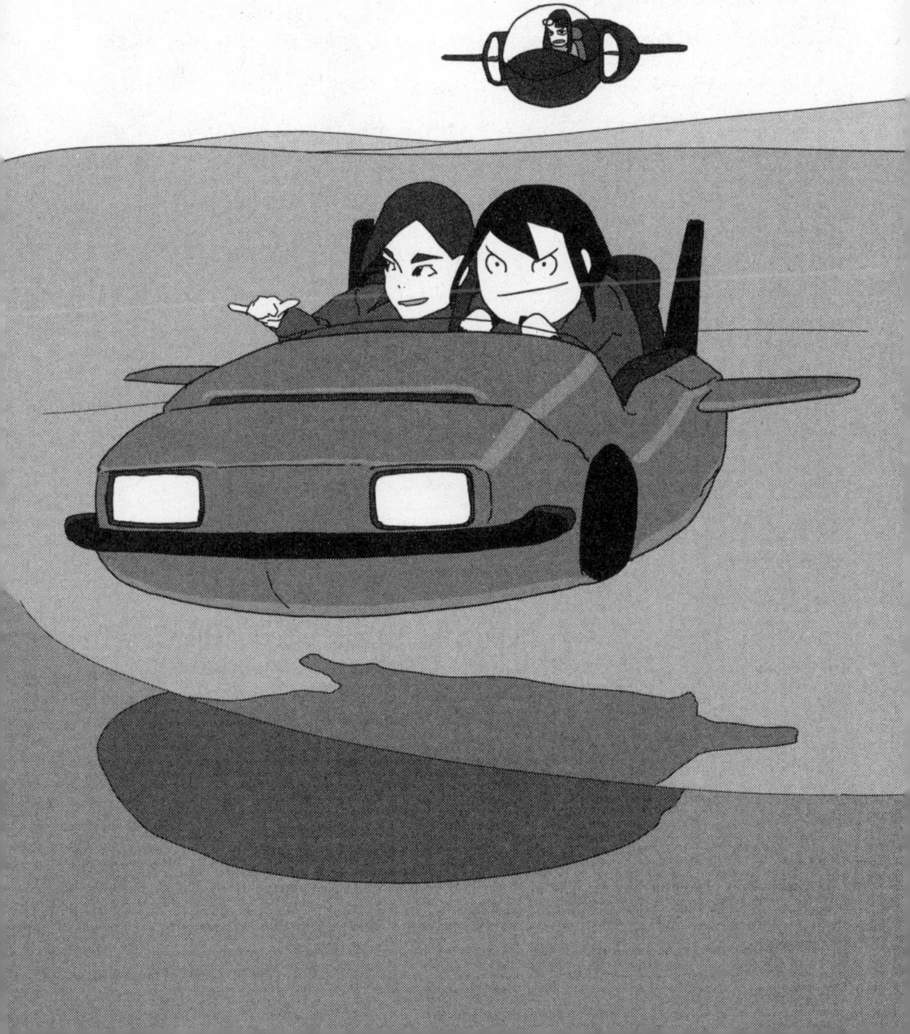

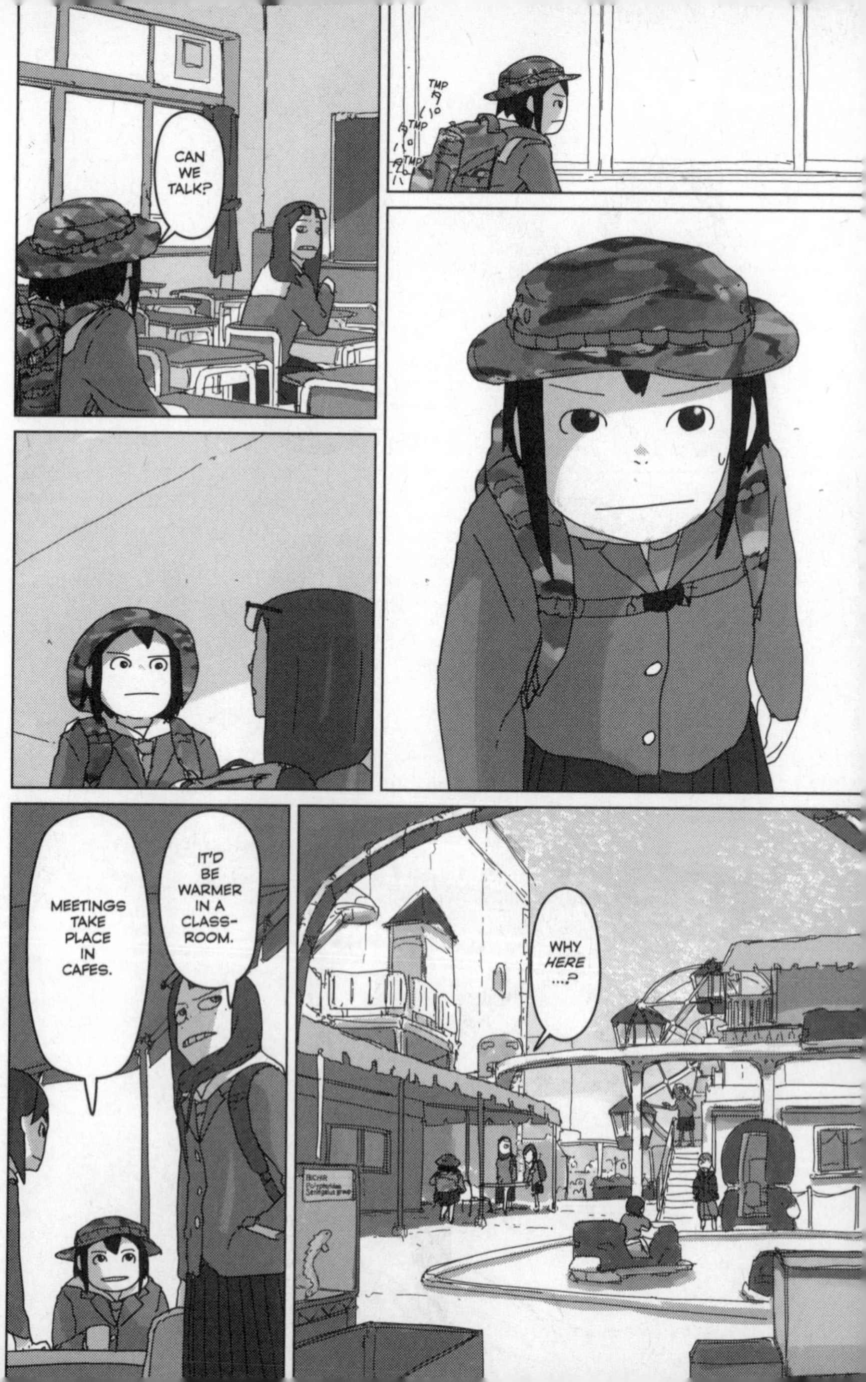
TMP
TMP
TMP
CAN WE TALK?
WHY *HERE* ...?
IT'D BE WARMER IN A CLASS-ROOM.
MEETINGS TAKE PLACE IN CAFES.

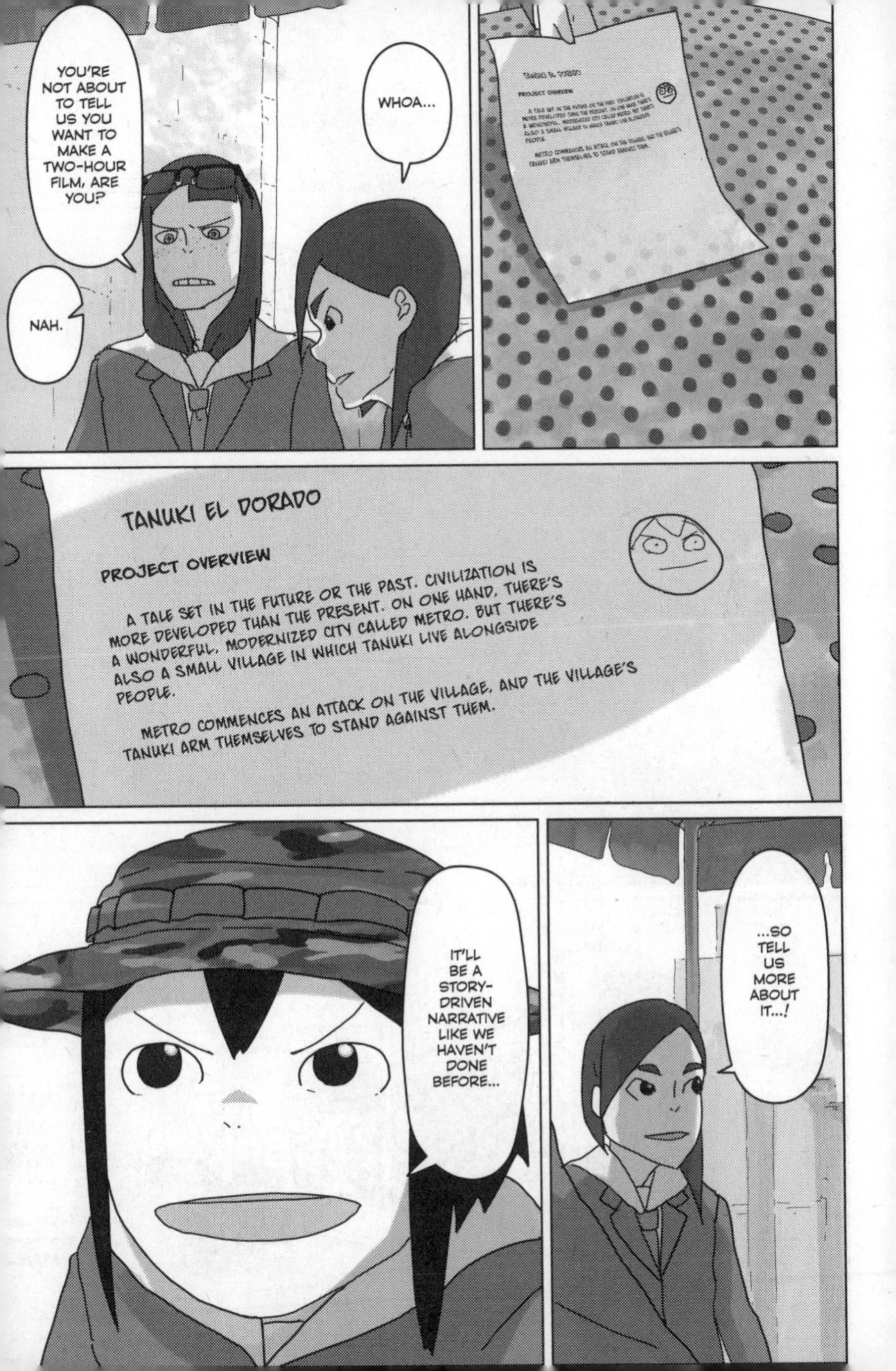
WHOA...
YOU'RE NOT ABOUT TO TELL US YOU WANT TO MAKE A TWO-HOUR FILM, ARE YOU?
NAH.
TANUKI EL DORADO
PROJECT OVERVIEW
A TALE SET IN THE FUTURE OR THE PAST. CIVILIZATION IS MORE DEVELOPED THAN THE PRESENT. ON ONE HAND, THERE'S A WONDERFUL, MODERNIZED CITY CALLED METRO. BUT THERE'S ALSO A SMALL VILLAGE IN WHICH TANUKI LIVE ALONGSIDE PEOPLE.
METRO COMMENCES AN ATTACK ON THE VILLAGE, AND THE VILLAGE'S TANUKI ARM THEMSELVES TO STAND AGAINST THEM.
...SO TELL US MORE ABOUT IT...!
IT'LL BE A STORY-DRIVEN NARRATIVE LIKE WE HAVEN'T DONE BEFORE...

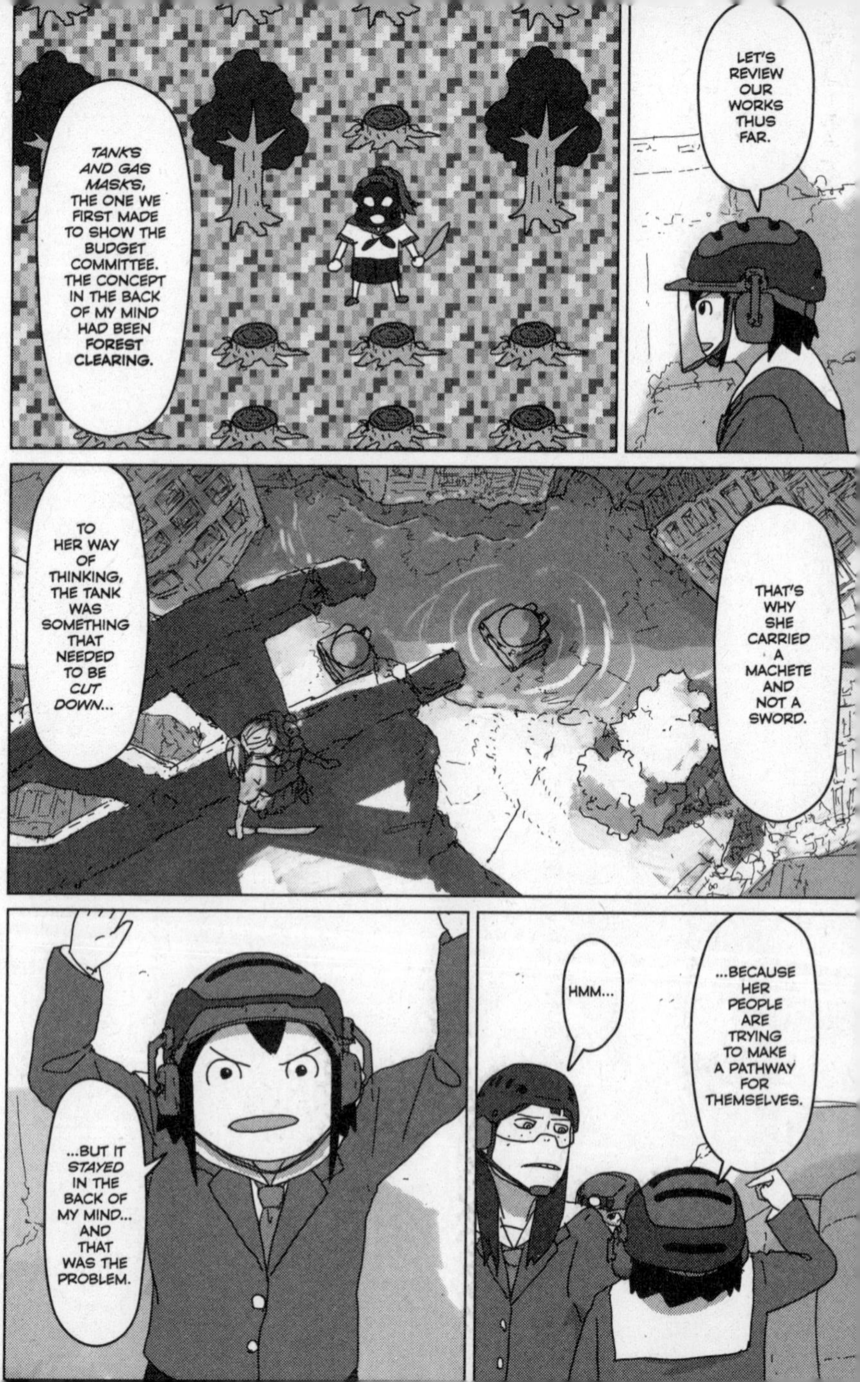
LET'S REVIEW OUR WORKS THUS FAR.
TANKS AND GAS MASKS, THE ONE WE FIRST MADE TO SHOW THE BUDGET COMMITTEE. THE CONCEPT IN THE BACK OF MY MIND HAD BEEN FOREST CLEARING.
TO HER WAY OF THINKING, THE TANK WAS SOMETHING THAT NEEDED TO BE *CUT DOWN*...
THAT'S WHY SHE CARRIED A MACHETE AND NOT A SWORD.
...BECAUSE HER PEOPLE ARE TRYING TO MAKE A PATHWAY FOR THEMSELVES.
HMM...
...BUT IT *STAYED* IN THE BACK OF MY MIND... AND THAT WAS THE PROBLEM.

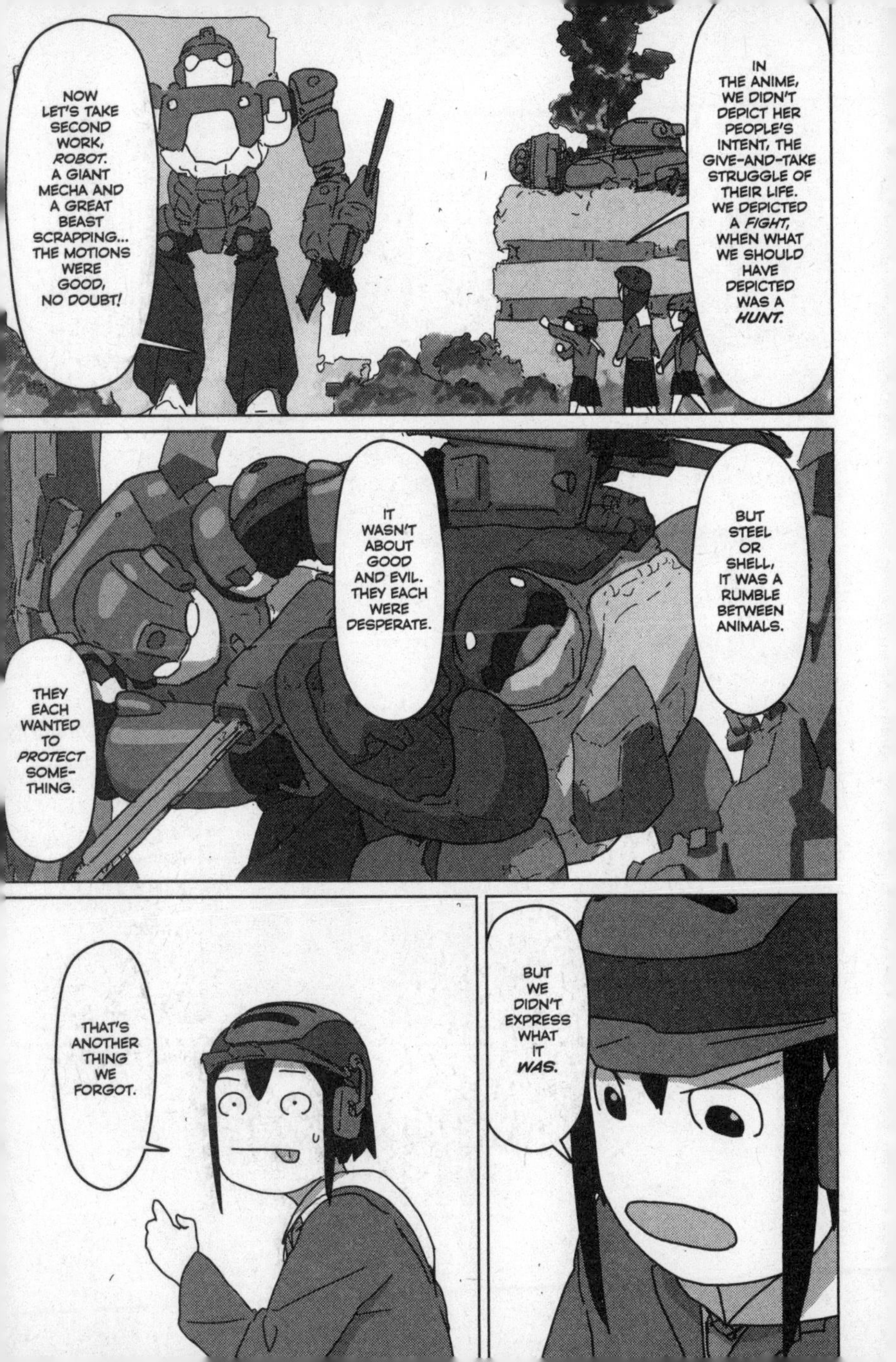
IN THE ANIME, WE DIDN'T DEPICT HER PEOPLE'S INTENT, THE GIVE-AND-TAKE STRUGGLE OF THEIR LIFE. WE DEPICTED A *FIGHT*, WHEN WHAT WE SHOULD HAVE DEPICTED WAS A ***HUNT***.
NOW LET'S TAKE SECOND WORK, *ROBOT*. A GIANT MECHA AND A GREAT BEAST SCRAPPING... THE MOTIONS WERE GOOD, NO DOUBT!
BUT STEEL OR SHELL, IT WAS A RUMBLE BETWEEN ANIMALS.
IT WASN'T ABOUT GOOD AND EVIL. THEY EACH WERE DESPERATE.
THEY EACH WANTED TO *PROTECT* SOME-THING.
BUT WE DIDN'T EXPRESS WHAT IT ***WAS***.
THAT'S ANOTHER THING WE FORGOT.

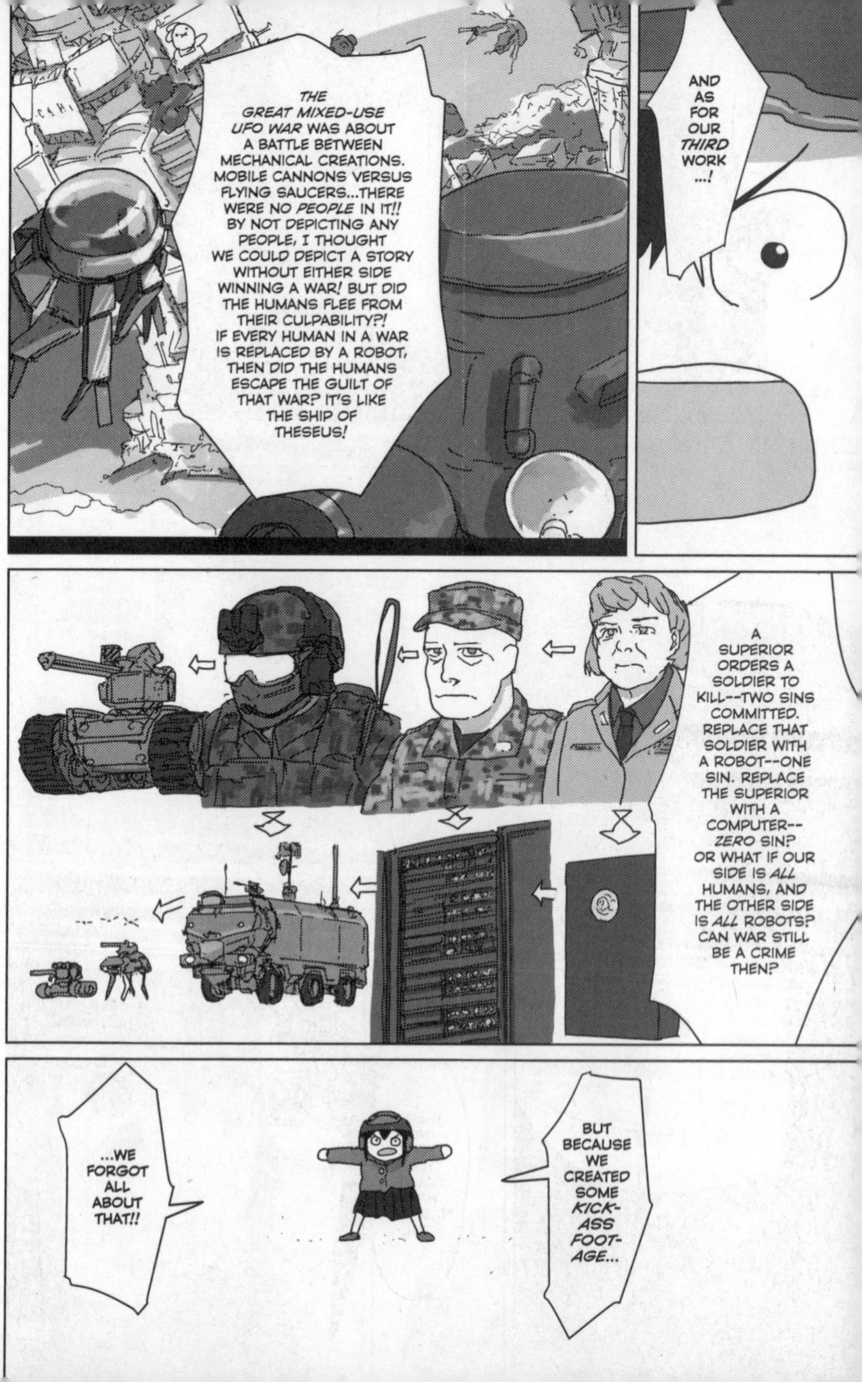
AND AS FOR OUR *THIRD* WORK ...!
THE GREAT MIXED-USE UFO WAR WAS ABOUT A BATTLE BETWEEN MECHANICAL CREATIONS. MOBILE CANNONS VERSUS FLYING SAUCERS...THERE WERE NO *PEOPLE* IN IT!! BY NOT DEPICTING ANY PEOPLE, I THOUGHT WE COULD DEPICT A STORY WITHOUT EITHER SIDE WINNING A WAR! BUT DID THE HUMANS FLEE FROM THEIR CULPABILITY?! IF EVERY HUMAN IN A WAR IS REPLACED BY A ROBOT, THEN DID THE HUMANS ESCAPE THE GUILT OF THAT WAR? IT'S LIKE THE SHIP OF THESEUS!
A SUPERIOR ORDERS A SOLDIER TO KILL--TWO SINS COMMITTED. REPLACE THAT SOLDIER WITH A ROBOT--ONE SIN. REPLACE THE SUPERIOR WITH A COMPUTER-- *ZERO* SIN? OR WHAT IF OUR SIDE IS *ALL* HUMANS, AND THE OTHER SIDE IS *ALL* ROBOTS? CAN WAR STILL BE A CRIME THEN?
BUT BECAUSE WE CREATED SOME *KICK-ASS* FOOT-AGE...
...WE FORGOT ALL ABOUT THAT!!

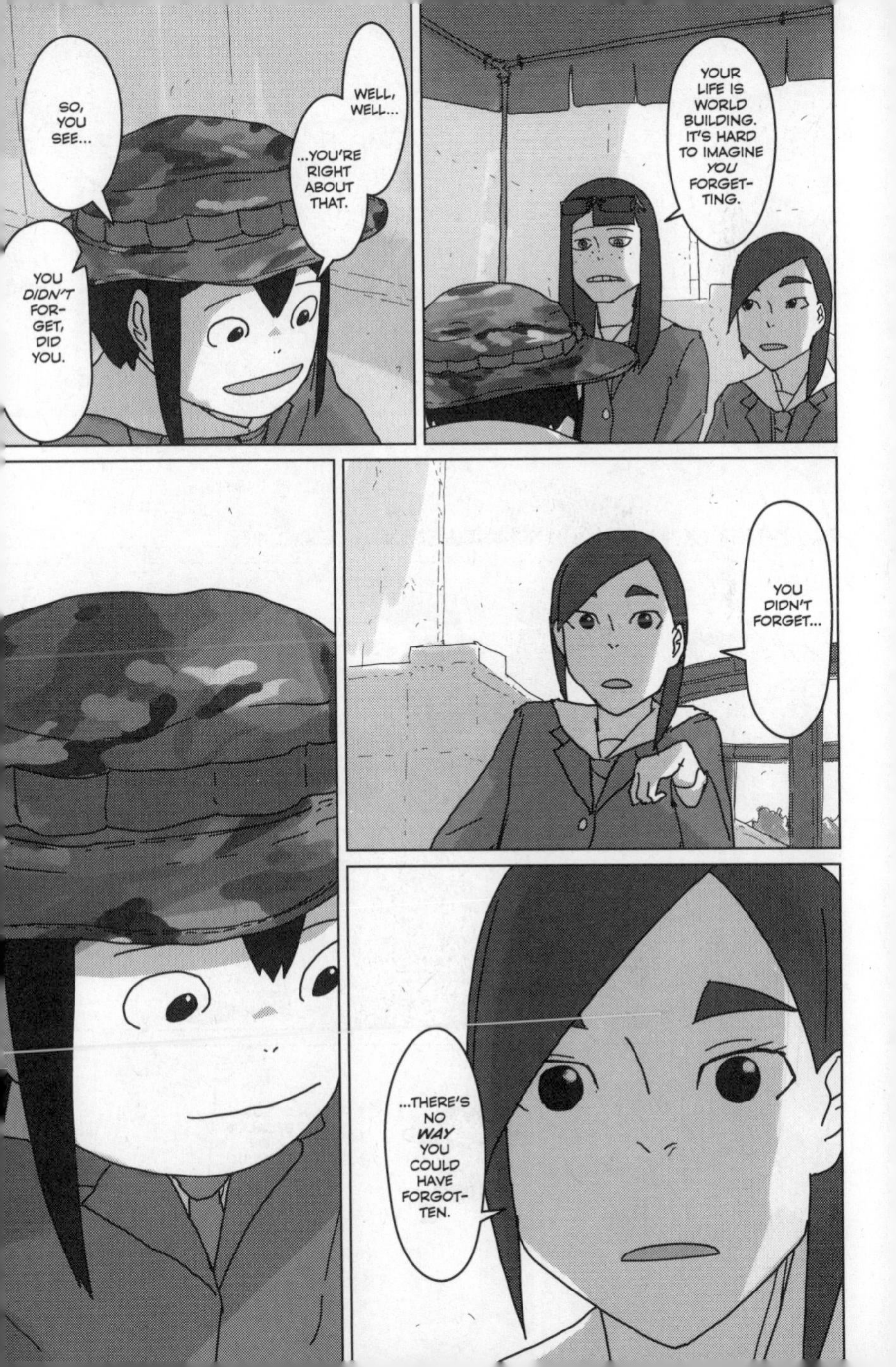
YOUR LIFE IS WORLD BUILDING. IT'S HARD TO IMAGINE *YOU* FORGET-TING.
WELL, WELL...
...YOU'RE RIGHT ABOUT THAT.
SO, YOU SEE...
YOU *DIDN'T* FOR-GET, DID YOU.
YOU DIDN'T FORGET...
...THERE'S NO ***WAY*** YOU COULD HAVE FORGOT-TEN.

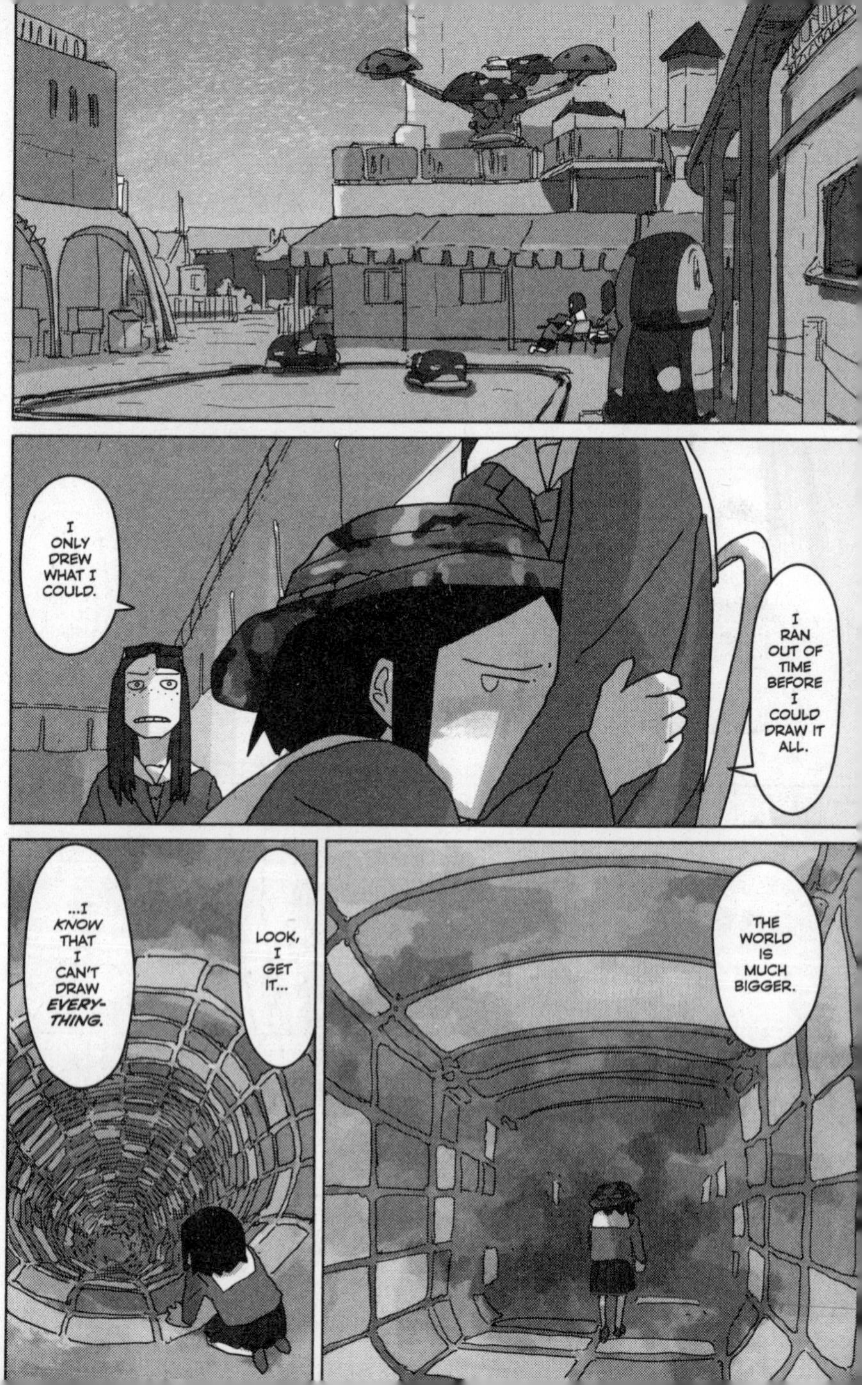
I RAN OUT OF TIME BEFORE I COULD DRAW IT ALL.
I ONLY DREW WHAT I COULD.
THE WORLD IS MUCH BIGGER.
LOOK, I GET IT...
...I *KNOW* THAT I CAN'T DRAW *EVERYTHING*.

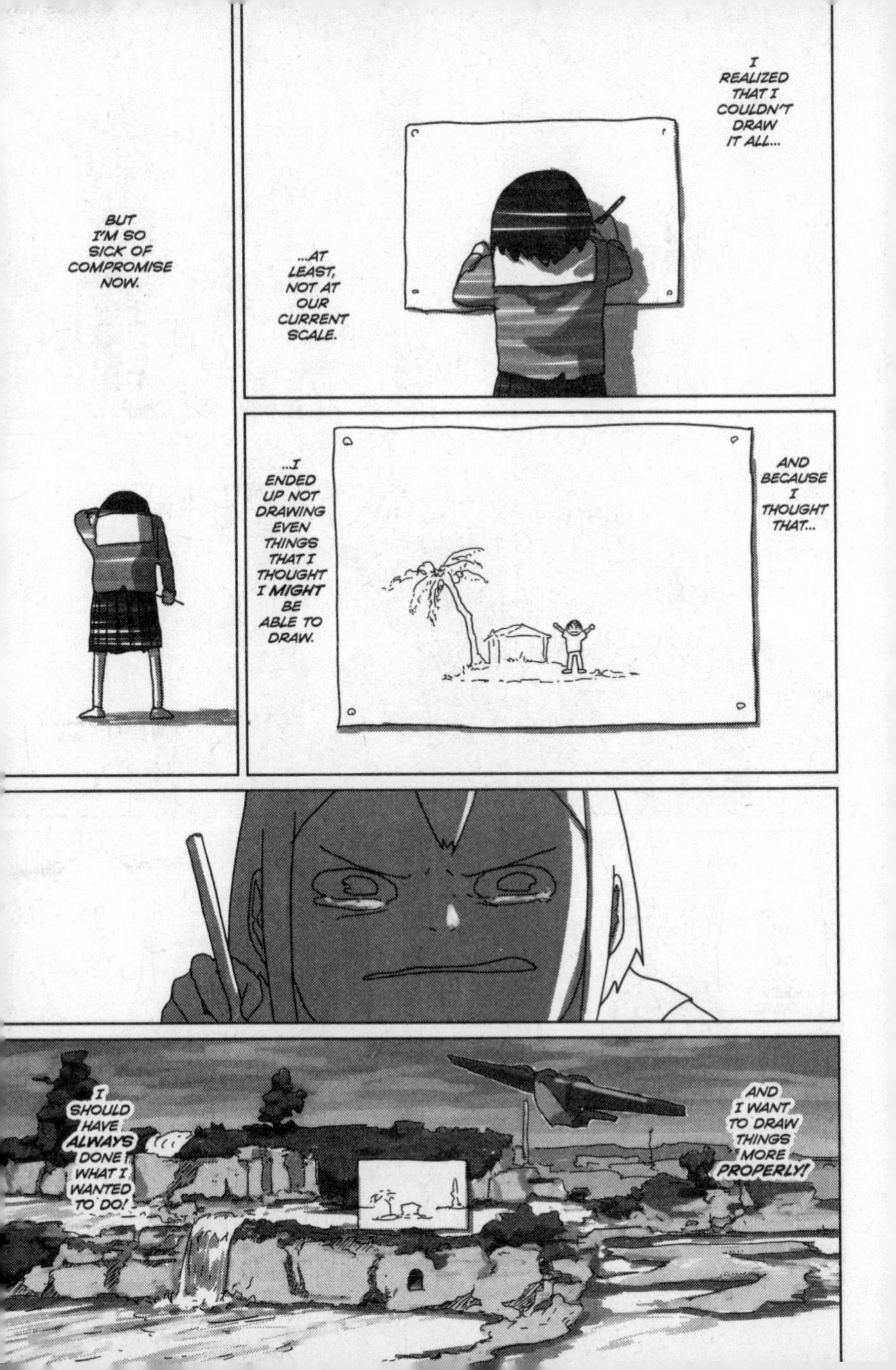
I REALIZED THAT I COULDN'T DRAW IT ALL...
...AT LEAST, NOT AT OUR CURRENT SCALE.
AND BECAUSE I THOUGHT THAT...
...I ENDED UP NOT DRAWING EVEN THINGS THAT I THOUGHT I MIGHT BE ABLE TO DRAW.
BUT I'M SO SICK OF COMPROMISE NOW.
AND I WANT TO DRAW THINGS MORE PROPERLY!
I SHOULD HAVE ALWAYS DONE WHAT I WANTED TO DO!

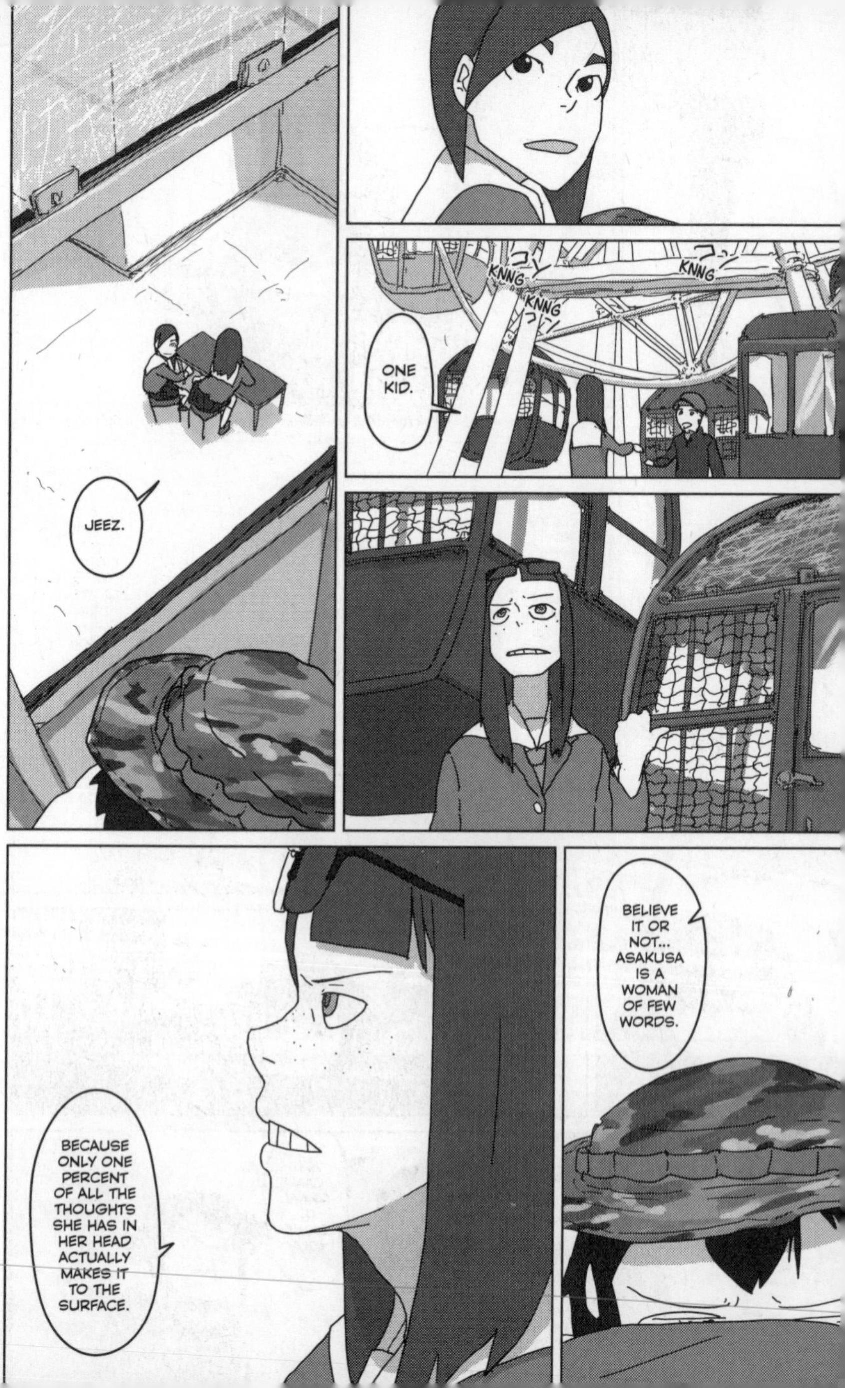
KNNG
KNNG
KNNG
ONE KID.
JEEZ.
BELIEVE IT OR NOT... ASAKUSA IS A WOMAN OF FEW WORDS.
BECAUSE ONLY ONE PERCENT OF ALL THE THOUGHTS SHE HAS IN HER HEAD ACTUALLY MAKES IT TO THE SURFACE.

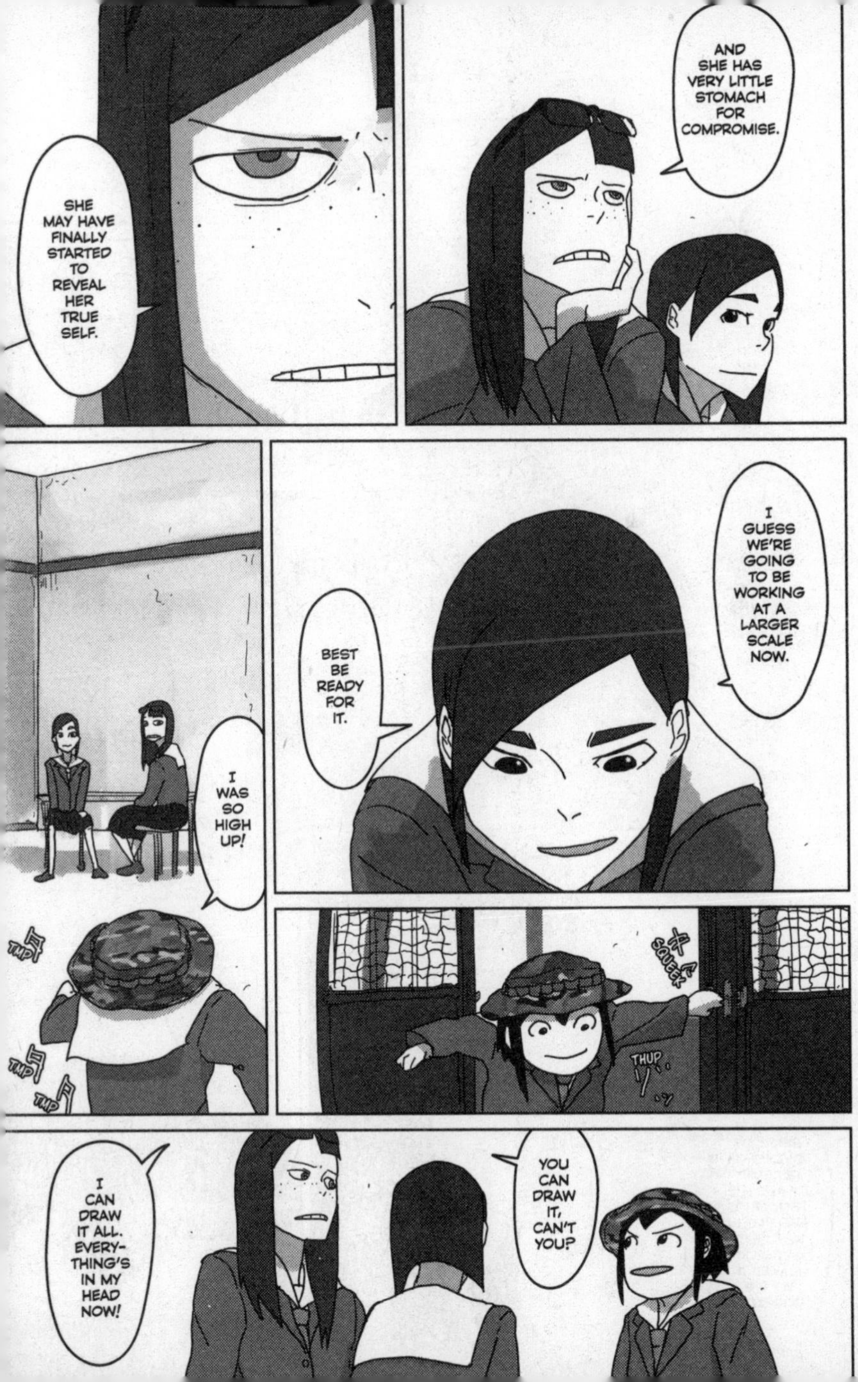
AND SHE HAS VERY LITTLE STOMACH FOR COMPROMISE.
SHE MAY HAVE FINALLY STARTED TO REVEAL HER TRUE SELF.
I GUESS WE'RE GOING TO BE WORKING AT A LARGER SCALE NOW.
BEST BE READY FOR IT.
I WAS SO HIGH UP!
SQUEEK
THUP
TMP
TMP
TMP
YOU CAN DRAW IT, CAN'T YOU?
I CAN DRAW IT ALL. EVERY-THING'S IN MY HEAD NOW!

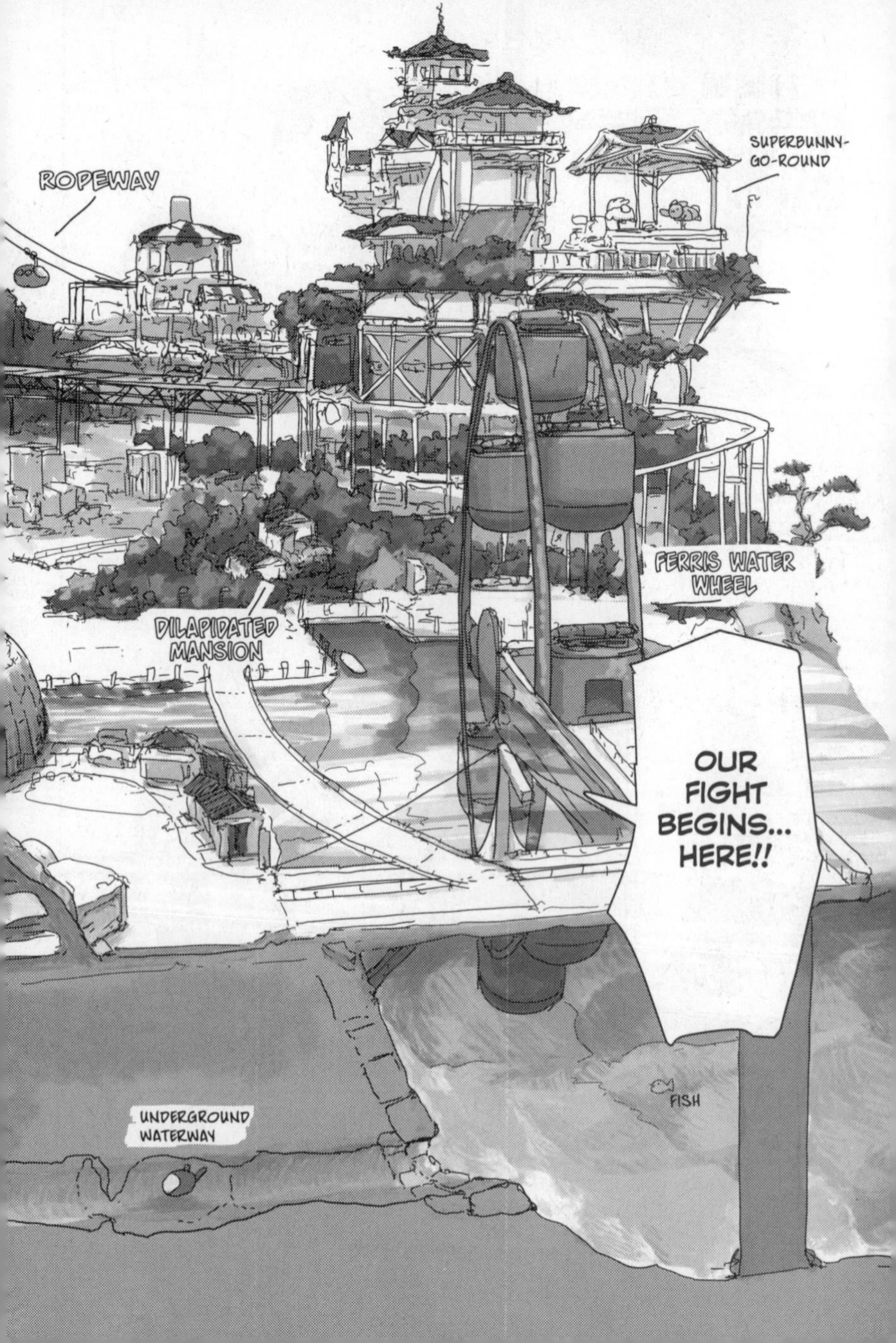
SUPERBUNNY-GO-ROUND
ROPEWAY
FERRIS WATER WHEEL
DILAPIDATED MANSION
OUR FIGHT BEGINS... HERE!!
FISH
UNDERGROUND WATERWAY

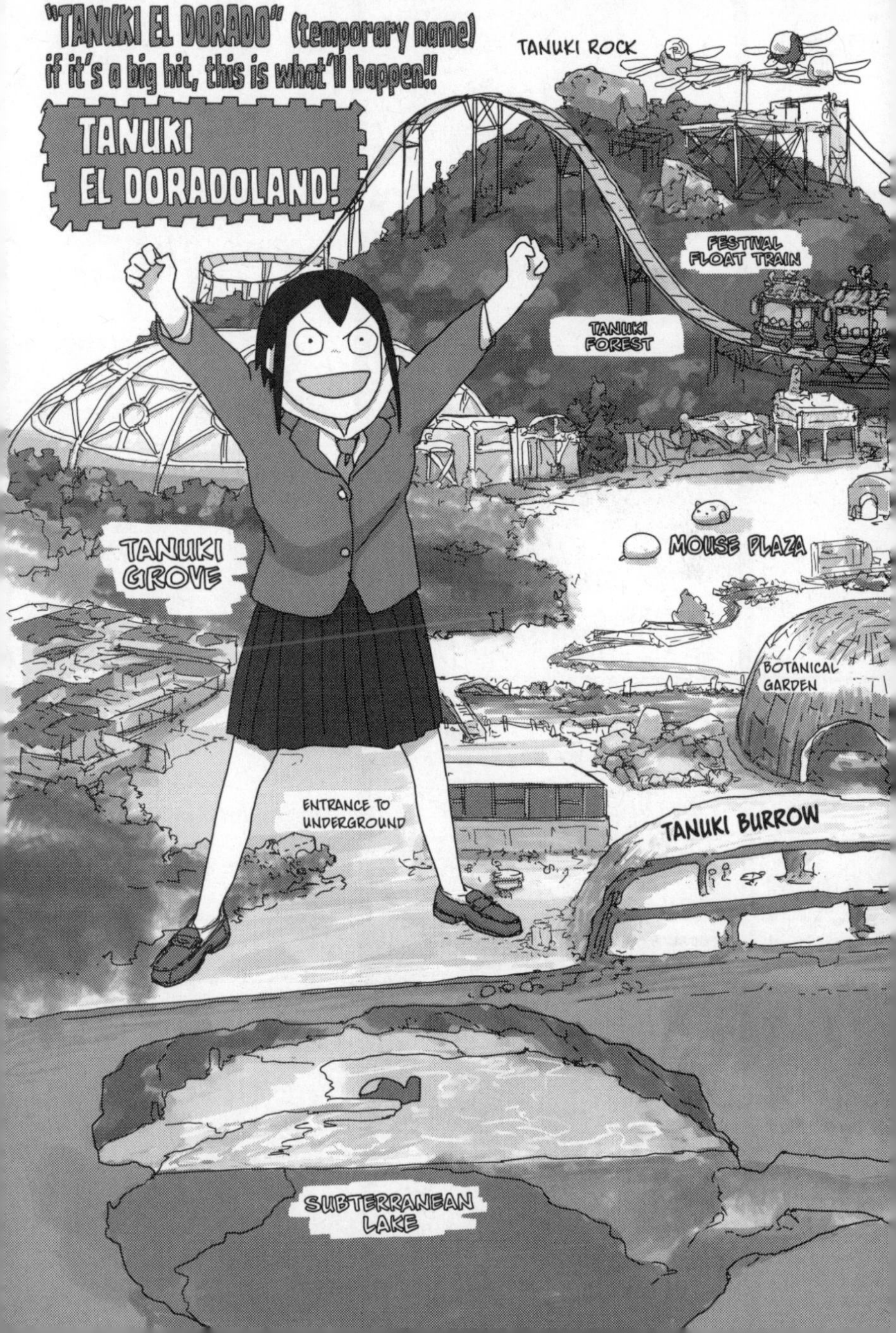
"TANUKI EL DORADO" (temporary name)
if it's a big hit, this is what'll happen!!
TANUKI EL DORADOLAND!
TANUKI ROCK
FESTIVAL FLOAT TRAIN
TANUKI FOREST
MOUSE PLAZA
TANUKI GROVE
BOTANICAL GARDEN
ENTRANCE TO UNDERGROUND
TANUKI BURROW
SUBTERRANEAN LAKE

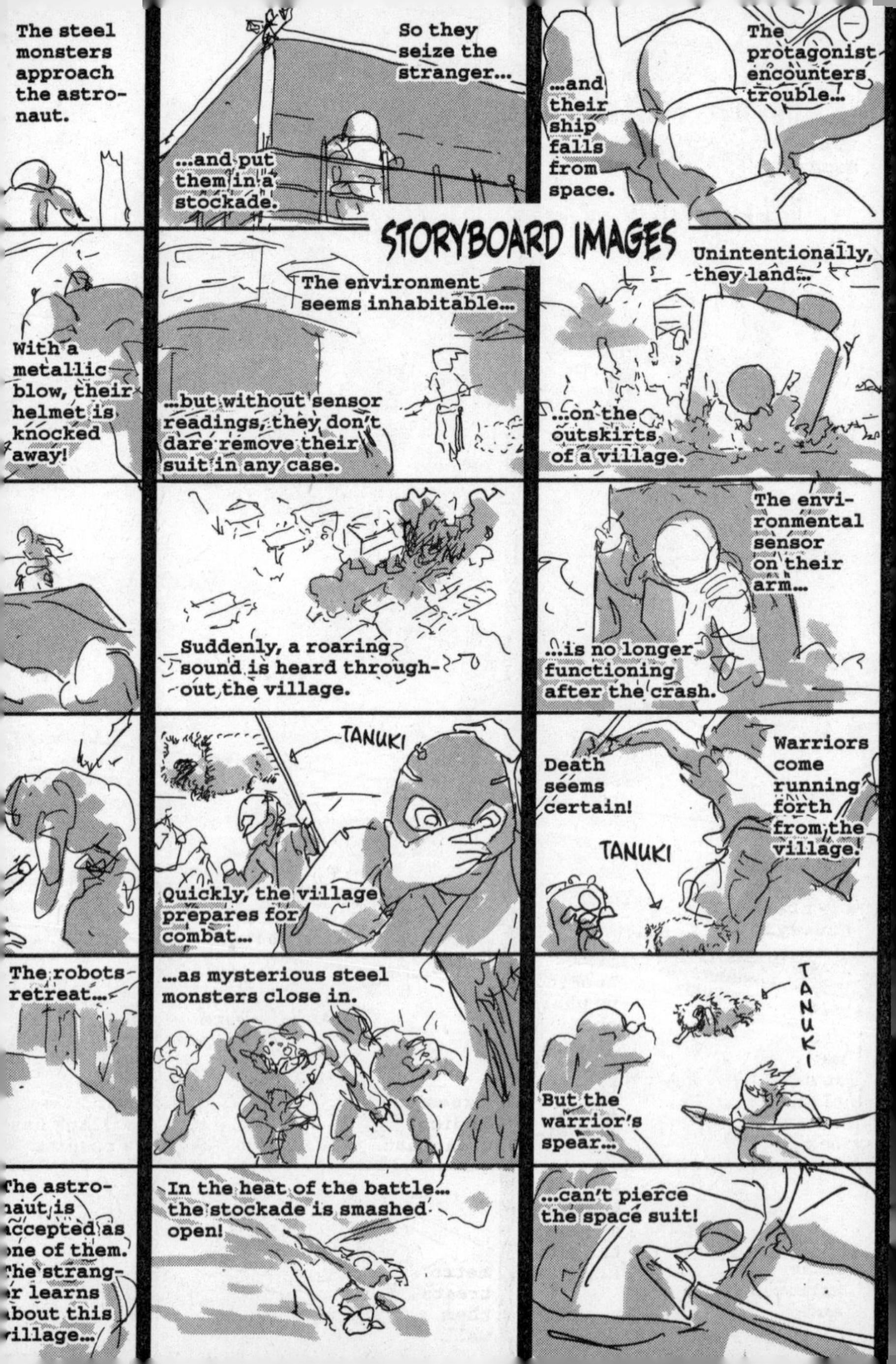
STORYBOARD IMAGES
The protagonist encounters trouble...
...and their ship falls from space.
Unintentionally, they land...
...on the outskirts of a village.
The environmental sensor on their arm...
...is no longer functioning after the crash.
Warriors come running forth from the village.
Death seems certain!
TANUKI
TANUKI
But the warrior's spear...
...can't pierce the space suit!
So they seize the stranger...
...and put them in a stockade.
The environment seems inhabitable...
...but without sensor readings, they don't dare remove their suit in any case.
Suddenly, a roaring sound is heard throughout the village.
TANUKI
Quickly, the village prepares for combat...
...as mysterious steel monsters close in.
In the heat of the battle... the stockade is smashed open!
The steel monsters approach the astronaut.
With a metallic blow, their helmet is knocked away!
The robots retreat...
The astronaut is accepted as one of them. The stranger learns about this village...

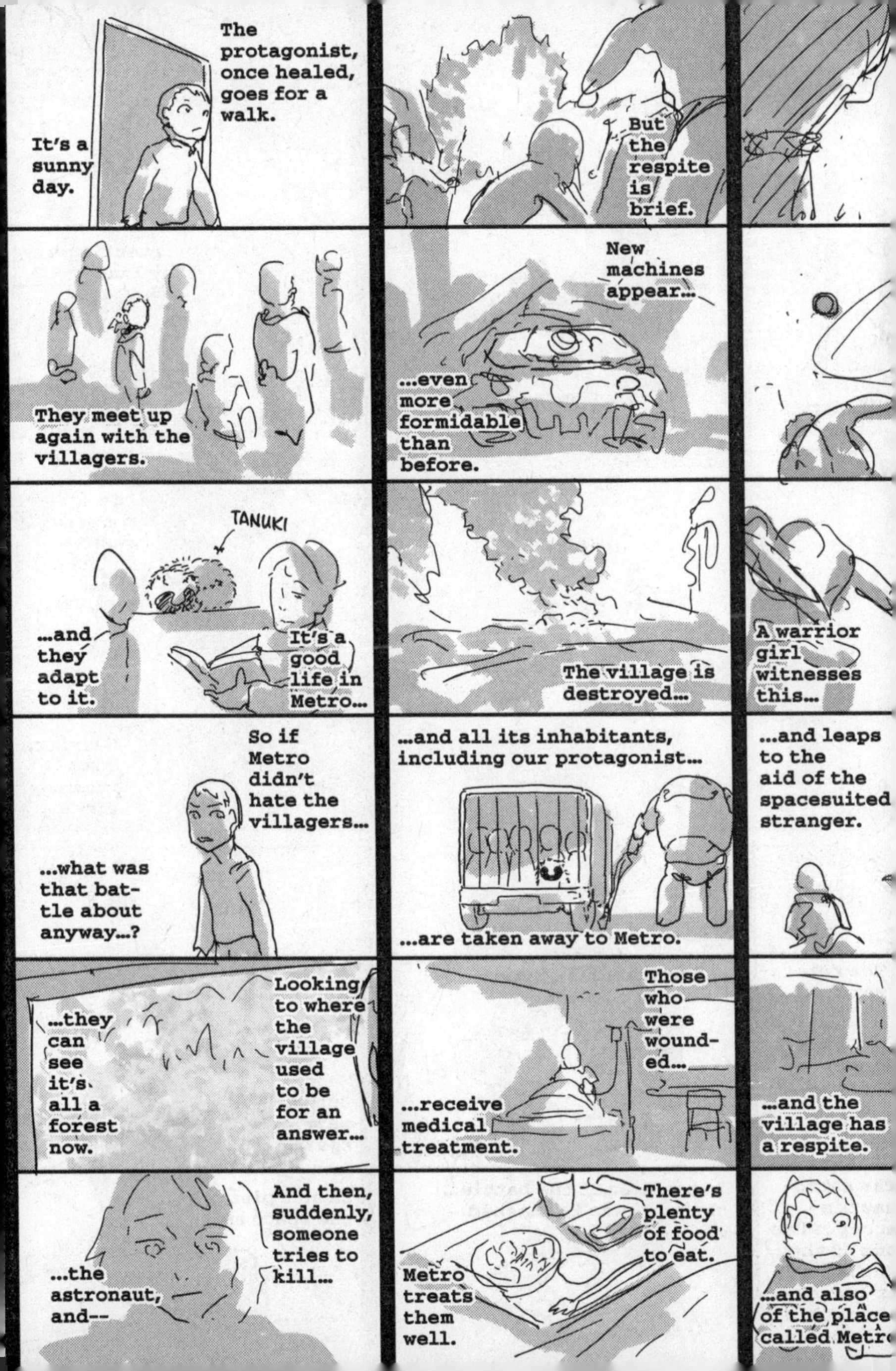
A warrior girl witnesses this...
...and leaps to the aid of the spacesuited stranger.
...and the village has a respite.
...and also of the place called Metr
But the respite is brief.
New machines appear...
...even more formidable than before.
The village is destroyed...
...and all its inhabitants, including our protagonist...
...are taken away to Metro.
Those who were wounded...
...receive medical treatment.
There's plenty of food to eat.
Metro treats them well.
The protagonist, once healed, goes for a walk.
It's a sunny day.
They meet up again with the villagers.
TANUKI
It's a good life in Metro...
...and they adapt to it.
So if Metro didn't hate the villagers...
...what was that battle about anyway...?
Looking to where the village used to be for an answer...
...they can see it's all a forest now.
And then, suddenly, someone tries to kill...
...the astronaut, and--

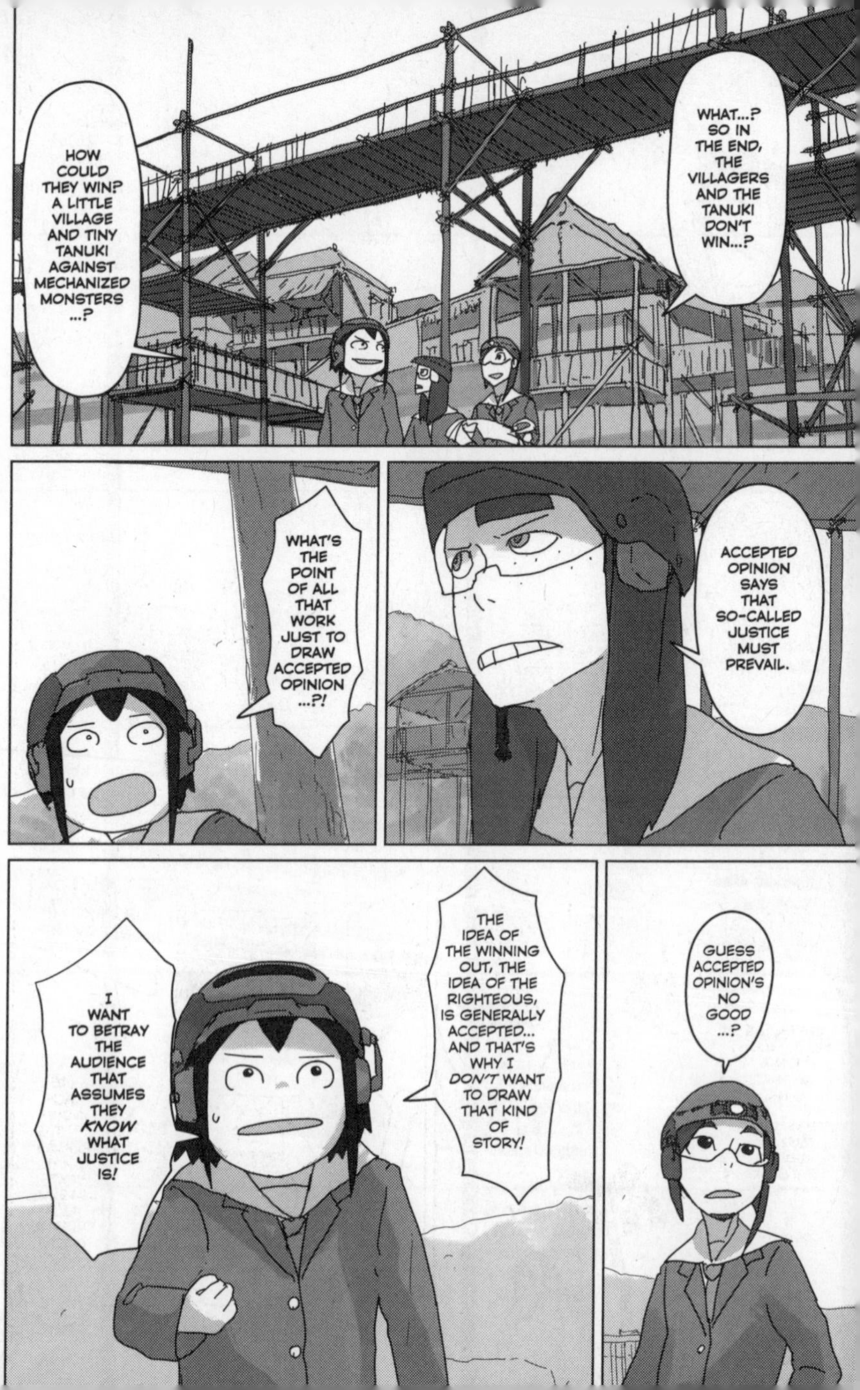
WHAT...? SO IN THE END, THE VILLAGERS AND THE TANUKI DON'T WIN...?
HOW COULD THEY WIN? A LITTLE VILLAGE AND TINY TANUKI AGAINST MECHANIZED MONSTERS ...?
ACCEPTED OPINION SAYS THAT SO-CALLED JUSTICE MUST PREVAIL.
WHAT'S THE POINT OF ALL THAT WORK JUST TO DRAW ACCEPTED OPINION ...?!
GUESS ACCEPTED OPINION'S NO GOOD ...?
THE IDEA OF THE WINNING OUT, THE IDEA OF THE RIGHTEOUS, IS GENERALLY ACCEPTED... AND THAT'S WHY I *DON'T* WANT TO DRAW THAT KIND OF STORY!
I WANT TO BETRAY THE AUDIENCE THAT ASSUMES THEY *KNOW* WHAT JUSTICE IS!

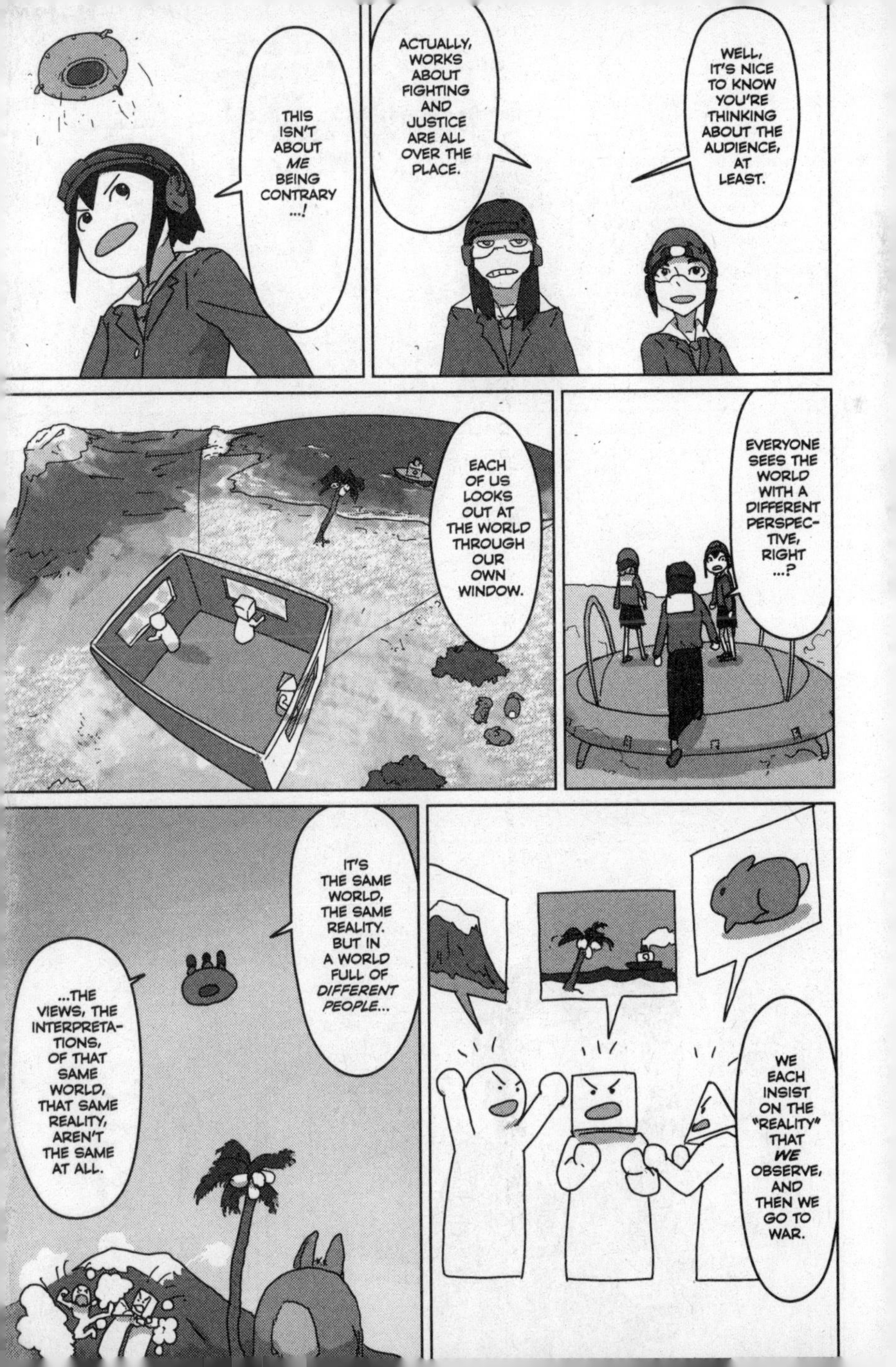
WELL, IT'S NICE TO KNOW YOU'RE THINKING ABOUT THE AUDIENCE, AT LEAST.
ACTUALLY, WORKS ABOUT FIGHTING AND JUSTICE ARE ALL OVER THE PLACE.
THIS ISN'T ABOUT *ME* BEING CONTRARY ...!
EVERYONE SEES THE WORLD WITH A DIFFERENT PERSPECTIVE, RIGHT ...?
EACH OF US LOOKS OUT AT THE WORLD THROUGH OUR OWN WINDOW.
WE EACH INSIST ON THE "REALITY" THAT *WE* OBSERVE, AND THEN WE GO TO WAR.
IT'S THE SAME WORLD, THE SAME REALITY. BUT IN A WORLD FULL OF *DIFFERENT PEOPLE*...
...THE VIEWS, THE INTERPRETATIONS, OF THAT SAME WORLD, THAT SAME REALITY, AREN'T THE SAME AT ALL.

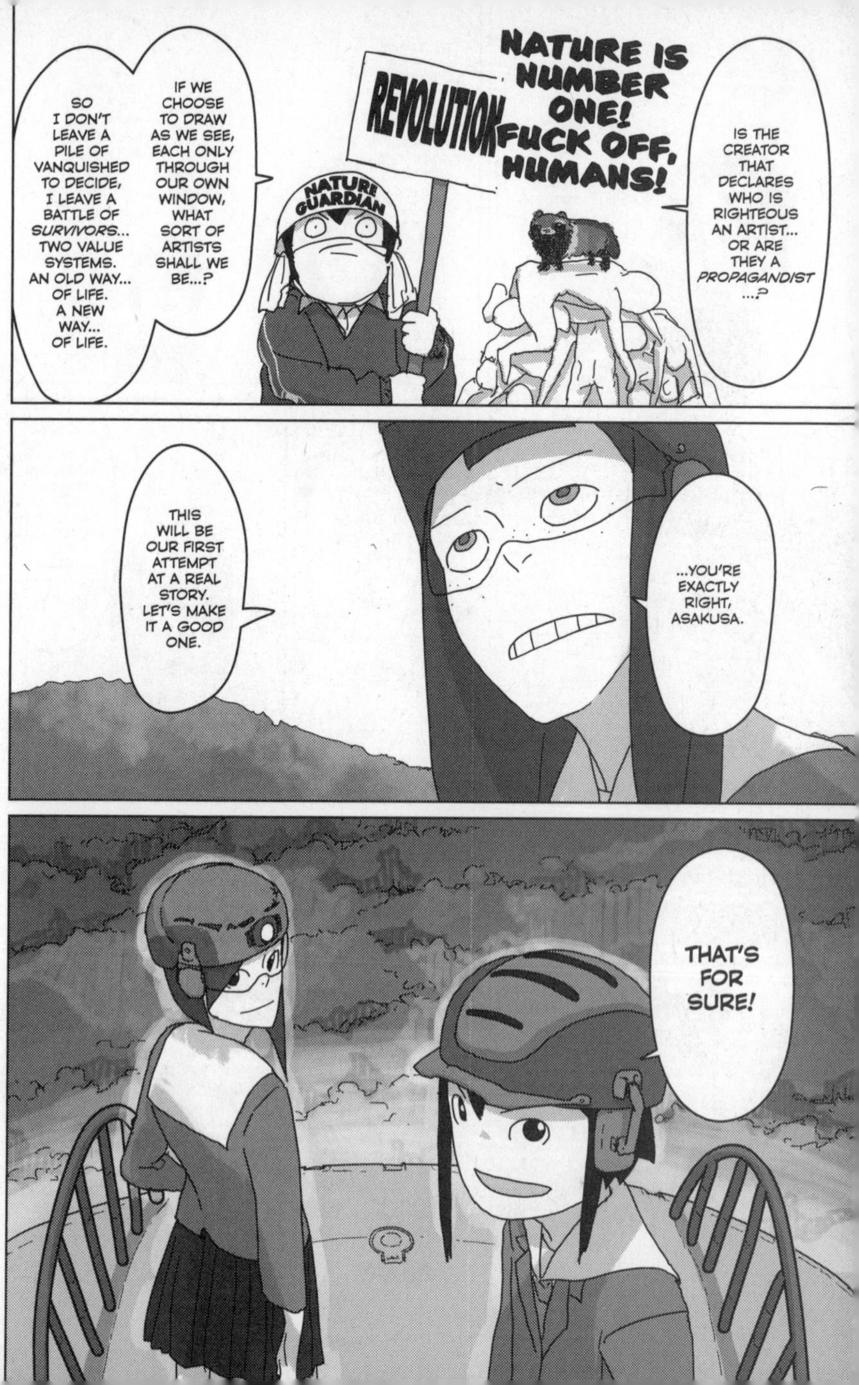
IS THE CREATOR THAT DECLARES WHO IS RIGHTEOUS AN ARTIST... OR ARE THEY A *PROPAGANDIST* ...?
NATURE IS NUMBER ONE! FUCK OFF, HUMANS!
REVOLUTION
NATURE GUARDIAN
IF WE CHOOSE TO DRAW AS WE SEE, EACH ONLY THROUGH OUR OWN WINDOW, WHAT SORT OF ARTISTS SHALL WE BE...?
SO I DON'T LEAVE A PILE OF VANQUISHED TO DECIDE, I LEAVE A BATTLE OF *SURVIVORS*... TWO VALUE SYSTEMS. AN OLD WAY... OF LIFE. A NEW WAY... OF LIFE.
...YOU'RE EXACTLY RIGHT, ASAKUSA.
THIS WILL BE OUR FIRST ATTEMPT AT A REAL STORY. LET'S MAKE IT A GOOD ONE.
THAT'S FOR SURE!

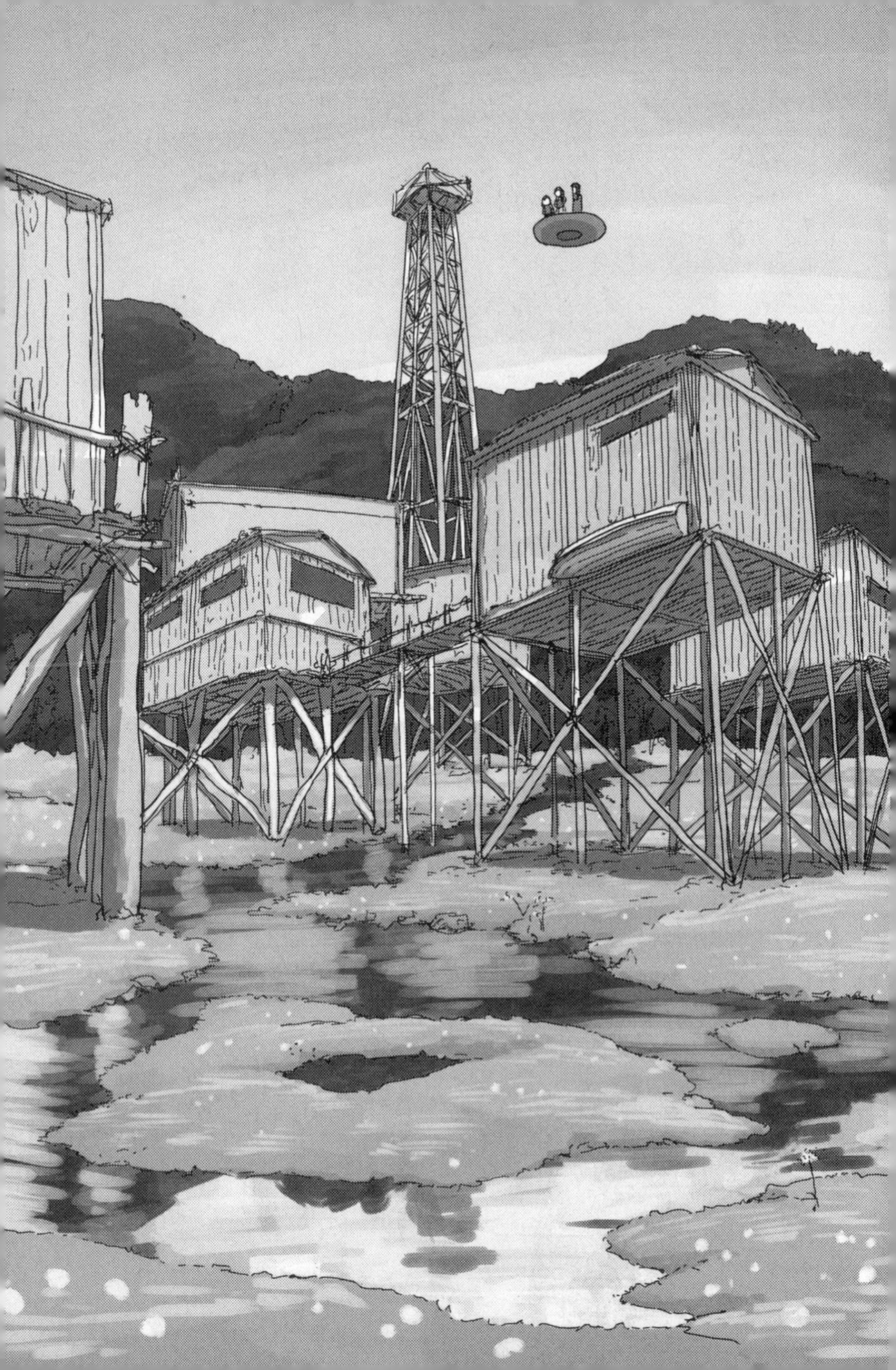

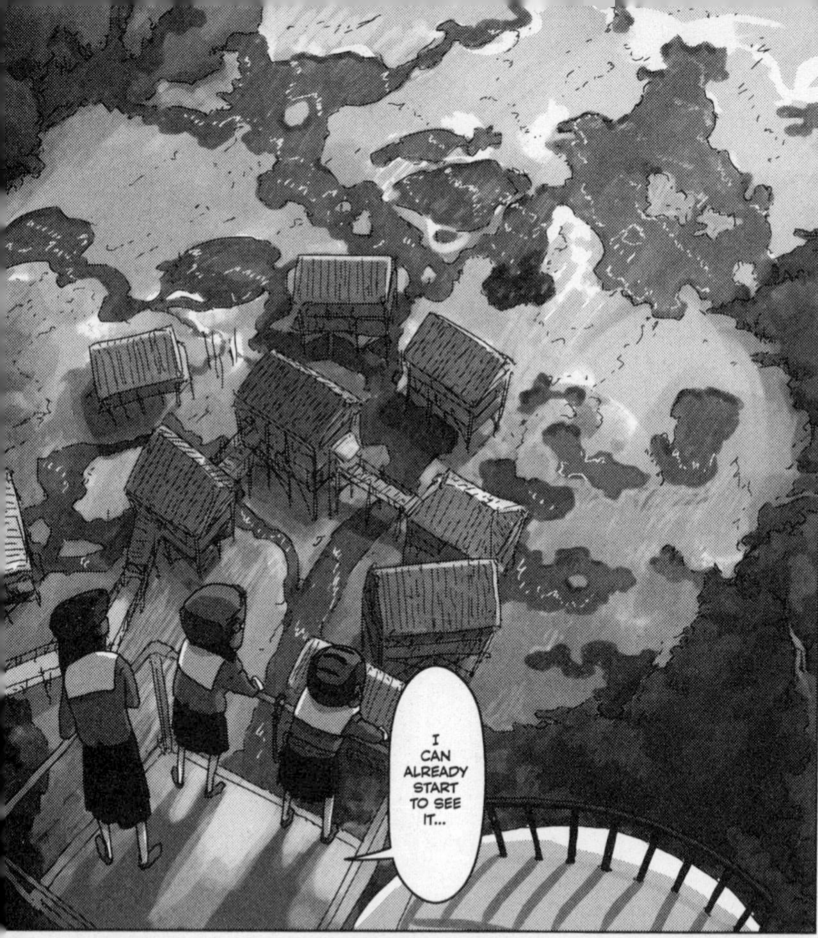
I CAN ALREADY START TO SEE IT...
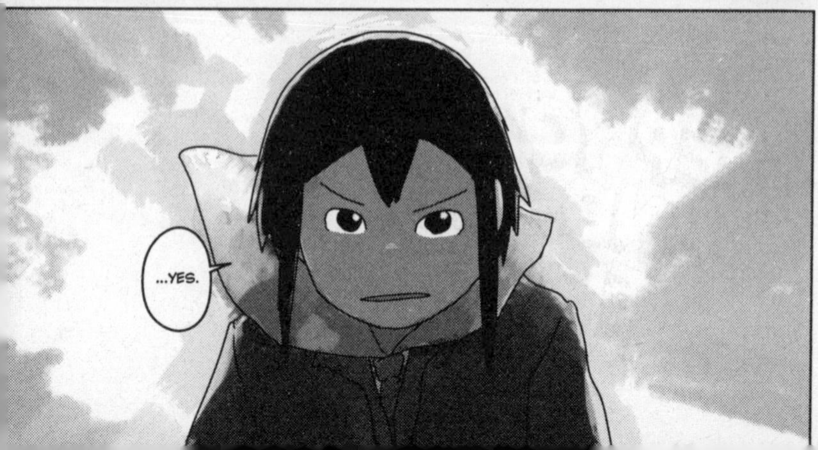
...YES.

KEEP YOUR HANDS OFF EIZOUKEN!

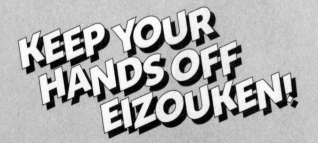

Memo from Mr. Oowara:

If one draws lurid battle scenes in a straightforward fashion, it communicates an unadulterated fear of war, and it can express an antiwar message.

However, if what you want to communicate is not an "antiwar message" but "thrilling combat action," then you have to put some macho soldiers in there and show some vigorous fighting.

Combat is an aspect of war. But if all you portray of war is combat, you're not addressing the underlying history, and questions arise such as "How did this war start, anyway?"

When working on a project with multiple different components like "script" and "footage," fellow travelers may put pressure on each other, and at times the core fundamentals of the project may be shaken.

Hang in there, Asakusa.

CHAPTER 27: BREAKTHROUGH FACE

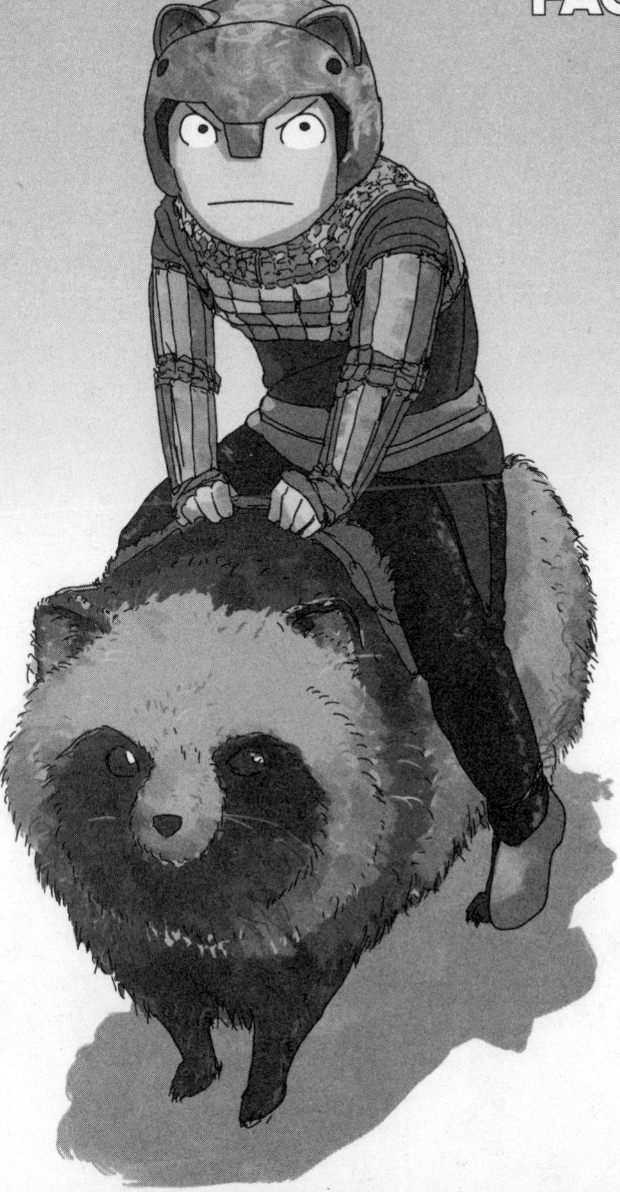

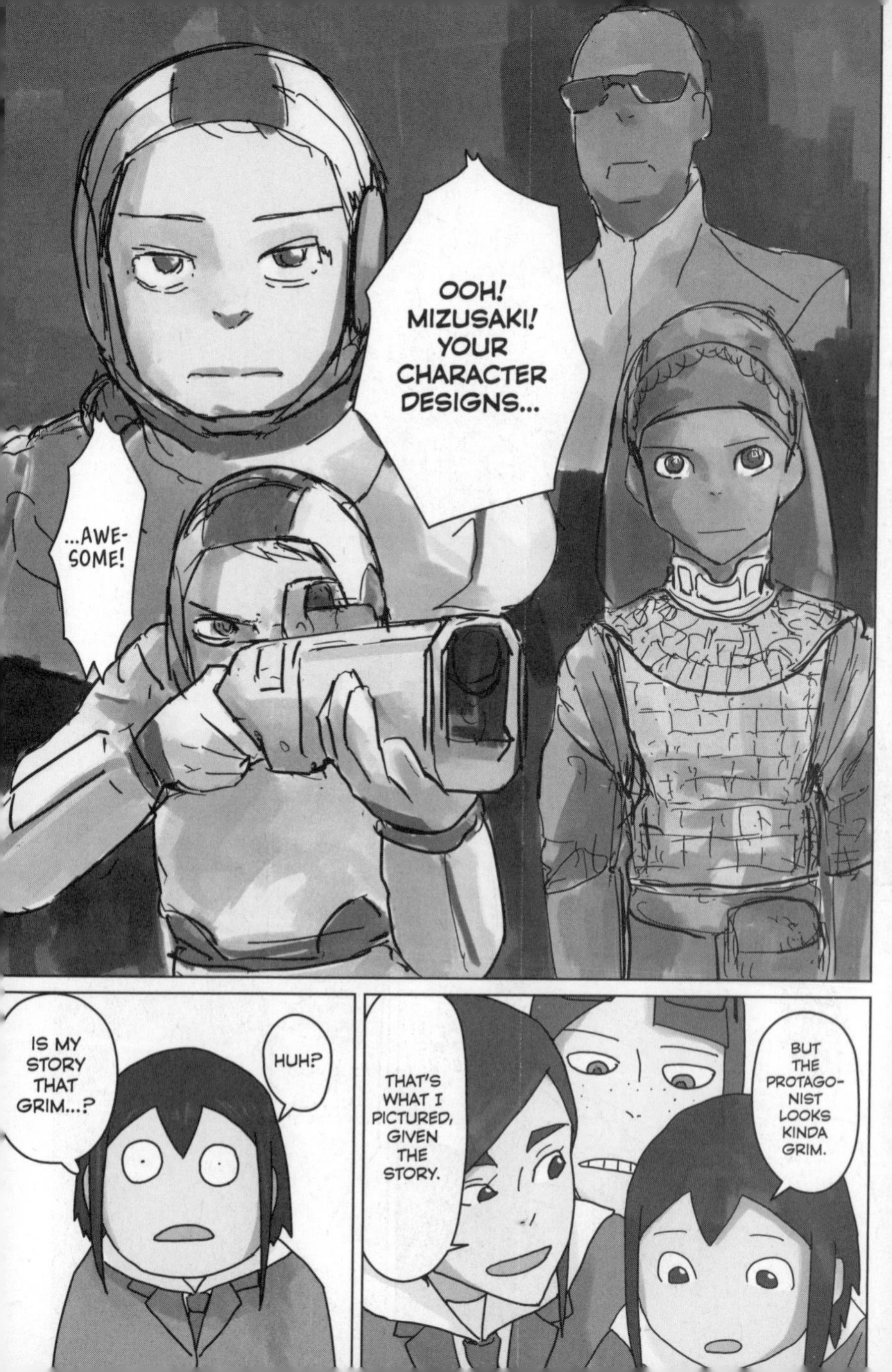
OOH! MIZUSAKI! YOUR CHARACTER DESIGNS...
...AWE-SOME!
BUT THE PROTAGO-NIST LOOKS KINDA GRIM.
THAT'S WHAT I PICTURED, GIVEN THE STORY.
HUH?
IS MY STORY THAT GRIM...?

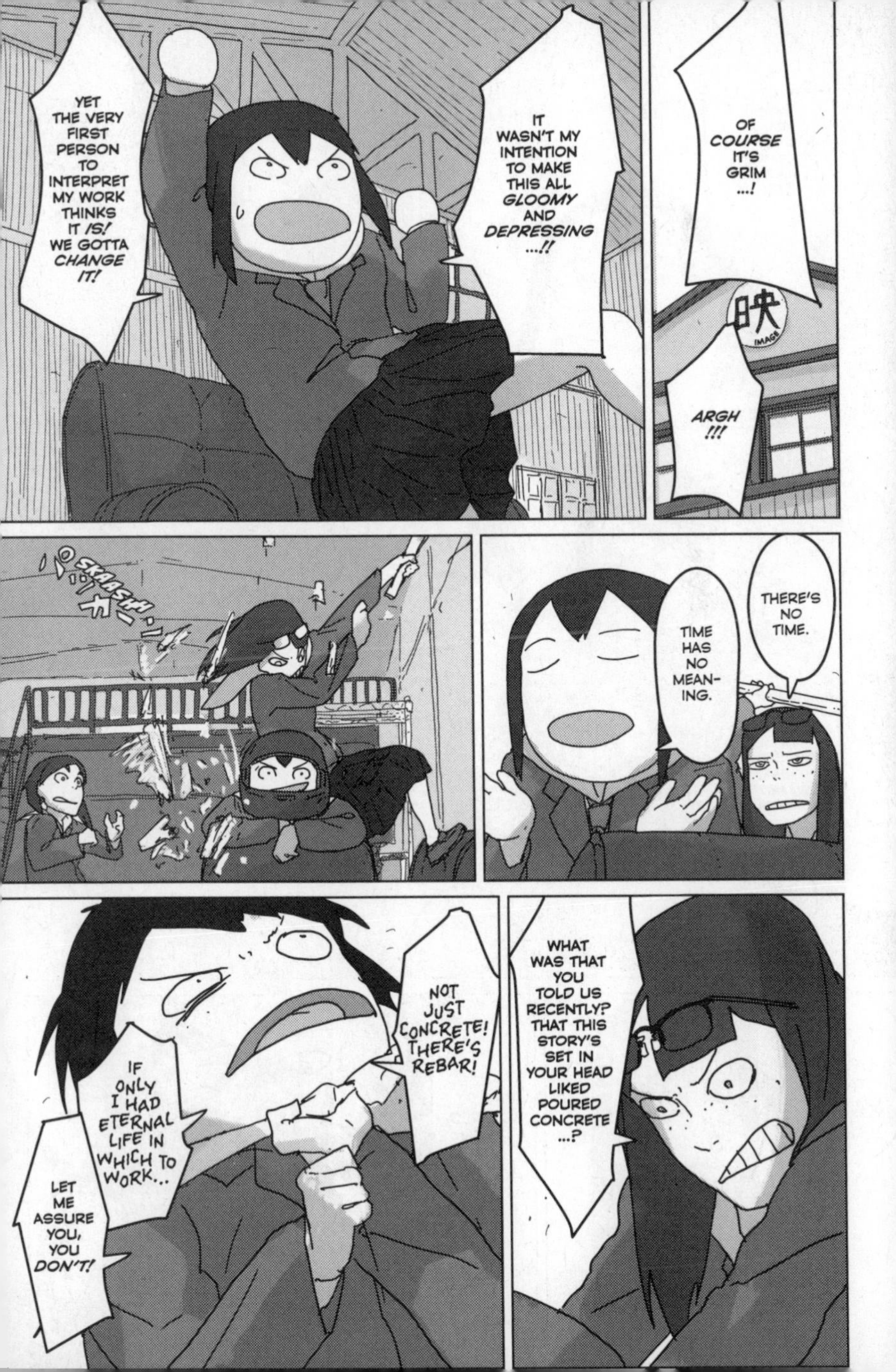
OF *COURSE* IT'S GRIM ...!
映 IMAGE
ARGH *!!!*
IT WASN'T MY INTENTION TO MAKE THIS ALL *GLOOMY* AND *DEPRESSING* ...!!
YET THE VERY FIRST PERSON TO INTERPRET MY WORK THINKS IT *IS!* WE GOTTA *CHANGE IT!*
THERE'S NO TIME.
TIME HAS NO MEAN-ING.
SKAASH
WHAT WAS THAT YOU TOLD US RECENTLY? THAT THIS STORY'S SET IN YOUR HEAD LIKED POURED CONCRETE ...?
NOT JUST CONCRETE! THERE'S REBAR!
IF ONLY I HAD ETERNAL LIFE IN WHICH TO WORK...
LET ME ASSURE YOU, YOU *DON'T!*

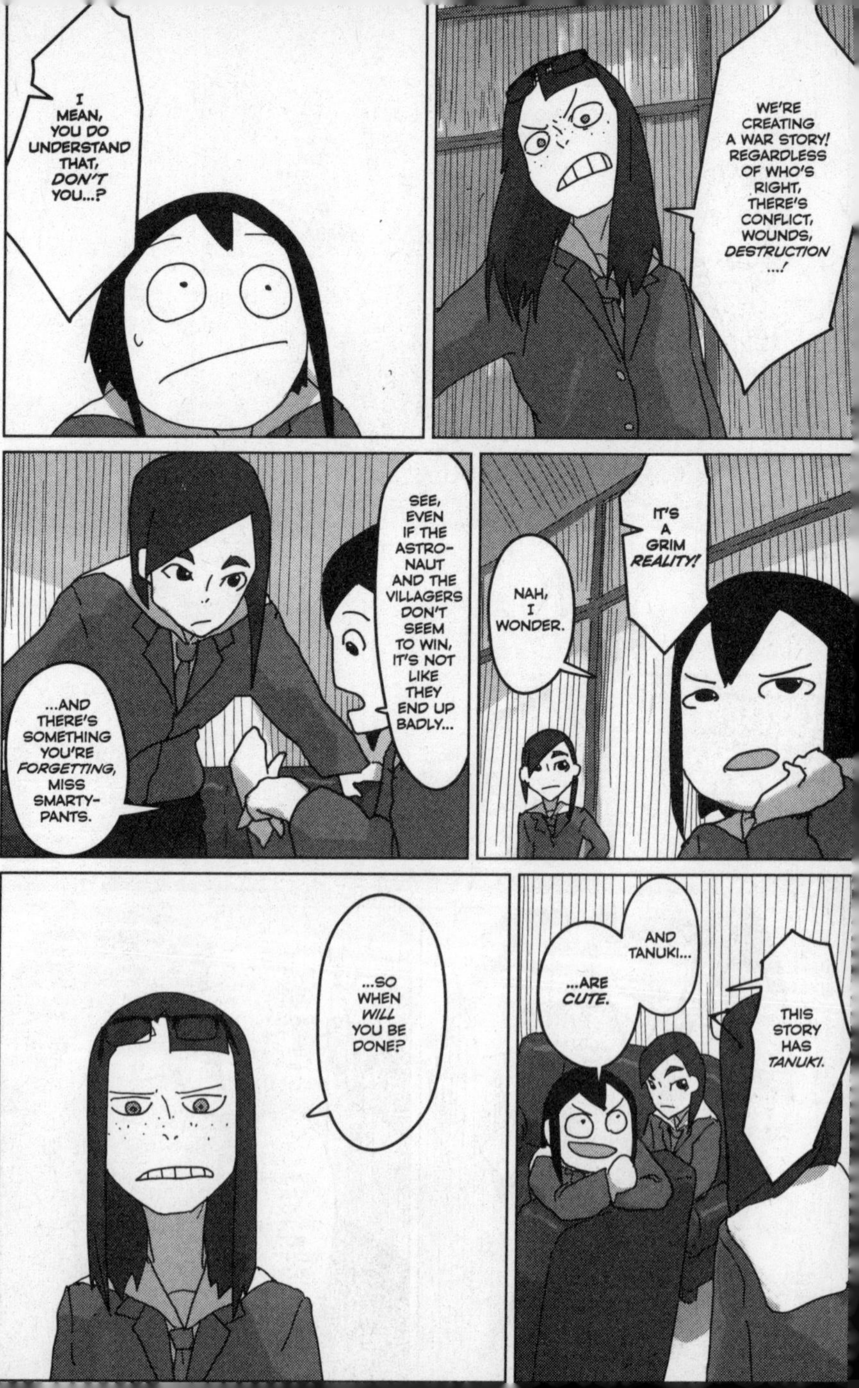
WE'RE CREATING A WAR STORY! REGARDLESS OF WHO'S RIGHT, THERE'S CONFLICT, WOUNDS, *DESTRUCTION* ...!
I MEAN, YOU DO UNDERSTAND THAT, *DON'T* YOU...?
IT'S A GRIM *REALITY!*
NAH, I WONDER.
SEE, EVEN IF THE ASTRONAUT AND THE VILLAGERS DON'T SEEM TO WIN, IT'S NOT LIKE THEY END UP BADLY...
...AND THERE'S SOMETHING YOU'RE *FORGETTING*, MISS SMARTY-PANTS.
THIS STORY HAS *TANUKI*.
AND TANUKI...
...ARE *CUTE*.
...SO WHEN *WILL* YOU BE DONE?

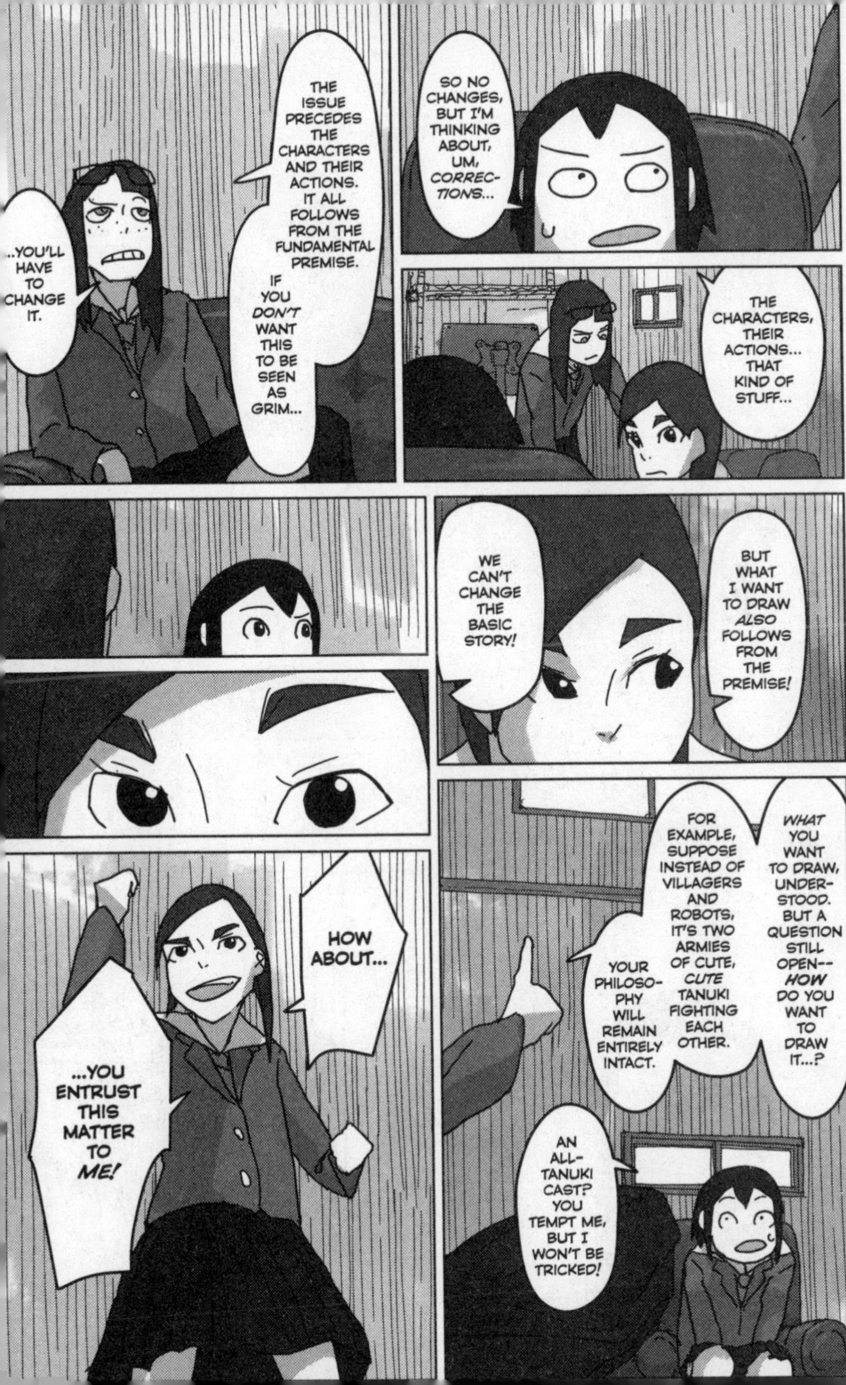
SO NO CHANGES, BUT I'M THINKING ABOUT, UM, *CORRECTIONS*...
THE CHARACTERS, THEIR ACTIONS... THAT KIND OF STUFF...
THE ISSUE PRECEDES THE CHARACTERS AND THEIR ACTIONS. IT ALL FOLLOWS FROM THE FUNDAMENTAL PREMISE.
IF YOU *DON'T* WANT THIS TO BE SEEN AS GRIM...
...YOU'LL HAVE TO CHANGE IT.
BUT WHAT I WANT TO DRAW *ALSO* FOLLOWS FROM THE PREMISE!
WE CAN'T CHANGE THE BASIC STORY!
WHAT YOU WANT TO DRAW, UNDERSTOOD. BUT A QUESTION STILL OPEN-- *HOW* DO YOU WANT TO DRAW IT...?
FOR EXAMPLE, SUPPOSE INSTEAD OF VILLAGERS AND ROBOTS, IT'S TWO ARMIES OF CUTE, *CUTE* TANUKI FIGHTING EACH OTHER.
YOUR PHILOSOPHY WILL REMAIN ENTIRELY INTACT.
AN ALL-TANUKI CAST? YOU TEMPT ME, BUT I WON'T BE TRICKED!
HOW ABOUT...
...YOU ENTRUST THIS MATTER TO *ME!*

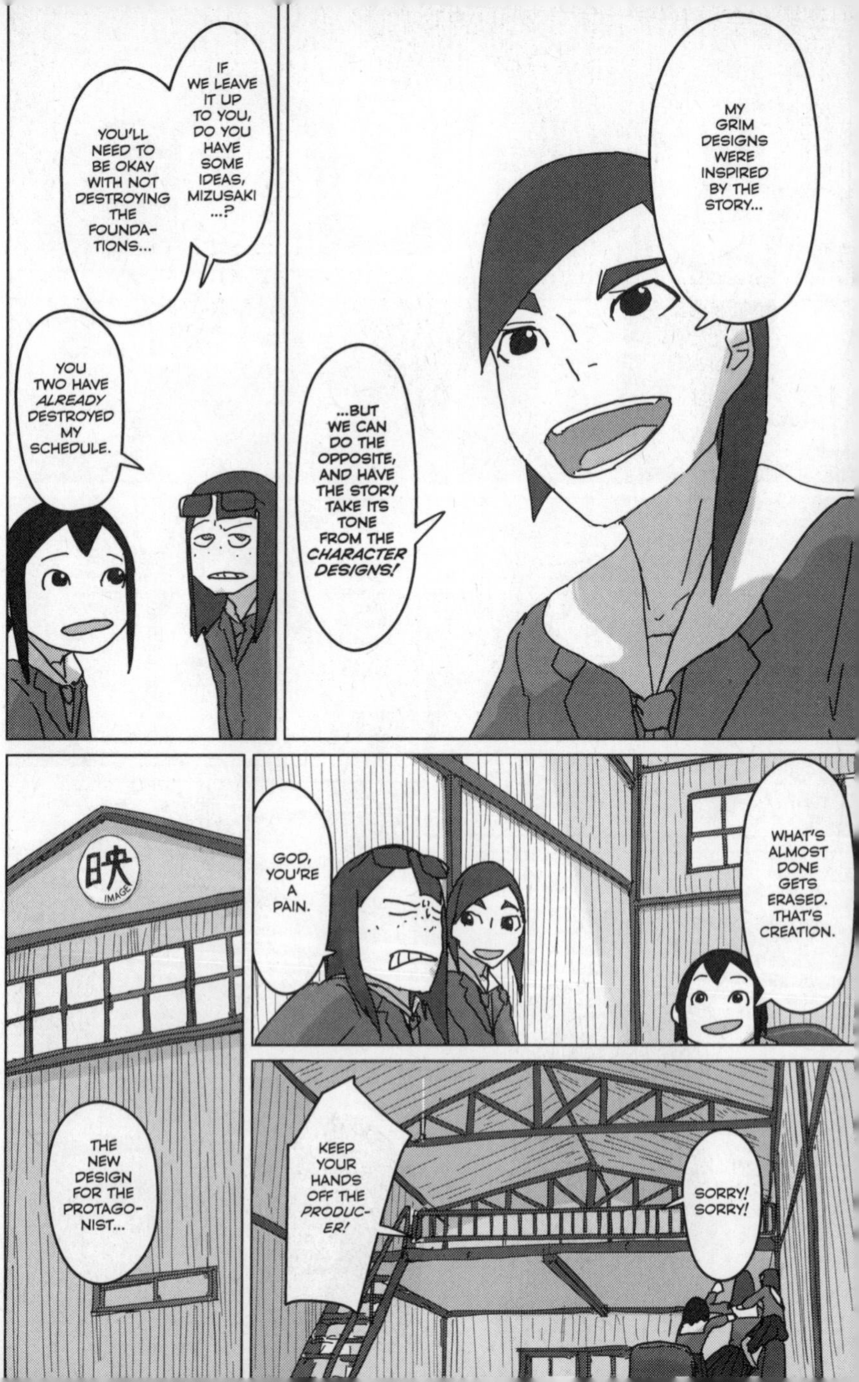
MY GRIM DESIGNS WERE INSPIRED BY THE STORY...
...BUT WE CAN DO THE OPPOSITE, AND HAVE THE STORY TAKE ITS TONE FROM THE *CHARACTER DESIGNS!*
IF WE LEAVE IT UP TO YOU, DO YOU HAVE SOME IDEAS, MIZUSAKI ...?
YOU'LL NEED TO BE OKAY WITH NOT DESTROYING THE FOUNDATIONS...
YOU TWO HAVE *ALREADY* DESTROYED MY SCHEDULE.
WHAT'S ALMOST DONE GETS ERASED. THAT'S CREATION.
GOD, YOU'RE A PAIN.
SORRY! SORRY!
KEEP YOUR HANDS OFF THE *PRODUCER!*
映
IMAGE
THE NEW DESIGN FOR THE PROTAGONIST...

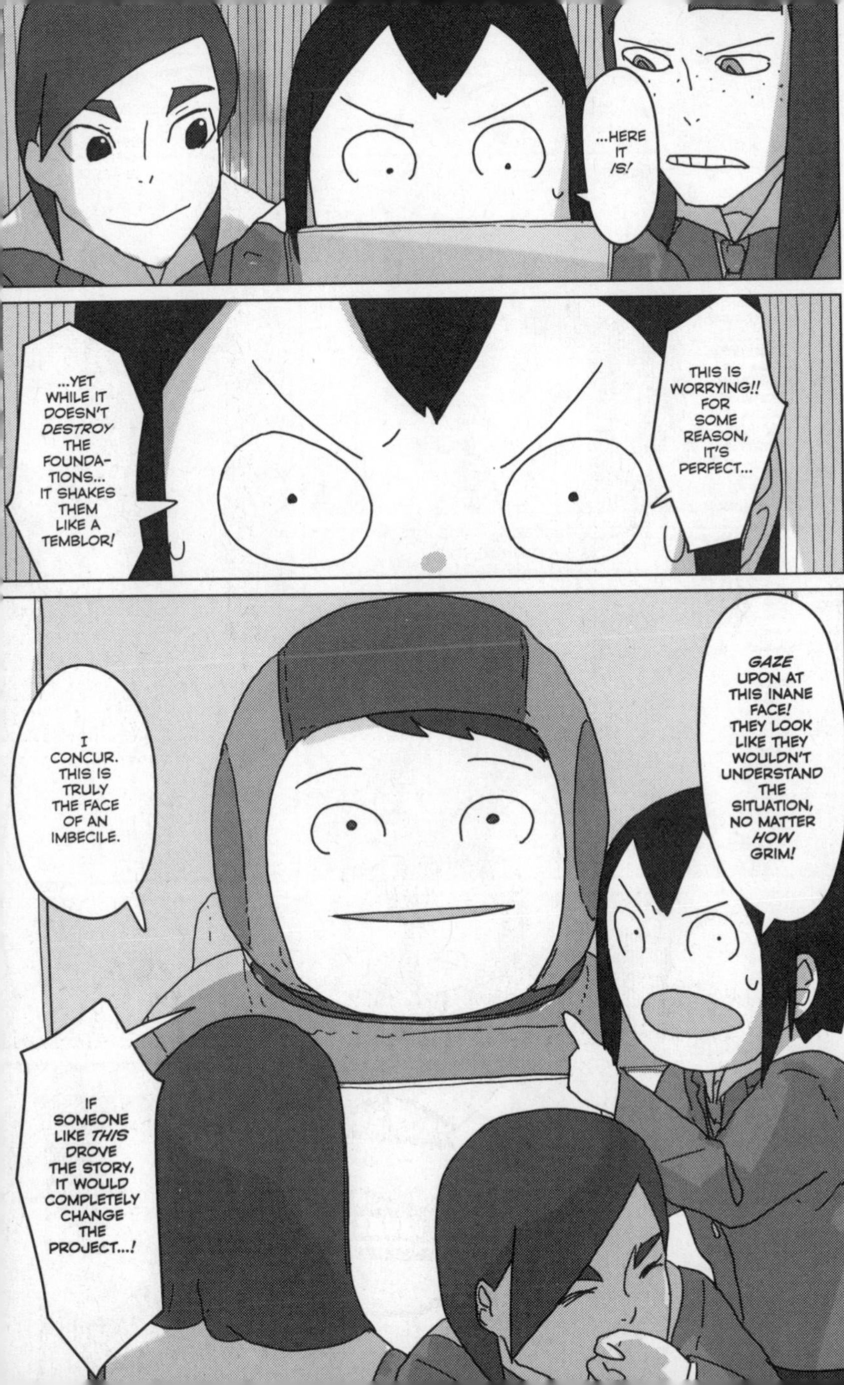
...HERE IT *IS!*
THIS IS WORRYING!! FOR SOME REASON, IT'S PERFECT...
...YET WHILE IT DOESN'T *DESTROY* THE FOUNDA-TIONS... IT SHAKES THEM LIKE A TEMBLOR!
GAZE UPON AT THIS INANE FACE! THEY LOOK LIKE THEY WOULDN'T UNDERSTAND THE SITUATION, NO MATTER *HOW* GRIM!
I CONCUR. THIS IS TRULY THE FACE OF AN IMBECILE.
IF SOMEONE LIKE *THIS* DROVE THE STORY, IT WOULD COMPLETELY CHANGE THE PROJECT...!

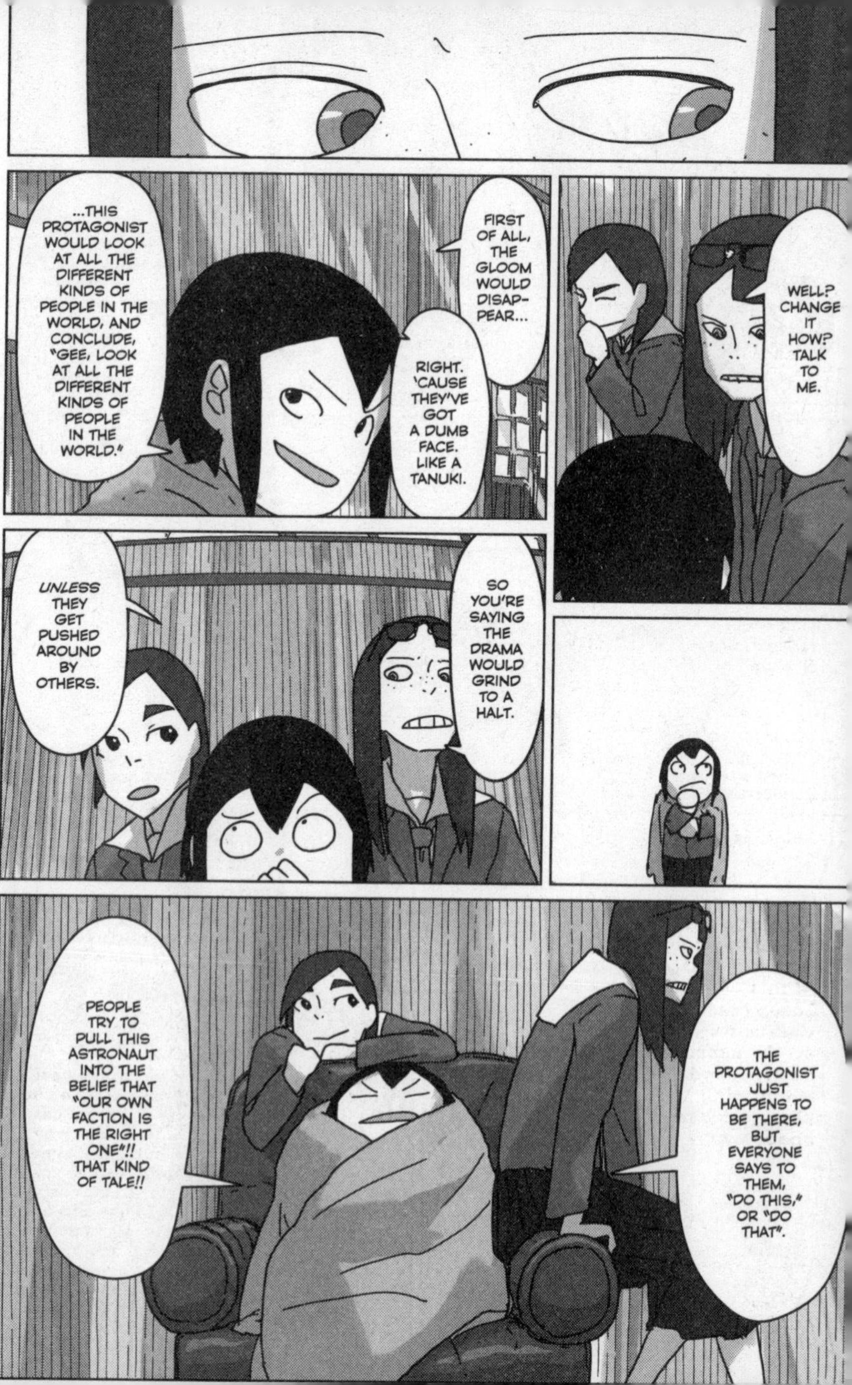
WELL? CHANGE IT HOW? TALK TO ME.
FIRST OF ALL, THE GLOOM WOULD DISAPPEAR...
...THIS PROTAGONIST WOULD LOOK AT ALL THE DIFFERENT KINDS OF PEOPLE IN THE WORLD, AND CONCLUDE, "GEE, LOOK AT ALL THE DIFFERENT KINDS OF PEOPLE IN THE WORLD."
RIGHT. 'CAUSE THEY'VE GOT A DUMB FACE. LIKE A TANUKI.
SO YOU'RE SAYING THE DRAMA WOULD GRIND TO A HALT.
UNLESS THEY GET PUSHED AROUND BY OTHERS.
THE PROTAGONIST JUST HAPPENS TO BE THERE, BUT EVERYONE SAYS TO THEM, "DO THIS," OR "DO THAT".
PEOPLE TRY TO PULL THIS ASTRONAUT INTO THE BELIEF THAT "OUR OWN FACTION IS THE RIGHT ONE"!! THAT KIND OF TALE!!

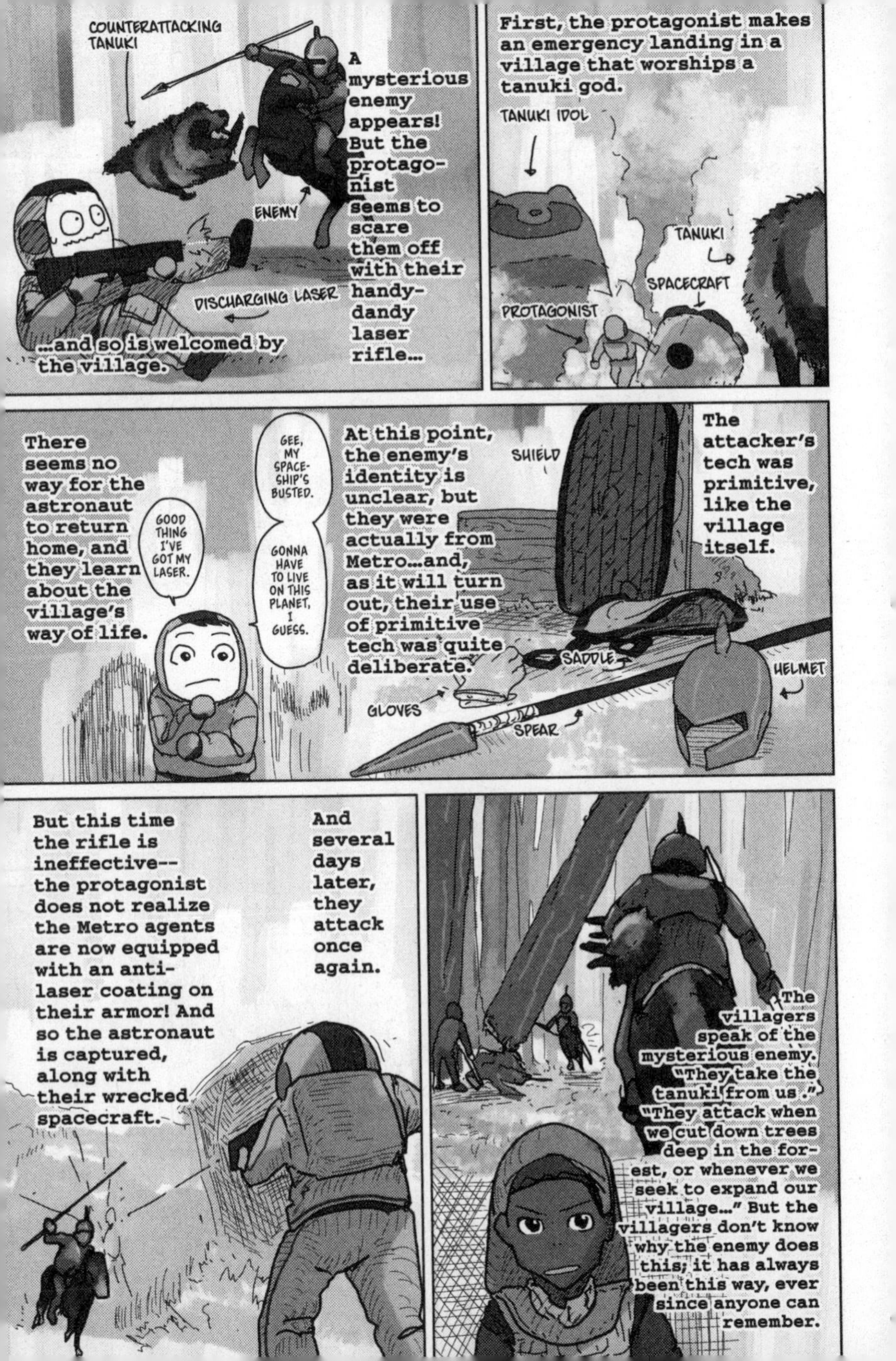
First, the protagonist makes an emergency landing in a village that worships a tanuki god.
TANUKI IDOL
TANUKI
SPACECRAFT
PROTAGONIST
A mysterious enemy appears! But the protago-nist seems to scare them off with their handy-dandy laser rifle...
COUNTERATTACKING TANUKI
ENEMY
DISCHARGING LASER
...and so is welcomed by the village.
The attacker's tech was primitive, like the village itself.
SHIELD
SADDLE
HELMET
SPEAR
GLOVES
At this point, the enemy's identity is unclear, but they were actually from Metro...and, as it will turn out, their use of primitive tech was quite deliberate.
GEE, MY SPACE-SHIP'S BUSTED.
GONNA HAVE TO LIVE ON THIS PLANET, I GUESS.
GOOD THING I'VE GOT MY LASER.
There seems no way for the astronaut to return home, and they learn about the village's way of life.
The villagers speak of the mysterious enemy. "They take the tanuki from us." "They attack when we cut down trees deep in the for-est, or whenever we seek to expand our village..." But the villagers don't know why the enemy does this; it has always been this way, ever since anyone can remember.
And several days later, they attack once again.
But this time the rifle is ineffective--the protagonist does not realize the Metro agents are now equipped with an anti-laser coating on their armor! And so the astronaut is captured, along with their wrecked spacecraft.

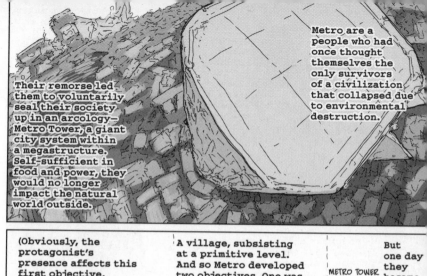

Metro are a people who had once thought themselves the only survivors of a civilization that collapsed due to environmental destruction.
Their remorse led them to voluntarily seal their society up in an arcology—Metro Tower, a giant city system within a megastructure. Self-sufficient in food and power, they would no longer impact the natural world outside.
But one day they became aware that another group had survived.
METRO TOWER
ALL METRONIANS LIVE HERE!
A village, subsisting at a primitive level. And so Metro developed two objectives. One was to protect this precious remnant and preserve its lifestyle...
THE VILLAGE AND METRO ARE SEPARATED BY MOUNTAINS
(Obviously, the protagonist's presence affects this first objective, as they, like Metro, represent a technological civilization, even if the astronaut is a bit of a dope).
VILLAGE
WETLAND
...but the other was to keep the village from altering the natural environment. That included logging the forests, expanding the village, and domesticating tanuki instead of letting them run wild.
Metro thought they could defuse the threat posed by the astronaut... their technology could repair their spaceship, and let them leave this world.
BEING SERVICED

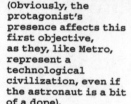

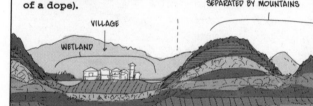

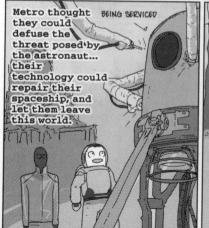

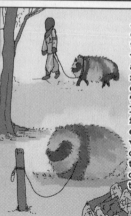

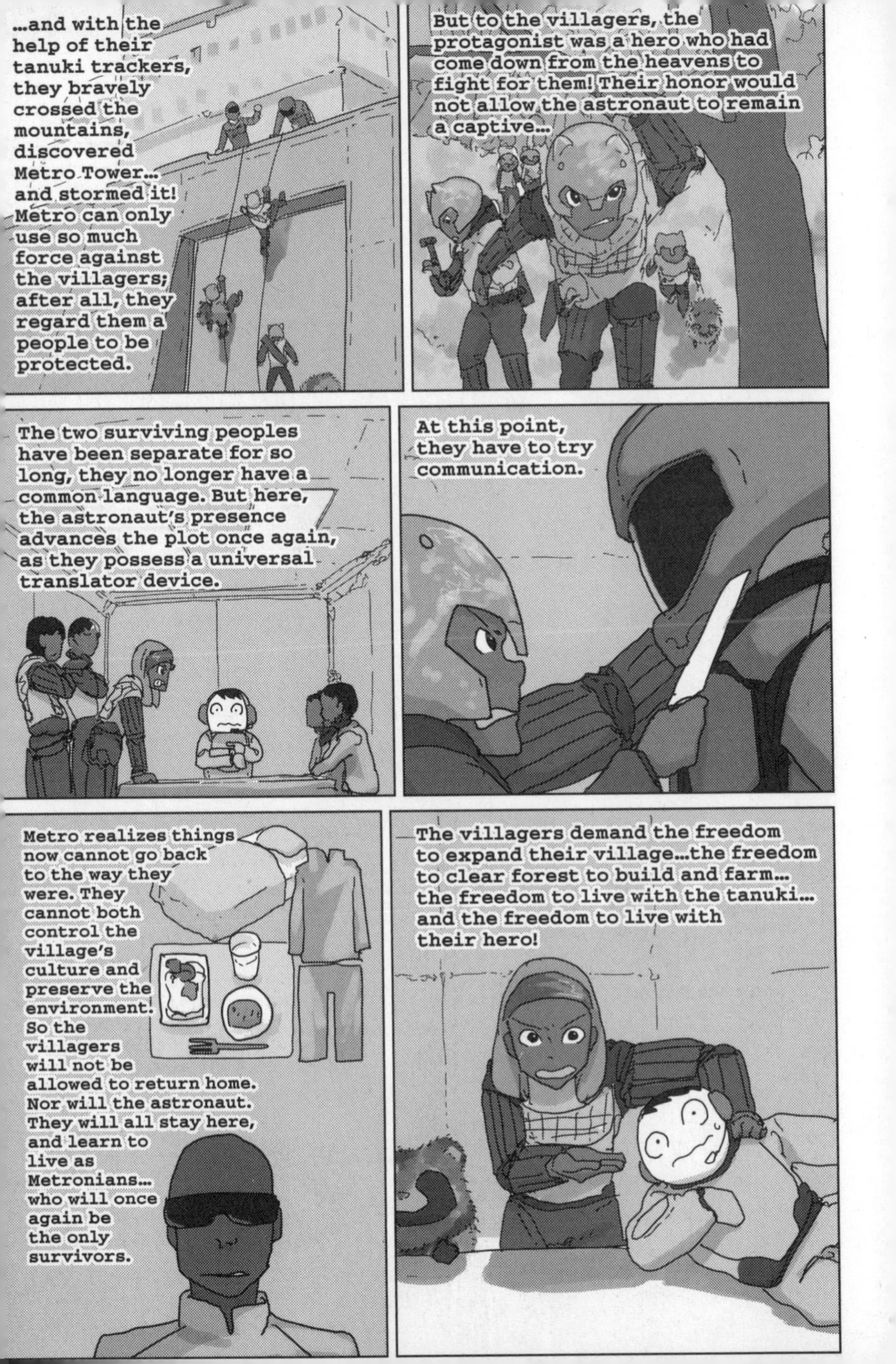
But to the villagers, the protagonist was a hero who had come down from the heavens to fight for them! Their honor would not allow the astronaut to remain a captive...
...and with the help of their tanuki trackers, they bravely crossed the mountains, discovered Metro Tower... and stormed it! Metro can only use so much force against the villagers; after all, they regard them a people to be protected.
At this point, they have to try communication.
The two surviving peoples have been separate for so long, they no longer have a common language. But here, the astronaut's presence advances the plot once again, as they possess a universal translator device.
The villagers demand the freedom to expand their village...the freedom to clear forest to build and farm... the freedom to live with the tanuki... and the freedom to live with their hero!
Metro realizes things now cannot go back to the way they were. They cannot both control the village's culture and preserve the environment. So the villagers will not be allowed to return home. Nor will the astronaut. They will all stay here, and learn to live as Metronians... who will once again be the only survivors.

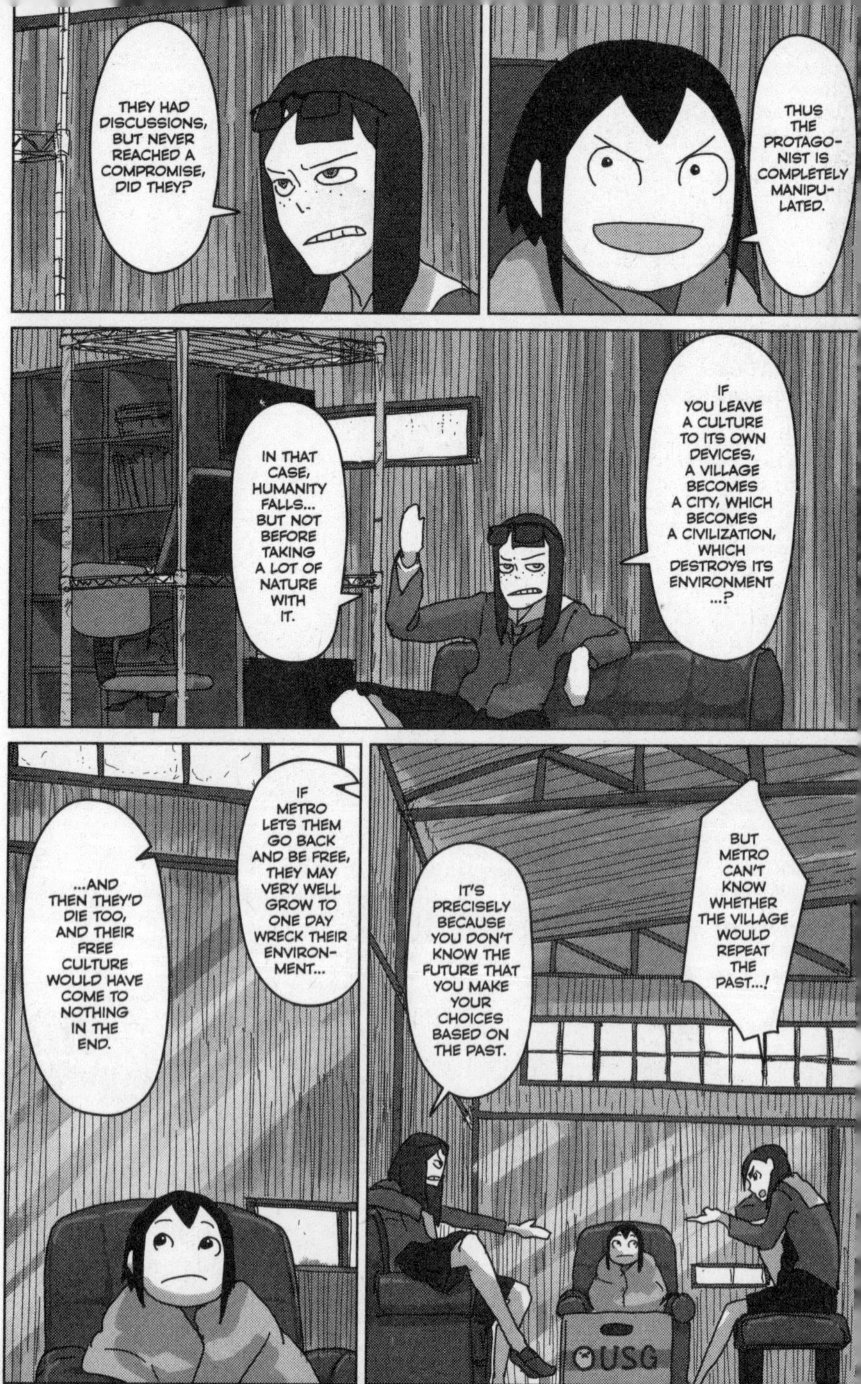
THUS THE PROTAGONIST IS COMPLETELY MANIPULATED.
THEY HAD DISCUSSIONS, BUT NEVER REACHED A COMPROMISE, DID THEY?
IF YOU LEAVE A CULTURE TO ITS OWN DEVICES, A VILLAGE BECOMES A CITY, WHICH BECOMES A CIVILIZATION, WHICH DESTROYS ITS ENVIRONMENT ...?
IN THAT CASE, HUMANITY FALLS... BUT NOT BEFORE TAKING A LOT OF NATURE WITH IT.
BUT METRO CAN'T KNOW WHETHER THE VILLAGE WOULD REPEAT THE PAST...!
IT'S PRECISELY BECAUSE YOU DON'T KNOW THE FUTURE THAT YOU MAKE YOUR CHOICES BASED ON THE PAST.
OUSG
IF METRO LETS THEM GO BACK AND BE FREE, THEY MAY VERY WELL GROW TO ONE DAY WRECK THEIR ENVIRONMENT...
...AND THEN THEY'D DIE TOO, AND THEIR FREE CULTURE WOULD HAVE COME TO NOTHING IN THE END.

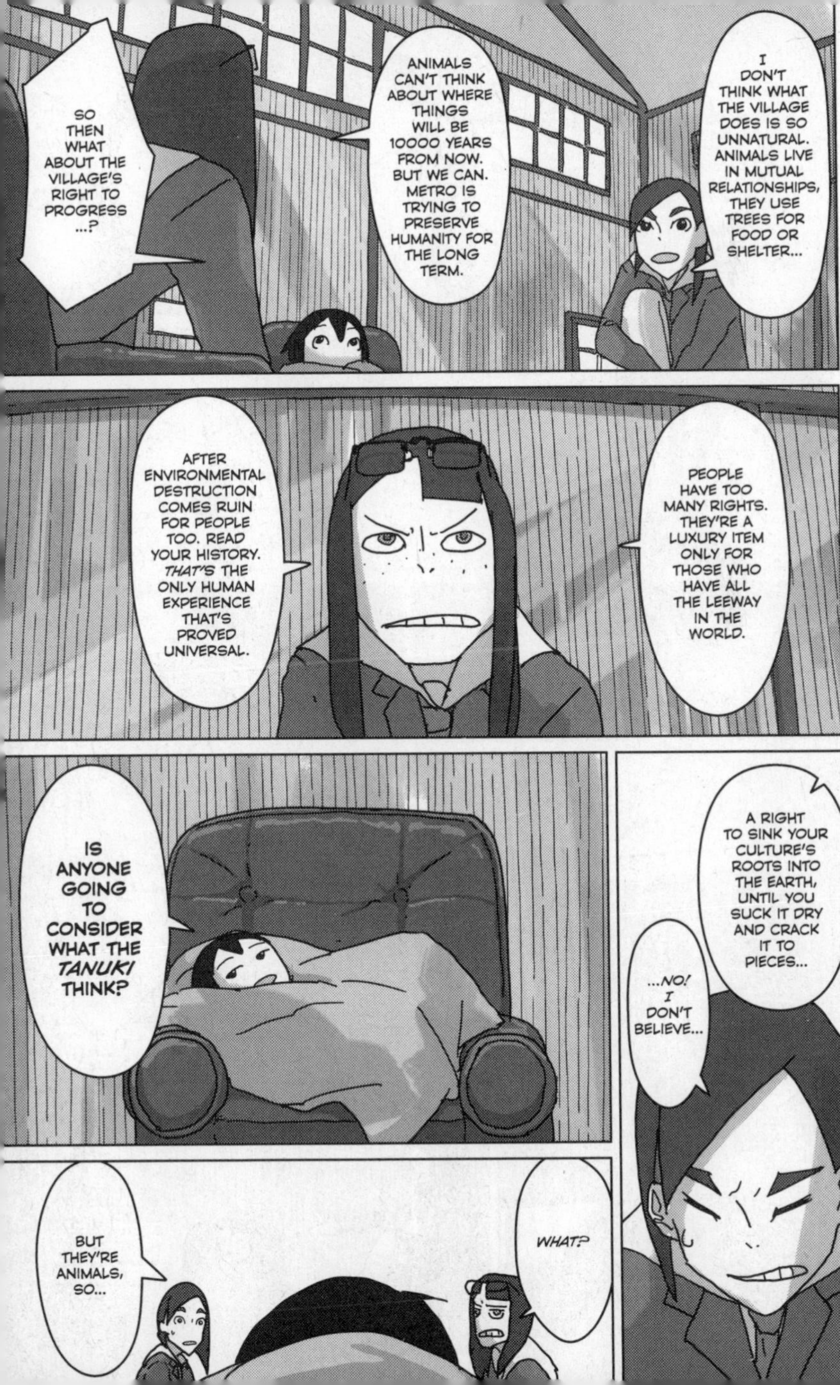
I DON'T THINK WHAT THE VILLAGE DOES IS SO UNNATURAL. ANIMALS LIVE IN MUTUAL RELATIONSHIPS, THEY USE TREES FOR FOOD OR SHELTER...
ANIMALS CAN'T THINK ABOUT WHERE THINGS WILL BE 10000 YEARS FROM NOW. BUT WE CAN. METRO IS TRYING TO PRESERVE HUMANITY FOR THE LONG TERM.
SO THEN WHAT ABOUT THE VILLAGE'S RIGHT TO PROGRESS ...?
PEOPLE HAVE TOO MANY RIGHTS. THEY'RE A LUXURY ITEM ONLY FOR THOSE WHO HAVE ALL THE LEEWAY IN THE WORLD.
AFTER ENVIRONMENTAL DESTRUCTION COMES RUIN FOR PEOPLE TOO. READ YOUR HISTORY. *THAT'S* THE ONLY HUMAN EXPERIENCE THAT'S PROVED UNIVERSAL.
A RIGHT TO SINK YOUR CULTURE'S ROOTS INTO THE EARTH, UNTIL YOU SUCK IT DRY AND CRACK IT TO PIECES...
...*NO! I* DON'T BELIEVE...
IS ANYONE GOING TO CONSIDER WHAT THE *TANUKI* THINK?
WHAT?
BUT THEY'RE ANIMALS, SO...

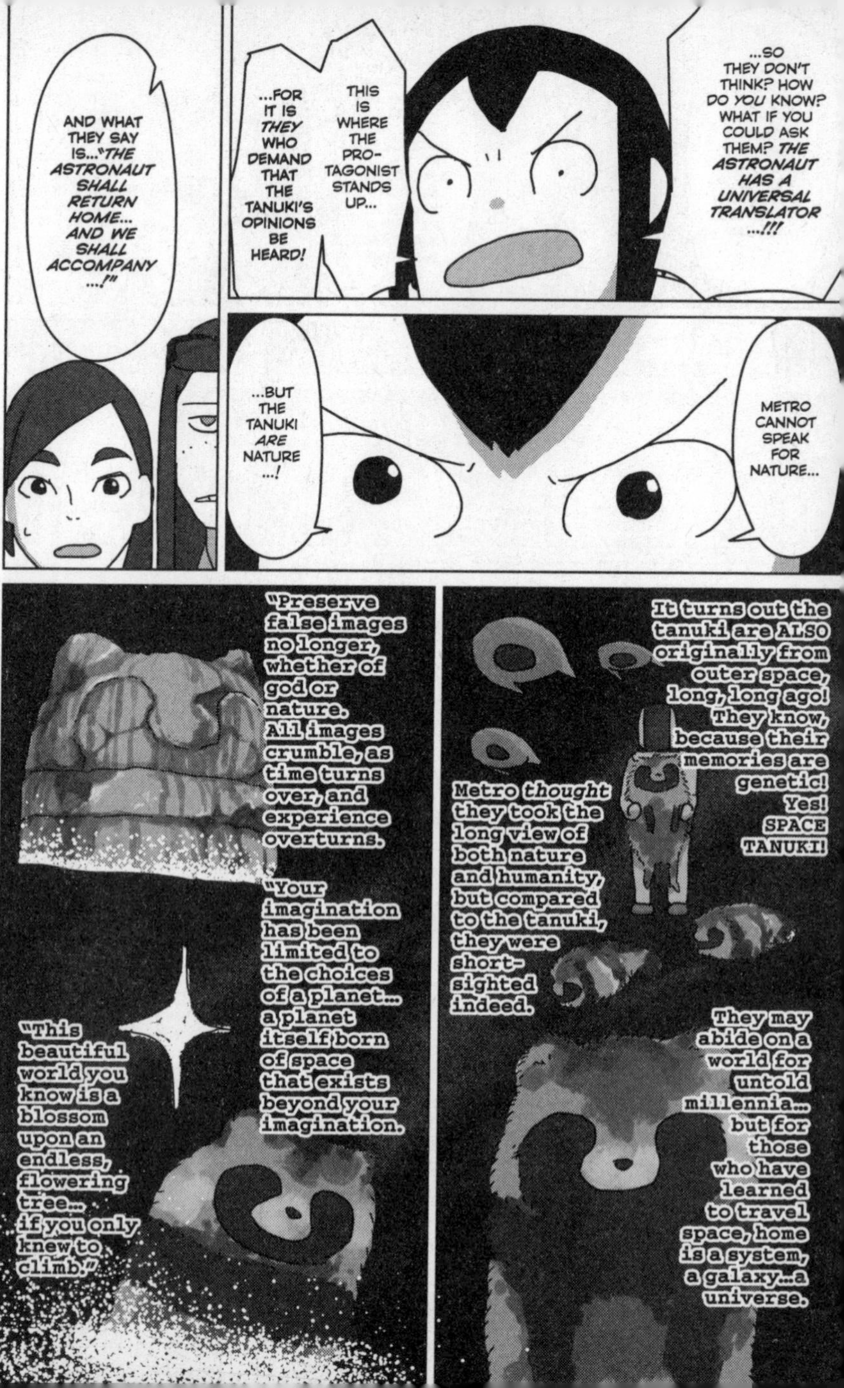
...SO THEY DON'T THINK? HOW DO *YOU* KNOW? WHAT IF YOU COULD ASK THEM? *THE ASTRONAUT HAS A UNIVERSAL TRANSLATOR* ...!!!
THIS IS WHERE THE PROTAGONIST STANDS UP...
...FOR IT IS *THEY* WHO DEMAND THAT THE TANUKI'S OPINIONS BE HEARD!
METRO CANNOT SPEAK FOR NATURE...
...BUT THE TANUKI *ARE* NATURE ...!
AND WHAT THEY SAY IS..."*THE ASTRONAUT SHALL RETURN HOME... AND WE SHALL ACCOMPANY* ...!"
It turns out the tanuki are ALSO originally from outer space, long, long ago! They know, because their memories are genetic! Yes! SPACE TANUKI!
Metro *thought* they took the long view of both nature and humanity, but compared to the tanuki, they were short-sighted indeed.
They may abide on a world for untold millennia... but for those who have learned to travel space, home is a system, a galaxy...a universe.
"Preserve false images no longer, whether of god or nature. All images crumble, as time turns over, and experience overturns.
"Your imagination has been limited to the choices of a planet... a planet itself born of space that exists beyond your imagination.
"This beautiful world you know is a blossom upon an endless, flowering tree... if you only knew to climb."

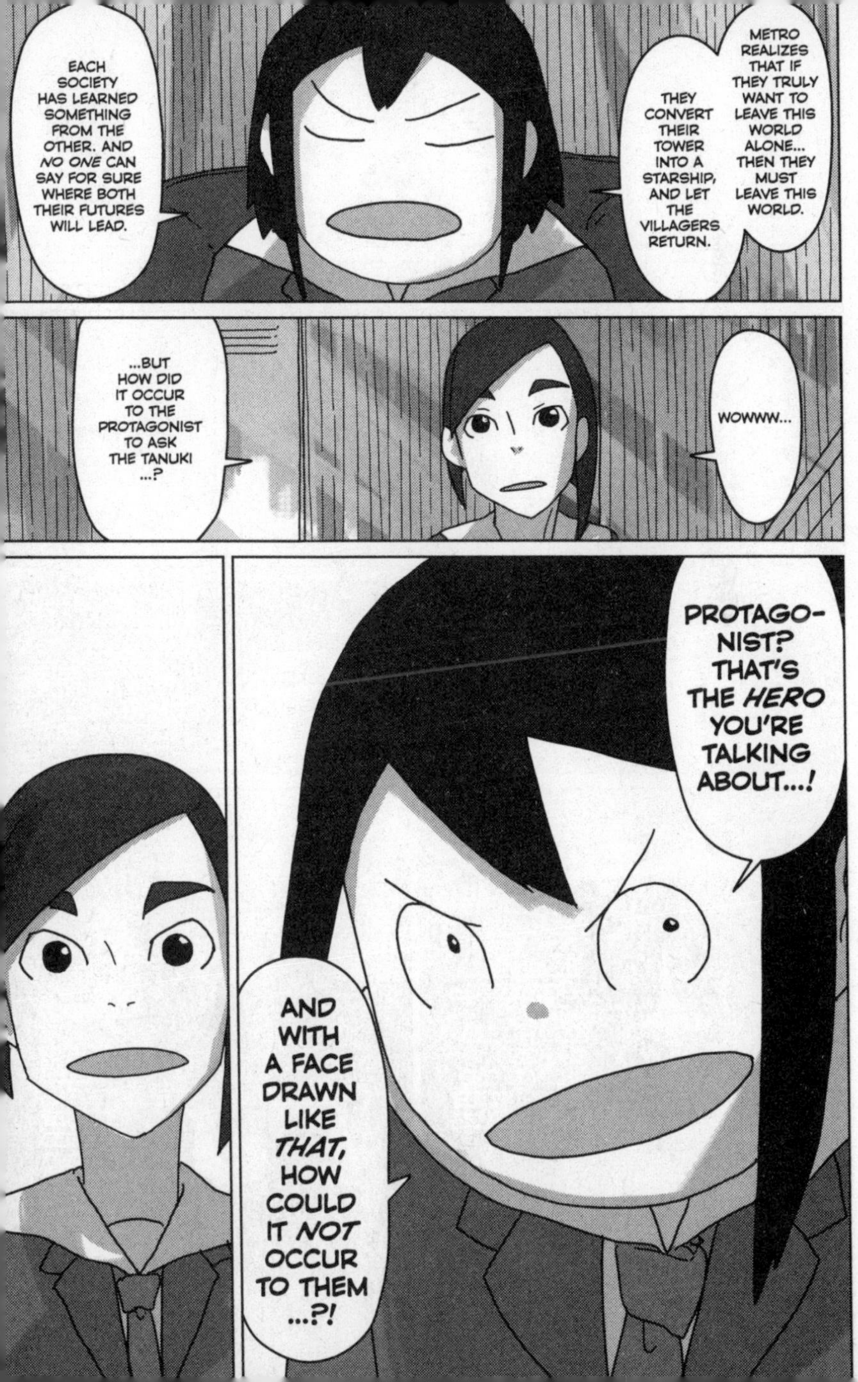
METRO REALIZES THAT IF THEY TRULY WANT TO LEAVE THIS WORLD ALONE... THEN THEY MUST LEAVE THIS WORLD.
THEY CONVERT THEIR TOWER INTO A STARSHIP, AND LET THE VILLAGERS RETURN.
EACH SOCIETY HAS LEARNED SOMETHING FROM THE OTHER. AND *NO ONE* CAN SAY FOR SURE WHERE BOTH THEIR FUTURES WILL LEAD.
WOWWW...
...BUT HOW DID IT OCCUR TO THE PROTAGONIST TO ASK THE TANUKI ...?
PROTAGO-NIST? THAT'S THE *HERO* YOU'RE TALKING ABOUT...!
AND WITH A FACE DRAWN LIKE *THAT,* HOW COULD IT *NOT* OCCUR TO THEM ...?!

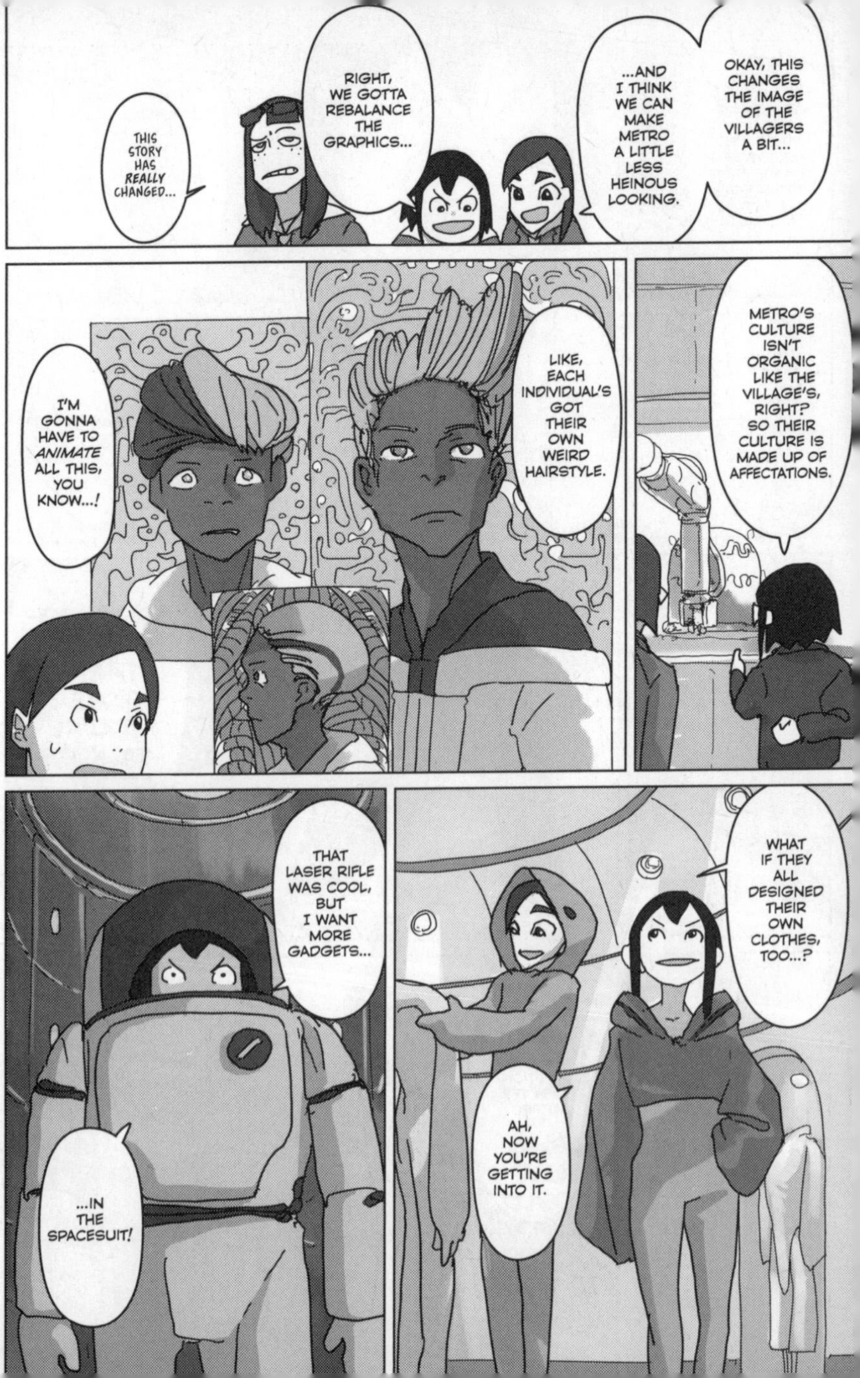
OKAY, THIS CHANGES THE IMAGE OF THE VILLAGERS A BIT...
...AND I THINK WE CAN MAKE METRO A LITTLE LESS HEINOUS LOOKING.
RIGHT, WE GOTTA REBALANCE THE GRAPHICS...
THIS STORY HAS *REALLY* CHANGED...
METRO'S CULTURE ISN'T ORGANIC LIKE THE VILLAGE'S, RIGHT? SO THEIR CULTURE IS MADE UP OF AFFECTATIONS.
LIKE, EACH INDIVIDUAL'S GOT THEIR OWN WEIRD HAIRSTYLE.
I'M GONNA HAVE TO *ANIMATE* ALL THIS, YOU KNOW...!
WHAT IF THEY ALL DESIGNED THEIR OWN CLOTHES, TOO...?
AH, NOW YOU'RE GETTING INTO IT.
THAT LASER RIFLE WAS COOL, BUT I WANT MORE GADGETS...
...IN THE SPACESUIT!

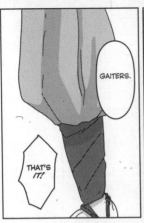

NOW, THE VILLAGERS! BECAUSE THEY LIVE IN WETLANDS, THEY KEEP THEIR CUFFS TIGHT AND USE LESS FABRIC.
YOU CALL THIS LESS FABRIC?
WE NEED... WHAT DO YOU CALL THEM ...?
KNICKER-BOCKERS?
GAITERS.
THAT'S *IT!*
LET'S LOSE SOME OF THE COPPER PLATES IN THIS ARMOR...
...WE'LL SWAP IT OUT FOR WOOD.
A LEATHER STRAP GOES OVER THE SHOULDER...
...WITH SLITS TO HANG TOOLS FROM.
WE PUT THESE TOGETHER, SIMPLIFY THE GEAR...
...AND REDUCE THE TOOL SET TO AN OVERALL OUTLINE.
DEFINE THE KNEE POSITION WITH THE GAITERS...

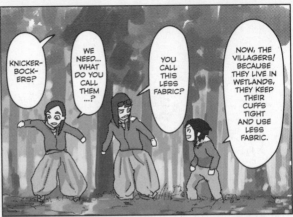

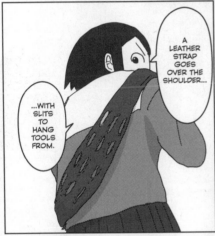

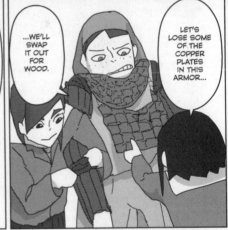

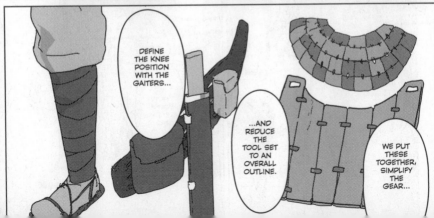

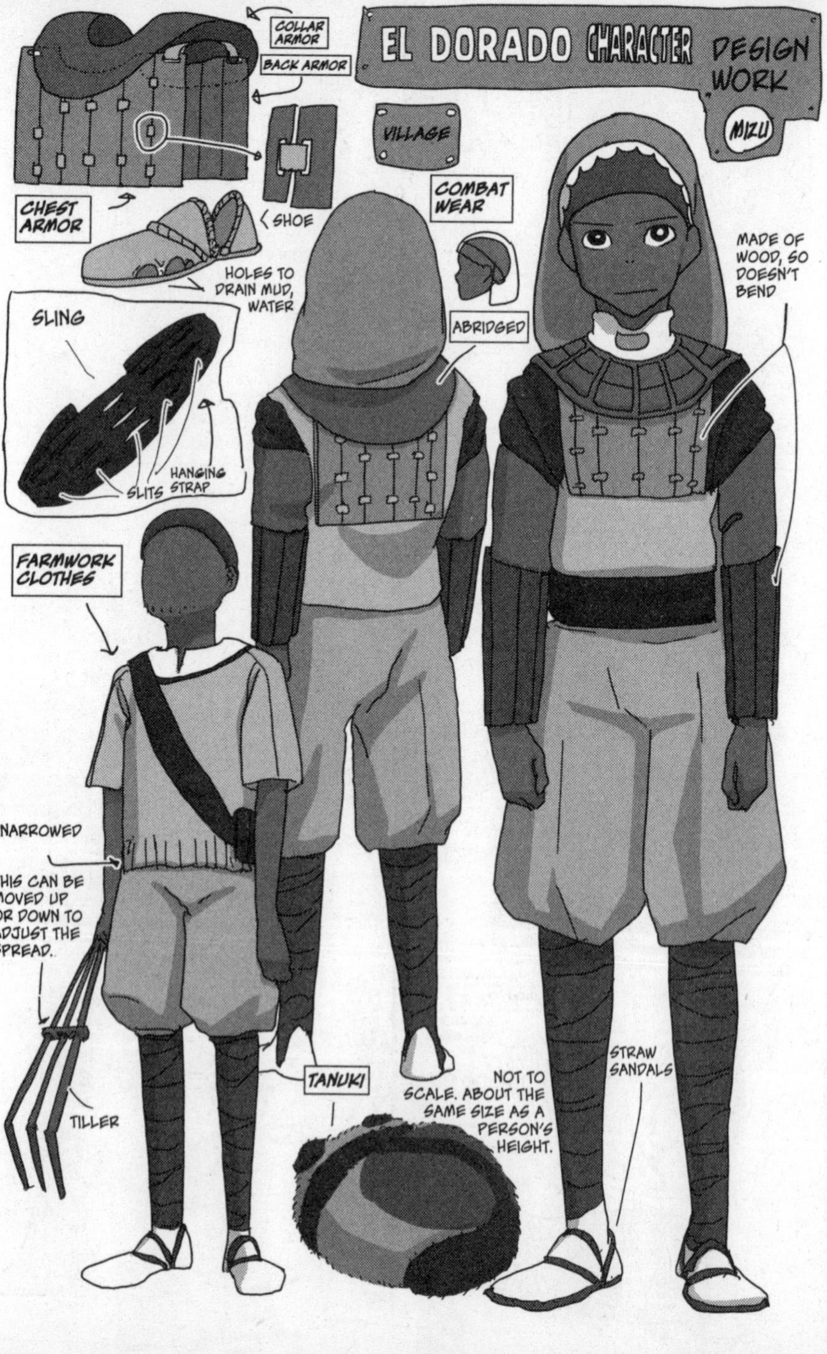
EL DORADO CHARACTER DESIGN WORK
MIZU
COLLAR ARMOR
BACK ARMOR
CHEST ARMOR
VILLAGE
COMBAT WEAR
SHOE
HOLES TO DRAIN MUD, WATER
SLING
HANGING STRAP
SLITS
ABRIDGED
MADE OF WOOD, SO DOESN'T BEND
FARMWORK CLOTHES
NARROWED
THIS CAN BE MOVED UP OR DOWN TO ADJUST THE SPREAD.
TILLER
TANUKI
NOT TO SCALE. ABOUT THE SAME SIZE AS A PERSON'S HEIGHT.
STRAW SANDALS

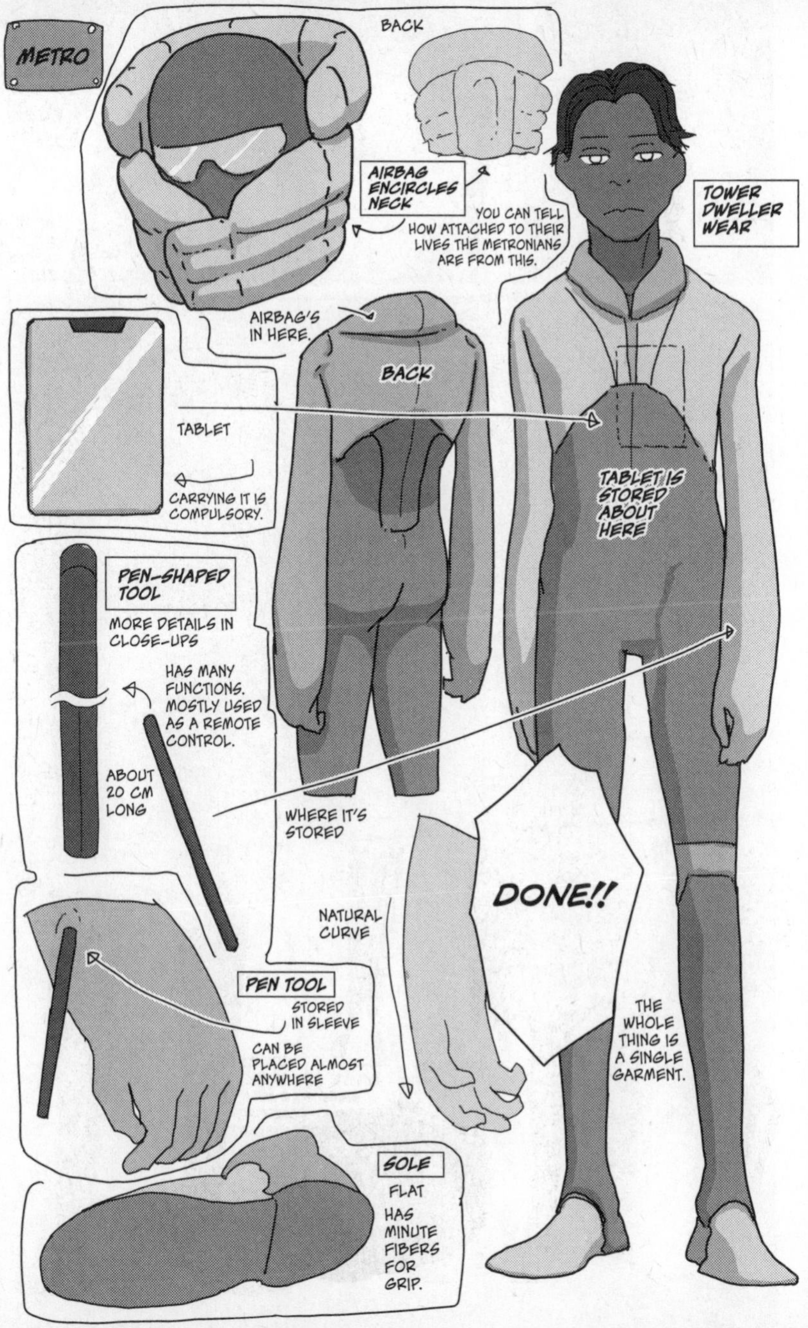

TOWER DWELLER WEAR
YOU CAN TELL HOW ATTACHED TO THEIR LIVES THE METRONIANS ARE FROM THIS.
BACK
AIRBAG ENCIRCLES NECK
METRO
AIRBAG'S IN HERE.
BACK
TABLET
CARRYING IT IS COMPULSORY.
TABLET IS STORED ABOUT HERE
PEN-SHAPED TOOL
MORE DETAILS IN CLOSE-UPS
HAS MANY FUNCTIONS. MOSTLY USED AS A REMOTE CONTROL.
ABOUT 20 CM LONG
WHERE IT'S STORED
DONE!!
NATURAL CURVE
THE WHOLE THING IS A SINGLE GARMENT.
PEN TOOL
STORED IN SLEEVE
CAN BE PLACED ALMOST ANYWHERE
SOLE
FLAT
HAS MINUTE FIBERS FOR GRIP.

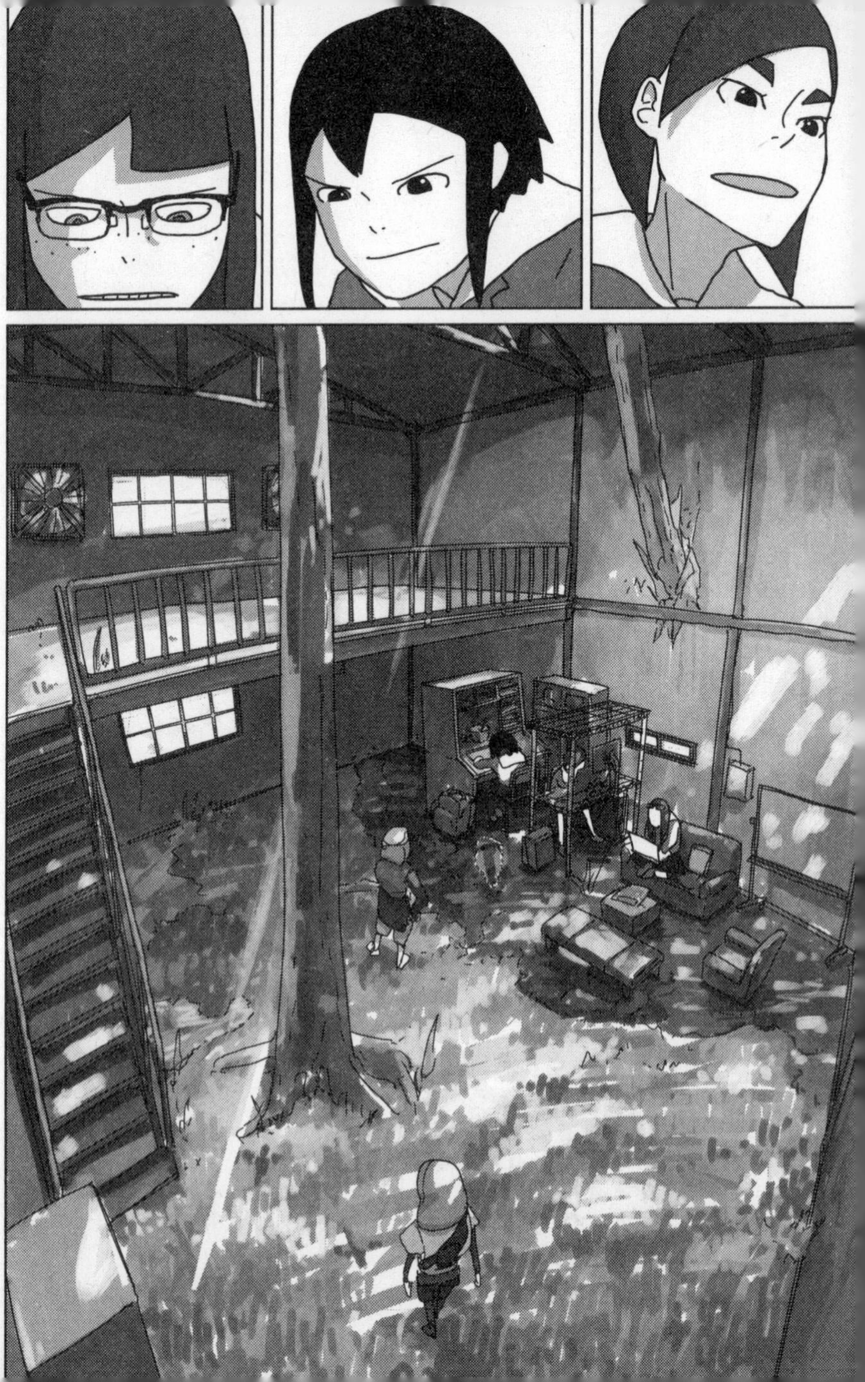

KEEP YOUR HANDS OFF EIZOUKEN!

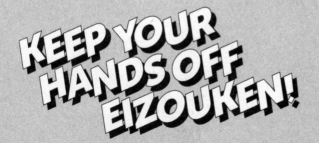

Memo from Mr. Oowara:

It would seem that if Asakusa and friends don't think through what they're portraying 100%, then they won't be able to create something of quality. But what percentage of all those things that they considered will be reflected in the finished work? That's the eternal question.

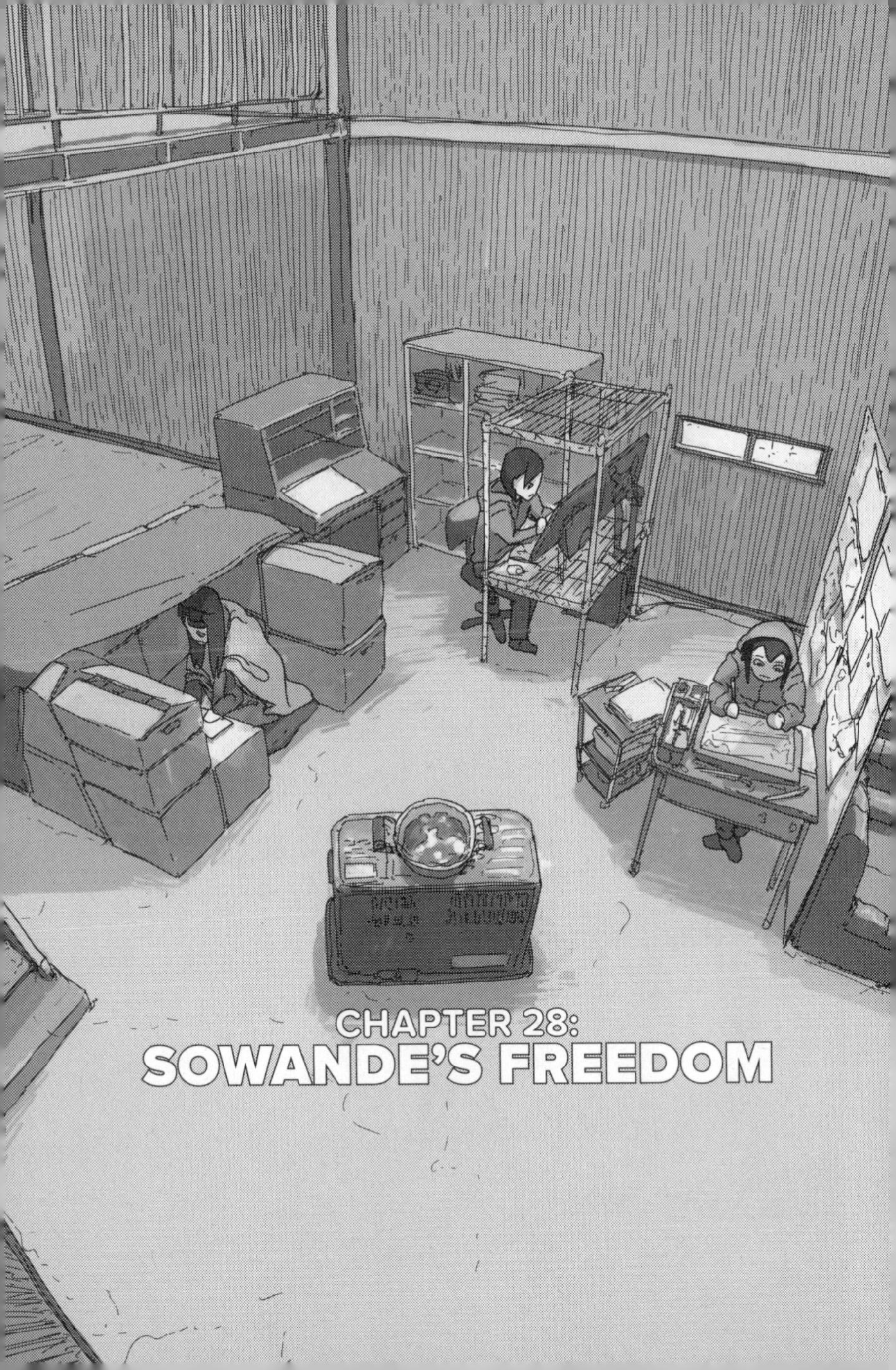

CHAPTER 28: SOWANDE'S FREEDOM

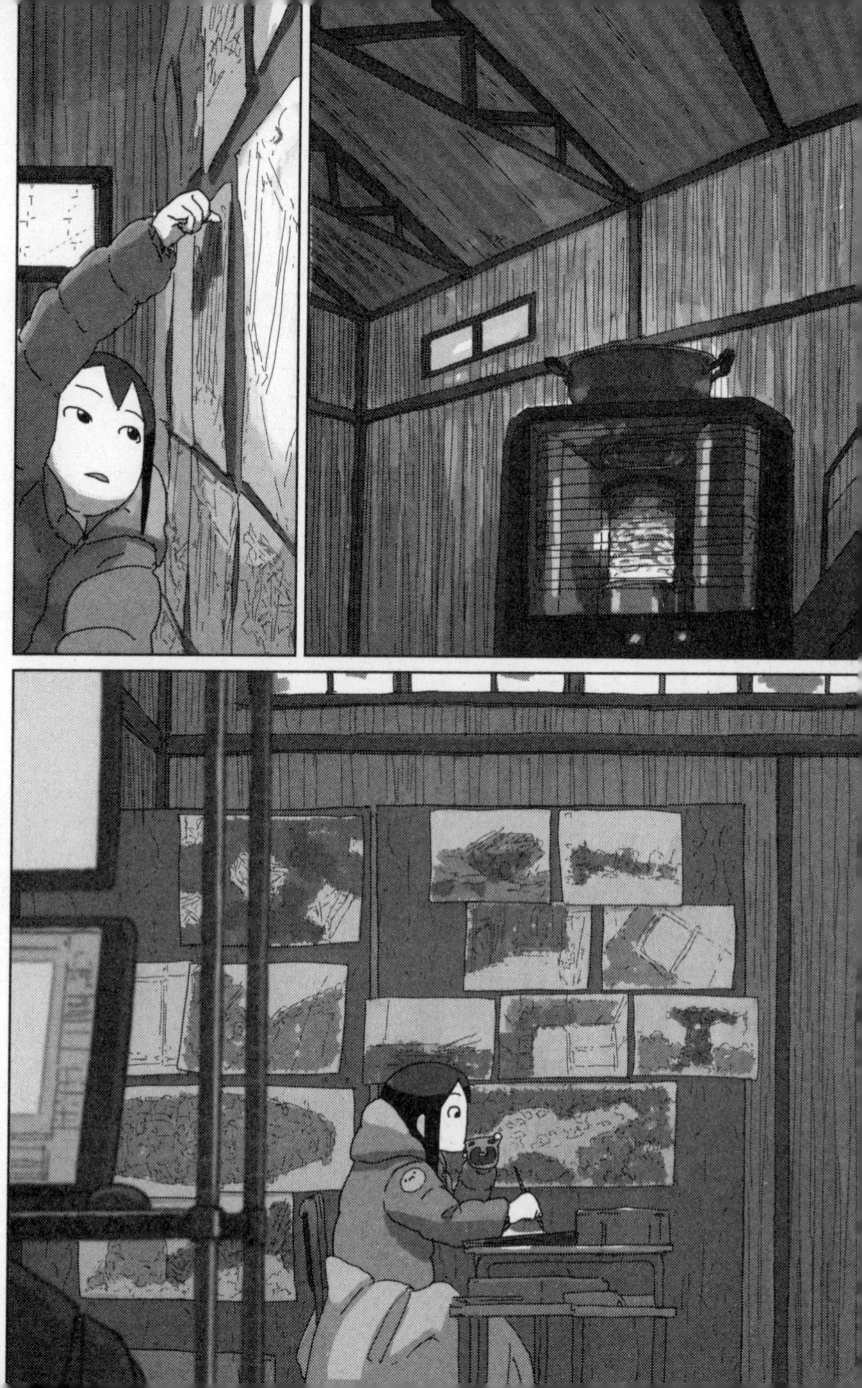

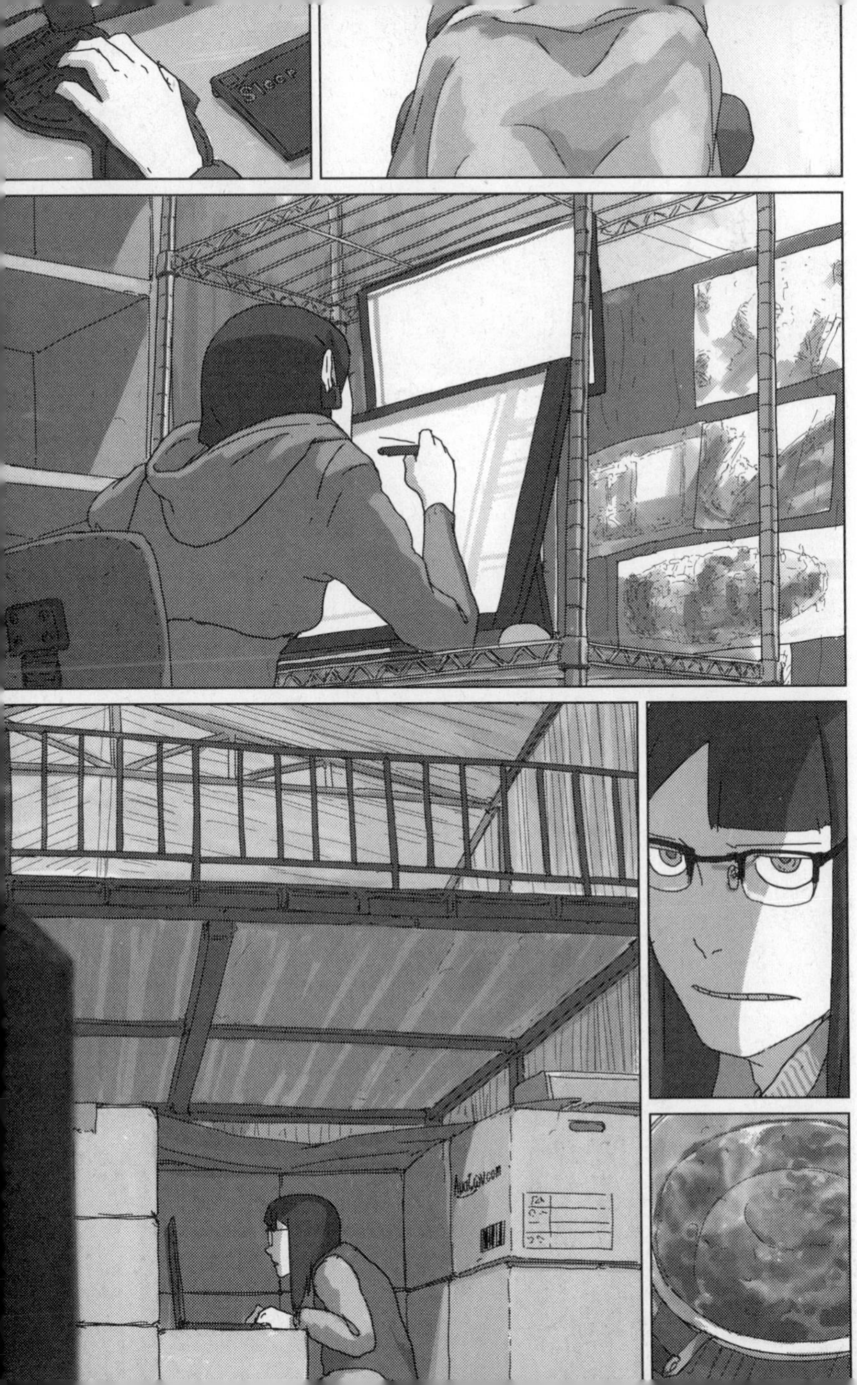

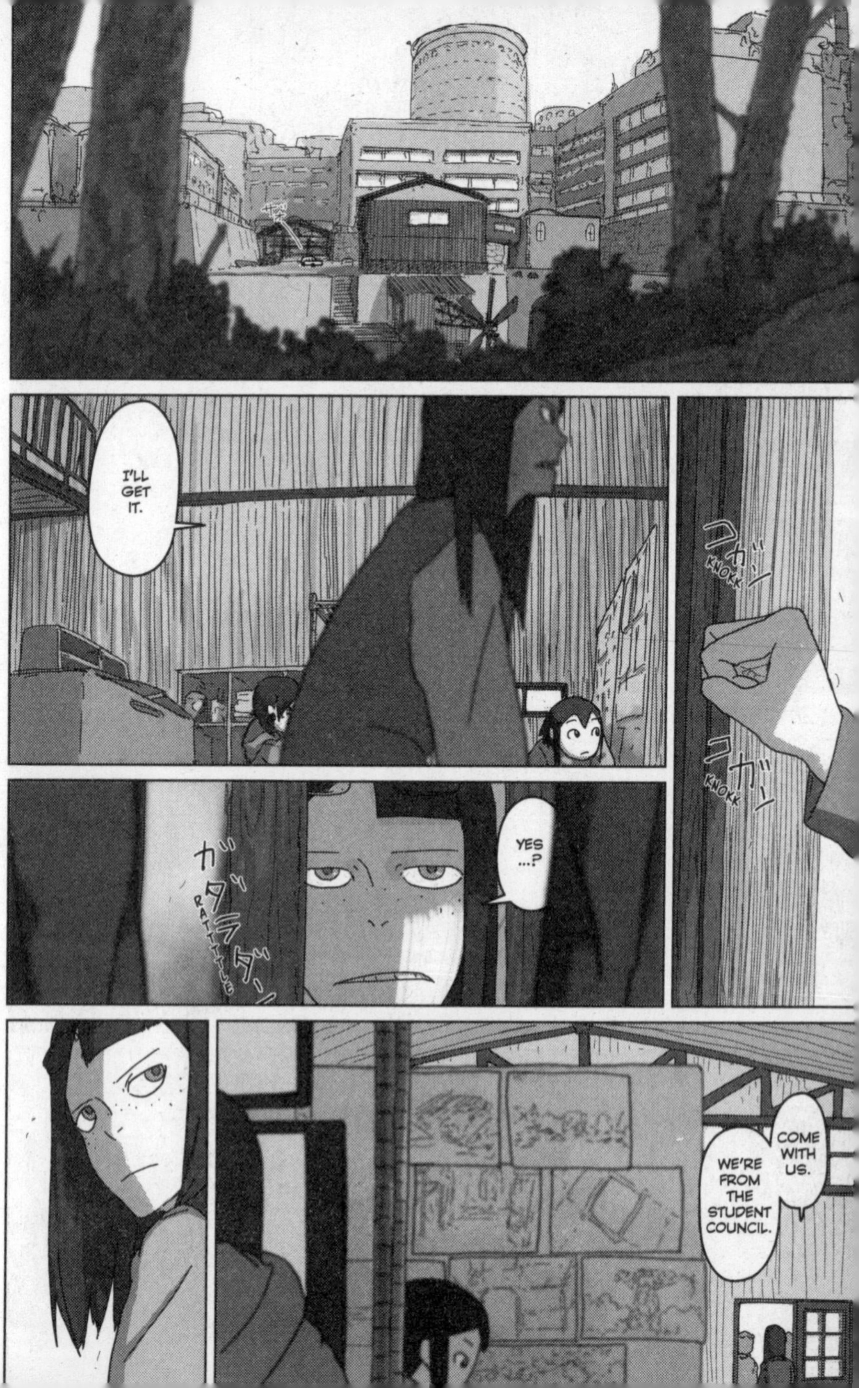
KNOKK
KNOKK
I'LL GET IT.
RATTTTLE
YES ...?
COME WITH US.
WE'RE FROM THE STUDENT COUNCIL.

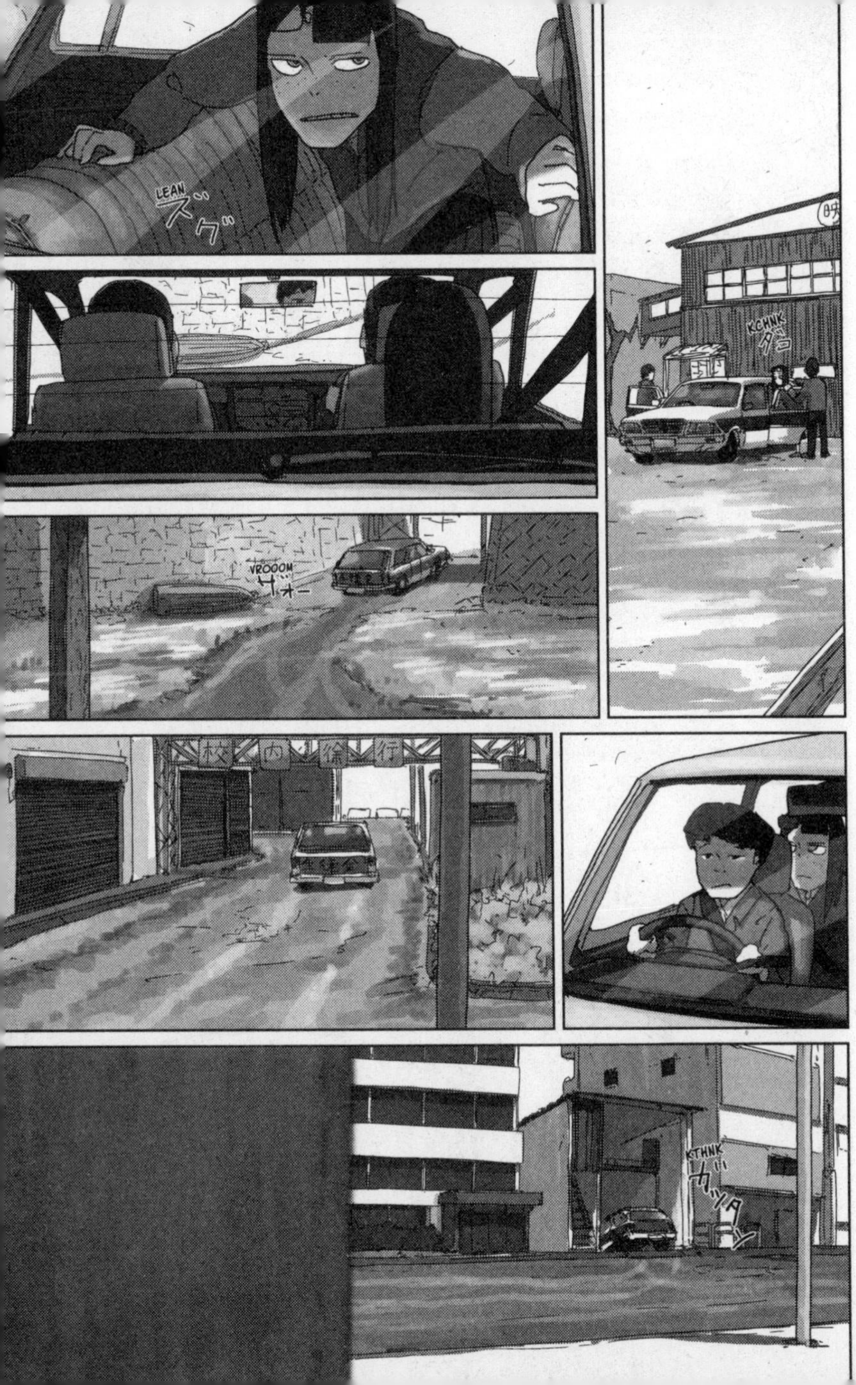
KCHNK
ダコ
LEAN
ズグ
VROOOM
校内徐行
KTHNK

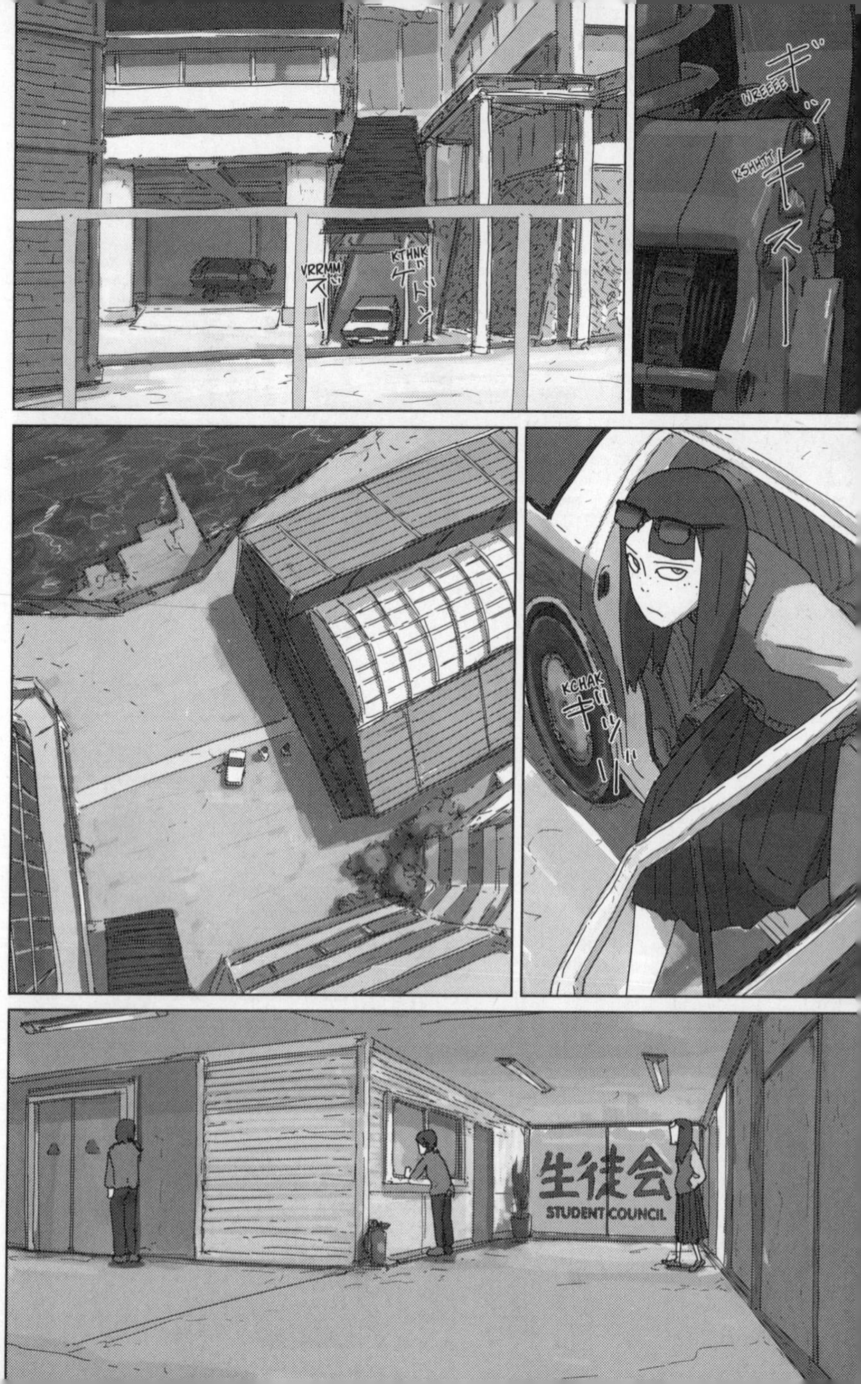
WREEEE
KSHHTT
KTHNK
VRRMM
KCHAK
生徒会
STUDENT COUNCIL

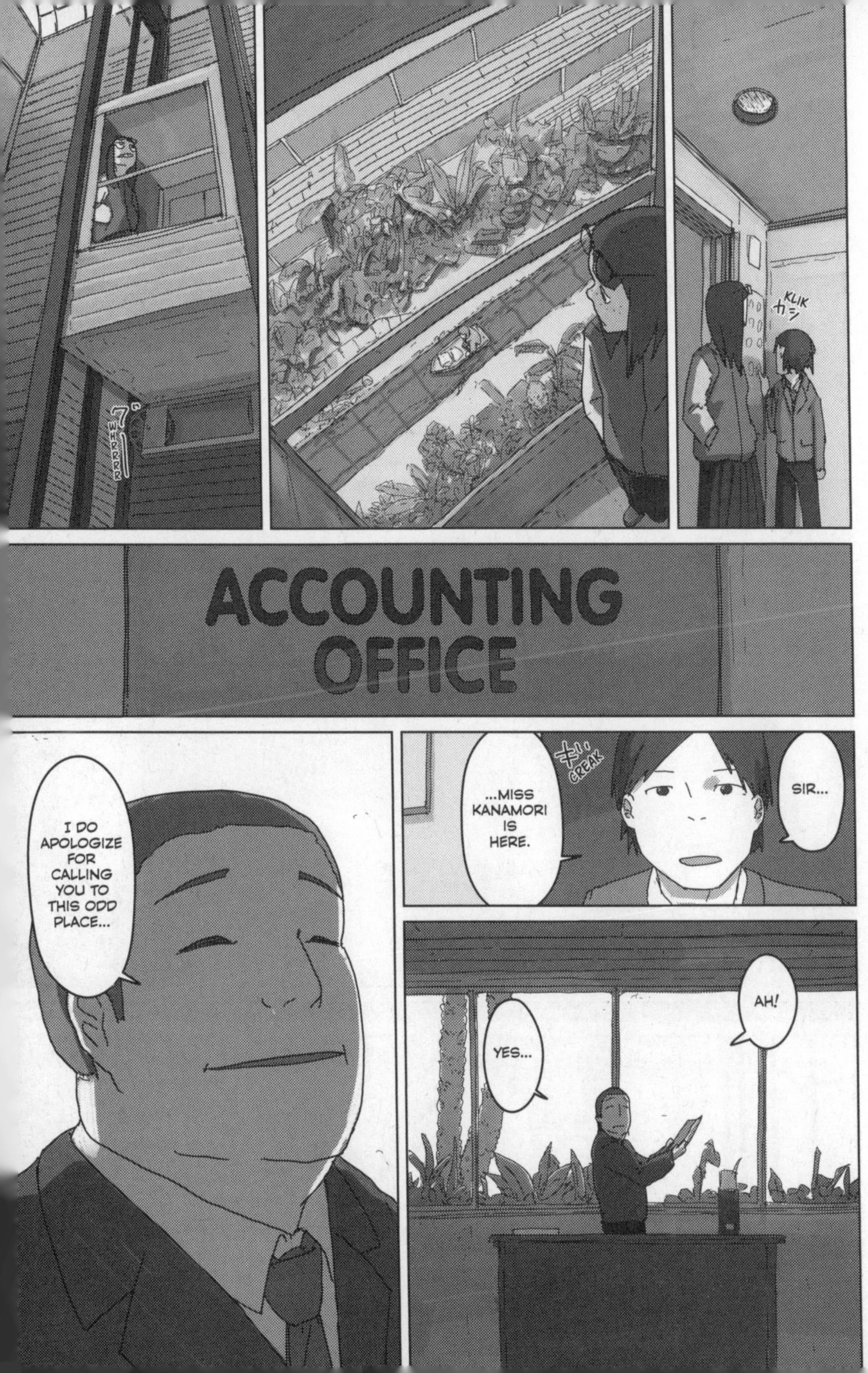
KLIK
カシ
WHRRRR
ACCOUNTING OFFICE
SIR...
CREAK
...MISS KANAMORI IS HERE.
AH!
YES...
I DO APOLOGIZE FOR CALLING YOU TO THIS ODD PLACE...

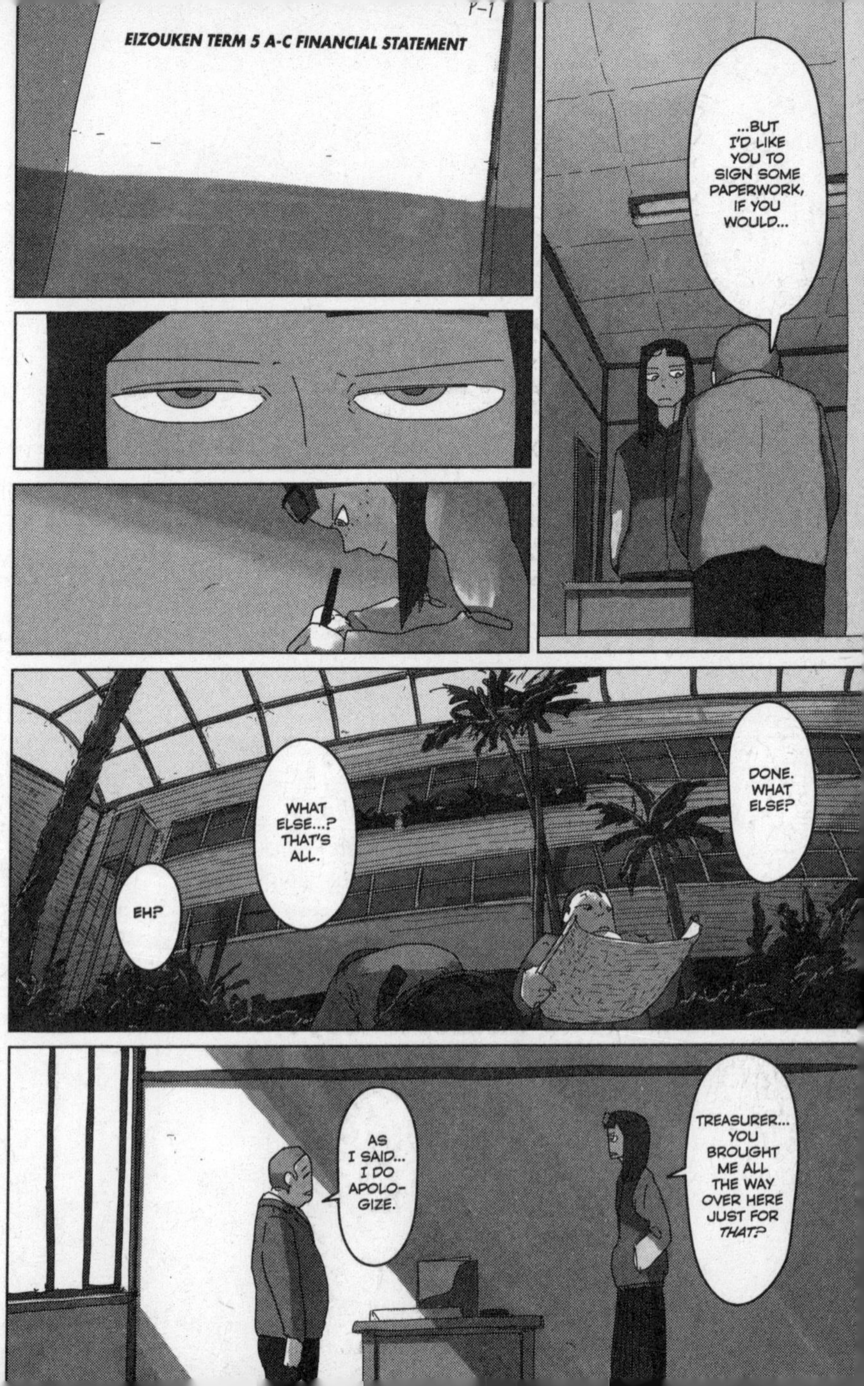
...BUT I'D LIKE YOU TO SIGN SOME PAPERWORK, IF YOU WOULD...
EIZOUKEN TERM 5 A-C FINANCIAL STATEMENT
DONE. WHAT ELSE?
WHAT ELSE...? THAT'S ALL.
EH?
TREASURER... YOU BROUGHT ME ALL THE WAY OVER HERE JUST FOR *THAT?*
AS I SAID... I DO APOLOGIZE.

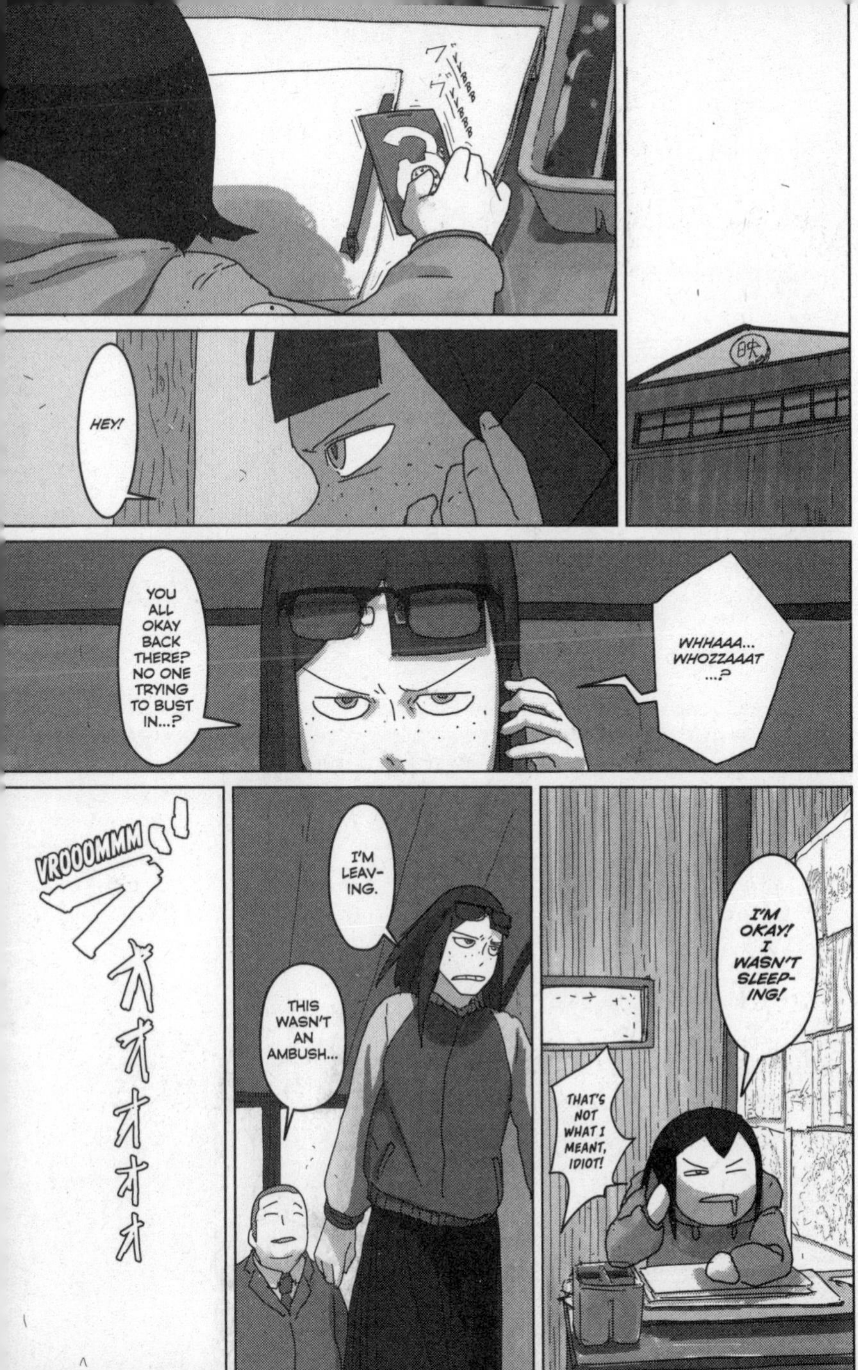VVVBBB
VVVBBB
HEY!
WHHAAA... WHOZZAAAT ...?
YOU ALL OKAY BACK THERE? NO ONE TRYING TO BUST IN...?
I'M OKAY! I WASN'T SLEEPING!
THAT'S NOT WHAT I MEANT, IDIOT!
I'M LEAVING.
THIS WASN'T AN AMBUSH...
VROOOMMM

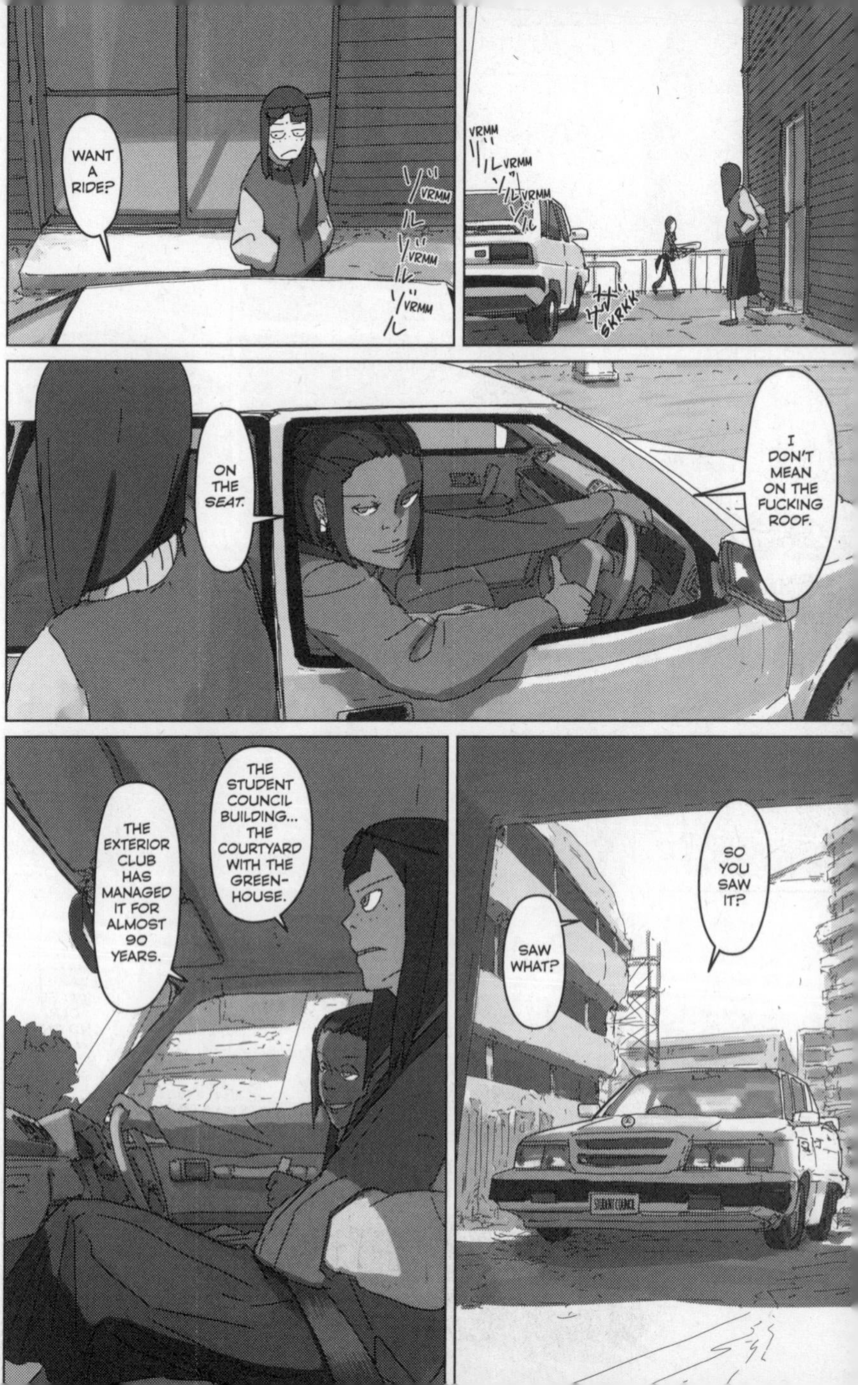
VRMM
VRMM
VRMM
SKRKK
WANT A RIDE?
VRMM
VRMM
VRMM
VRMM
I DON'T MEAN ON THE FUCKING ROOF.
ON THE SEAT.
SO YOU SAW IT?
SAW WHAT?
STUDENT COUNCIL
THE STUDENT COUNCIL BUILDING... THE COURTYARD WITH THE GREEN-HOUSE.
THE EXTERIOR CLUB HAS MANAGED IT FOR ALMOST 90 YEARS.

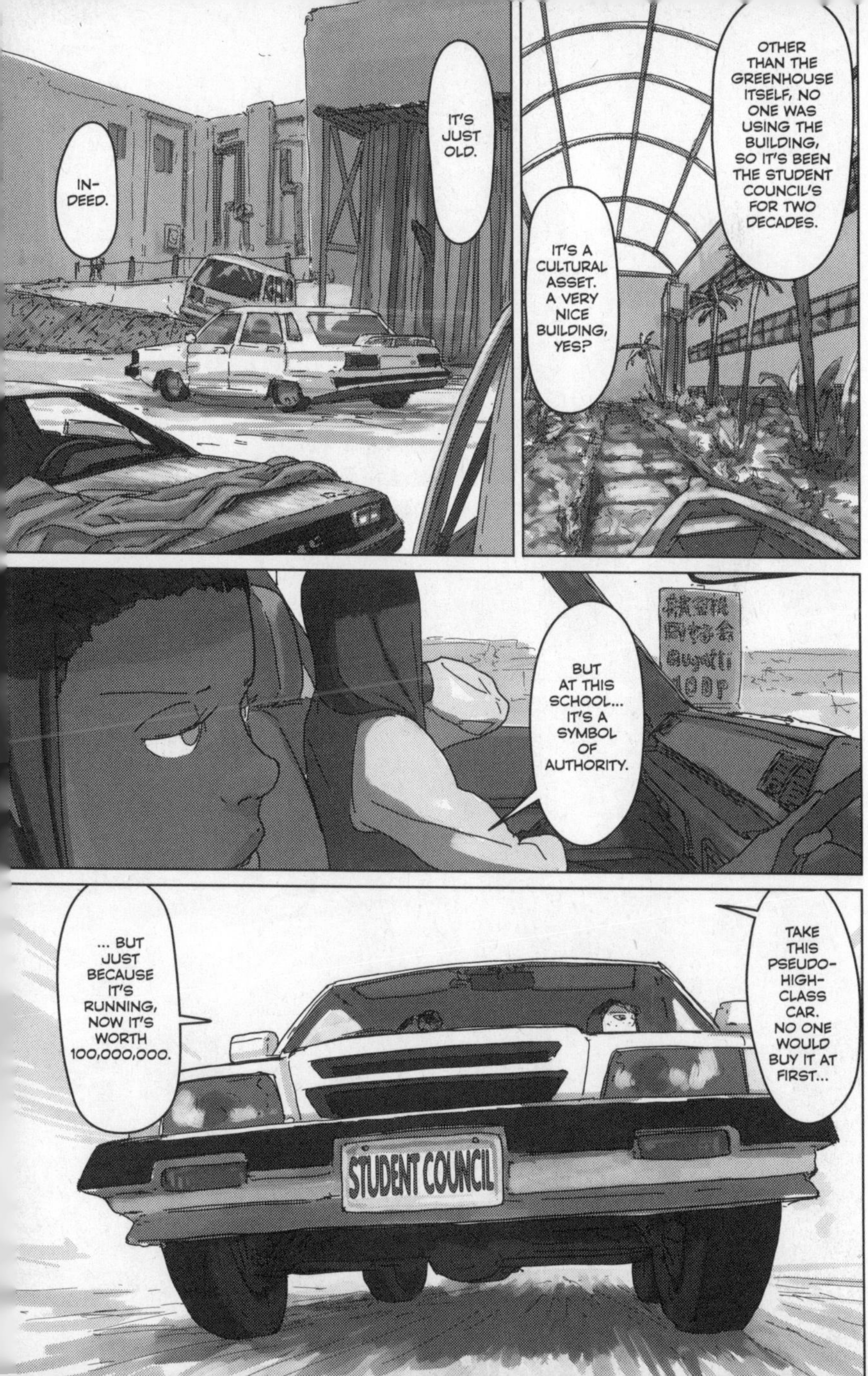
OTHER THAN THE GREENHOUSE ITSELF, NO ONE WAS USING THE BUILDING, SO IT'S BEEN THE STUDENT COUNCIL'S FOR TWO DECADES.
IT'S A CULTURAL ASSET. A VERY NICE BUILDING, YES?
IT'S JUST OLD.
IN-DEED.
BUT AT THIS SCHOOL... IT'S A SYMBOL OF AUTHORITY.
TAKE THIS PSEUDO-HIGH-CLASS CAR. NO ONE WOULD BUY IT AT FIRST...
... BUT JUST BECAUSE IT'S RUNNING, NOW IT'S WORTH 100,000,000.
STUDENT COUNCIL

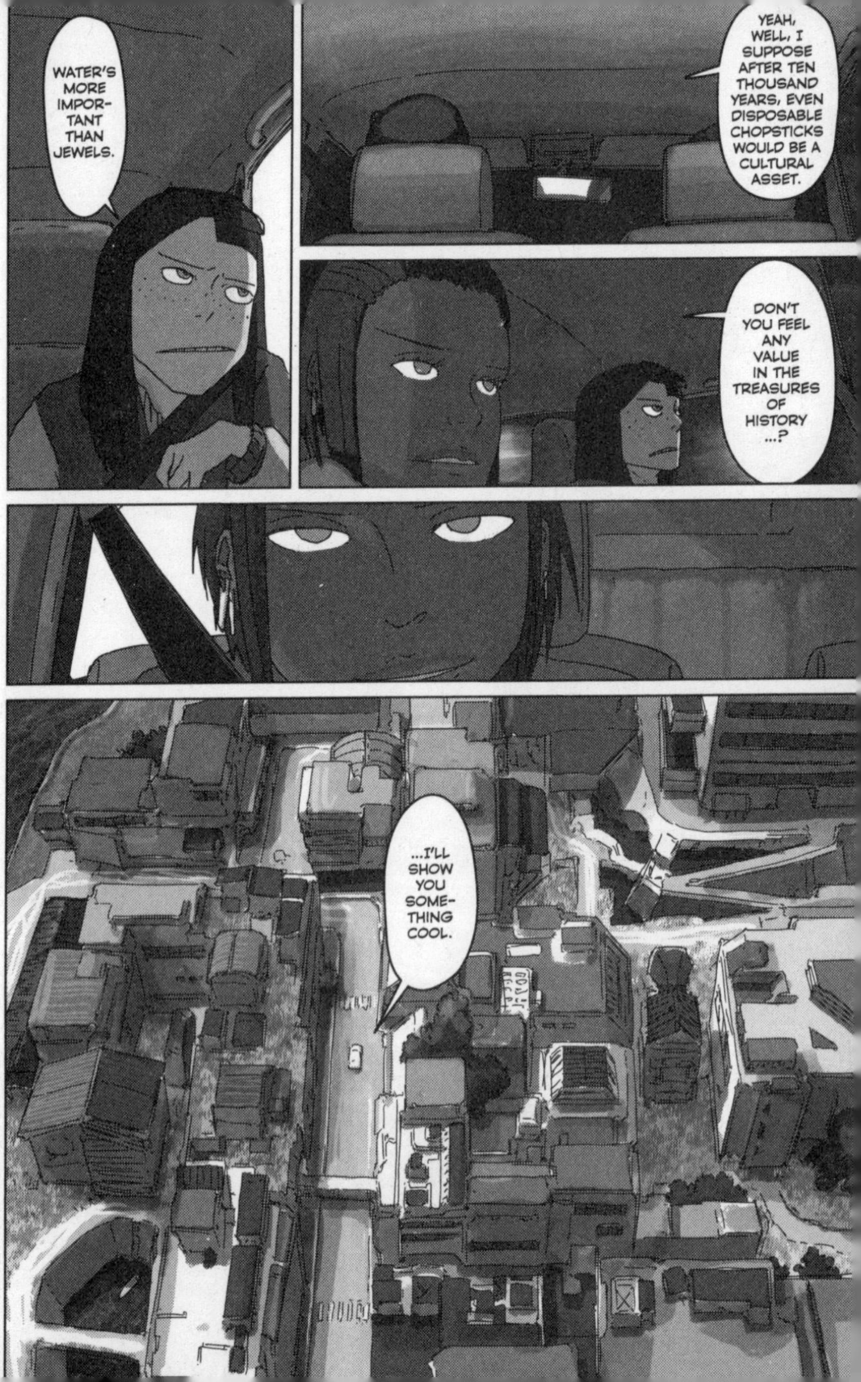
YEAH, WELL, I SUPPOSE AFTER TEN THOUSAND YEARS, EVEN DISPOSABLE CHOPSTICKS WOULD BE A CULTURAL ASSET.
DON'T YOU FEEL ANY VALUE IN THE TREASURES OF HISTORY ...?
WATER'S MORE IMPOR-TANT THAN JEWELS.
...I'LL SHOW YOU SOME-THING COOL.

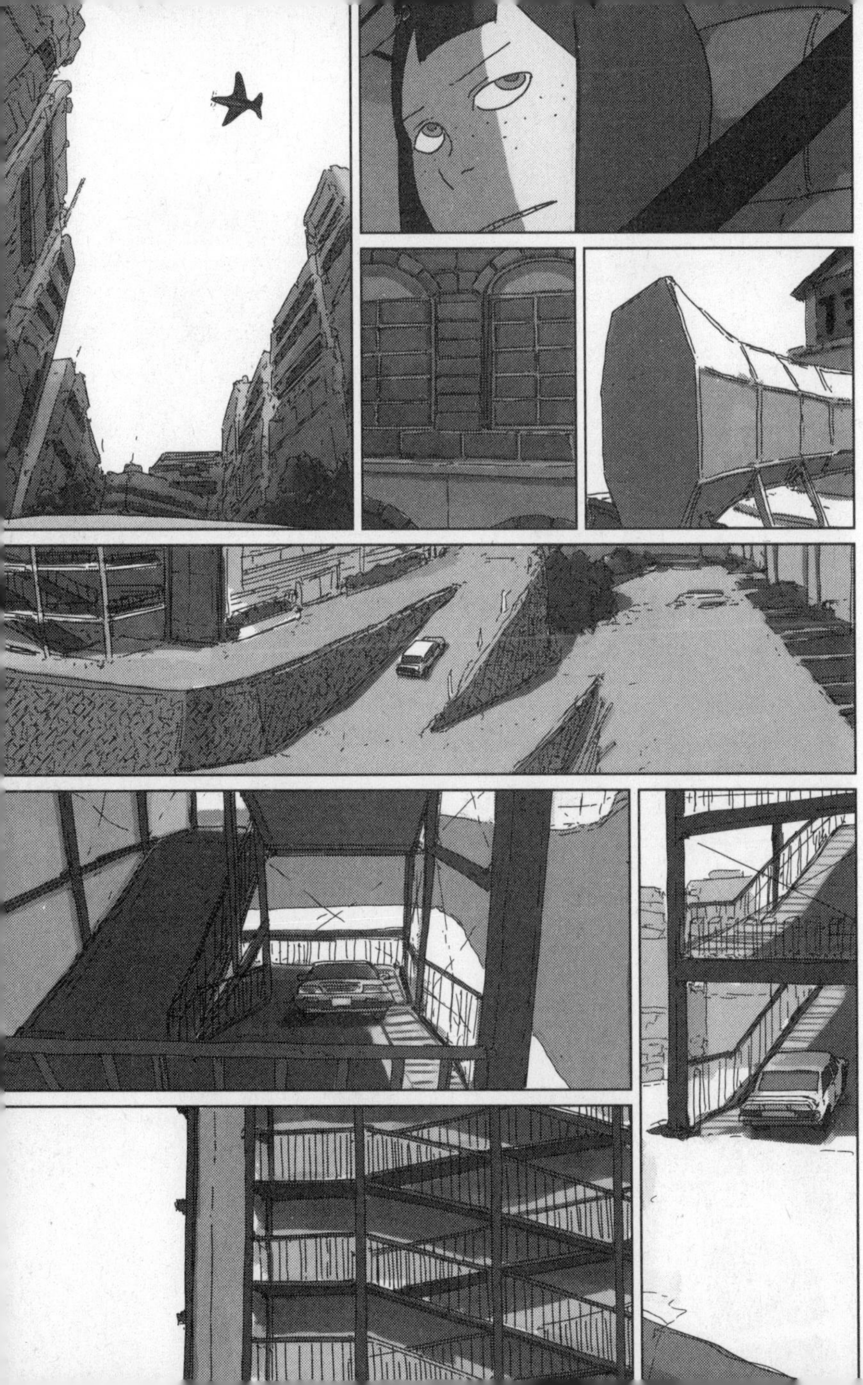

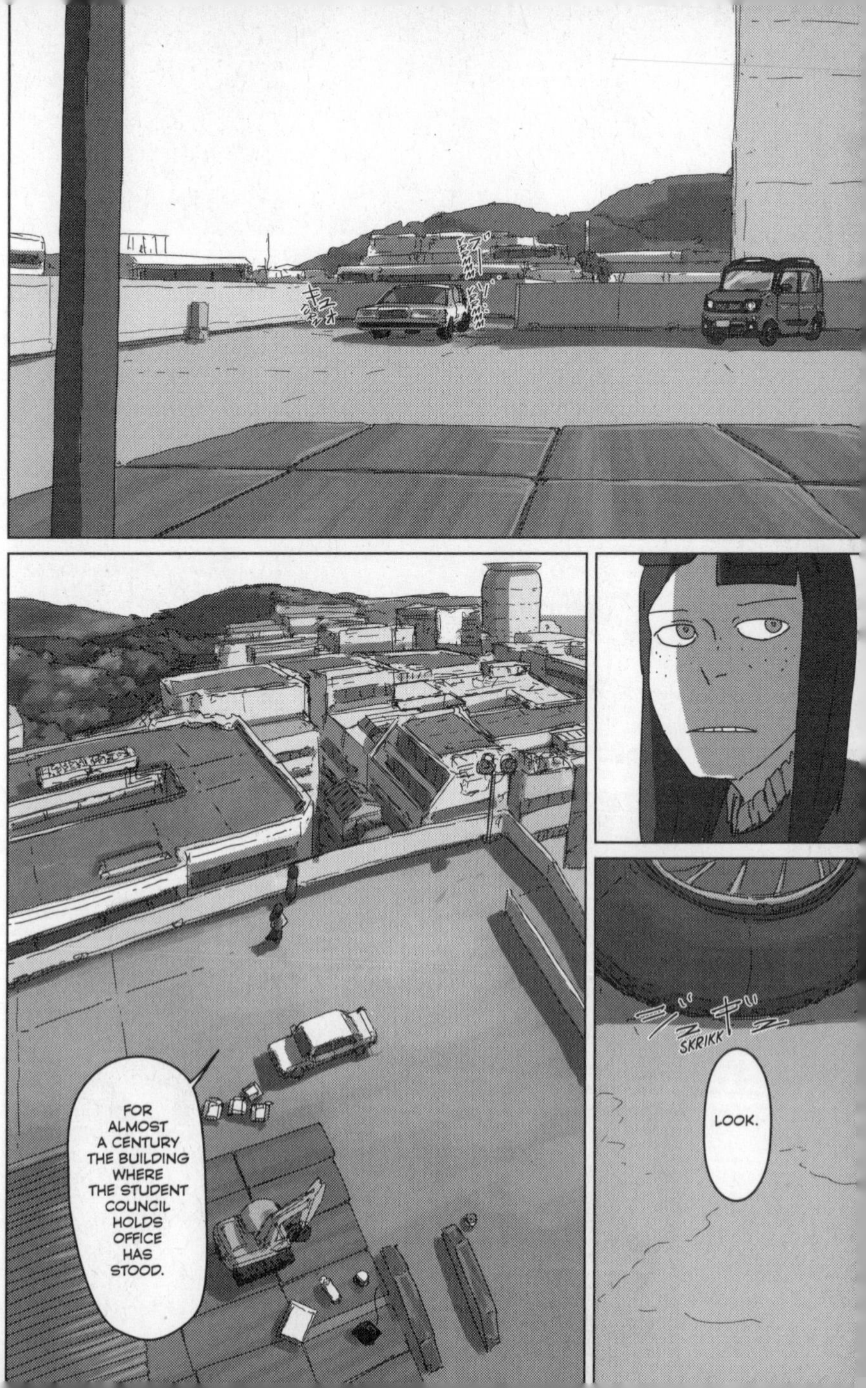
SKRIKK
LOOK.
FOR ALMOST A CENTURY THE BUILDING WHERE THE STUDENT COUNCIL HOLDS OFFICE HAS STOOD.

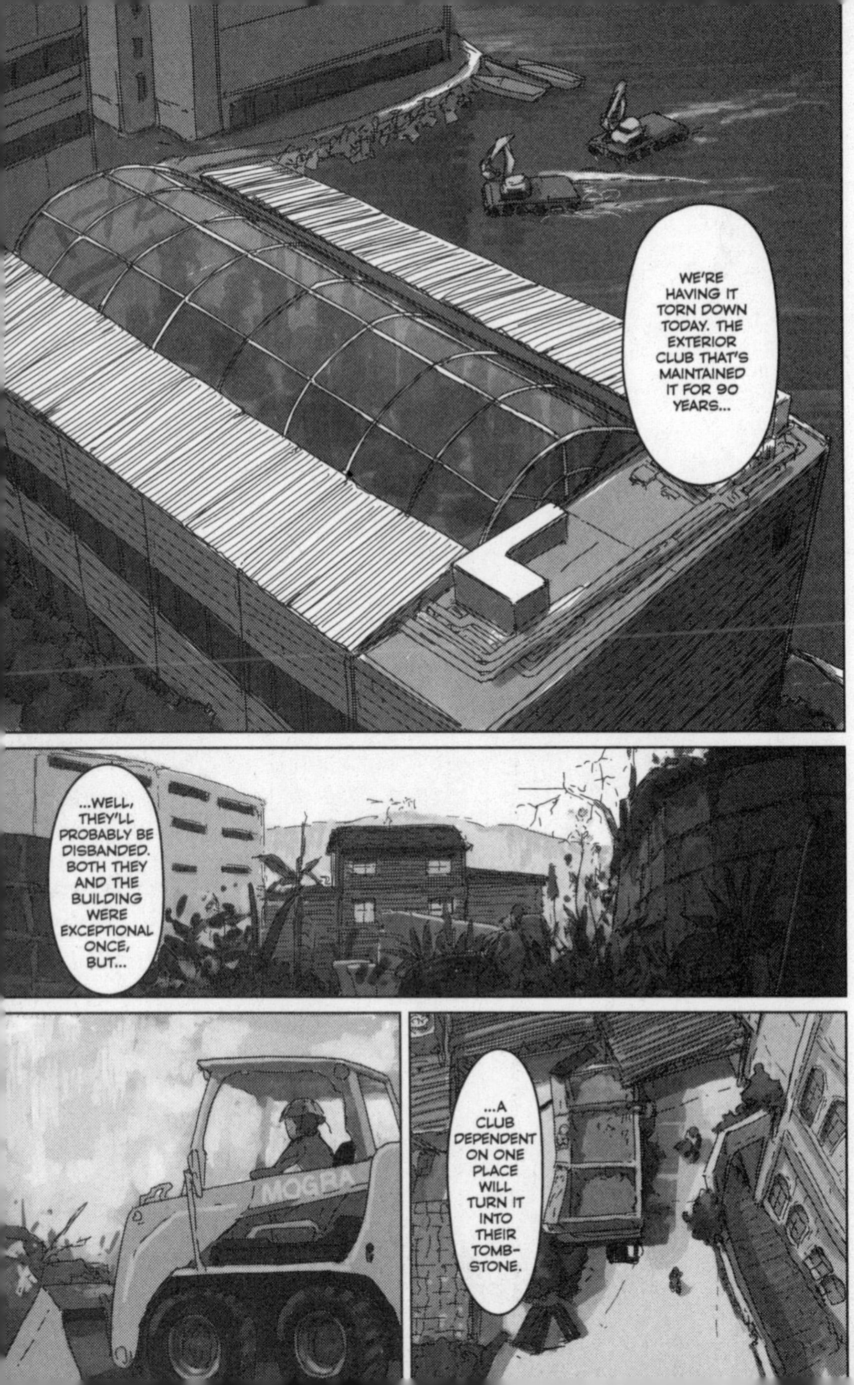
WE'RE HAVING IT TORN DOWN TODAY. THE EXTERIOR CLUB THAT'S MAINTAINED IT FOR 90 YEARS...
...WELL, THEY'LL PROBABLY BE DISBANDED. BOTH THEY AND THE BUILDING WERE EXCEPTIONAL ONCE, BUT...
...A CLUB DEPENDENT ON ONE PLACE WILL TURN IT INTO THEIR TOMB-STONE.
MOGRA

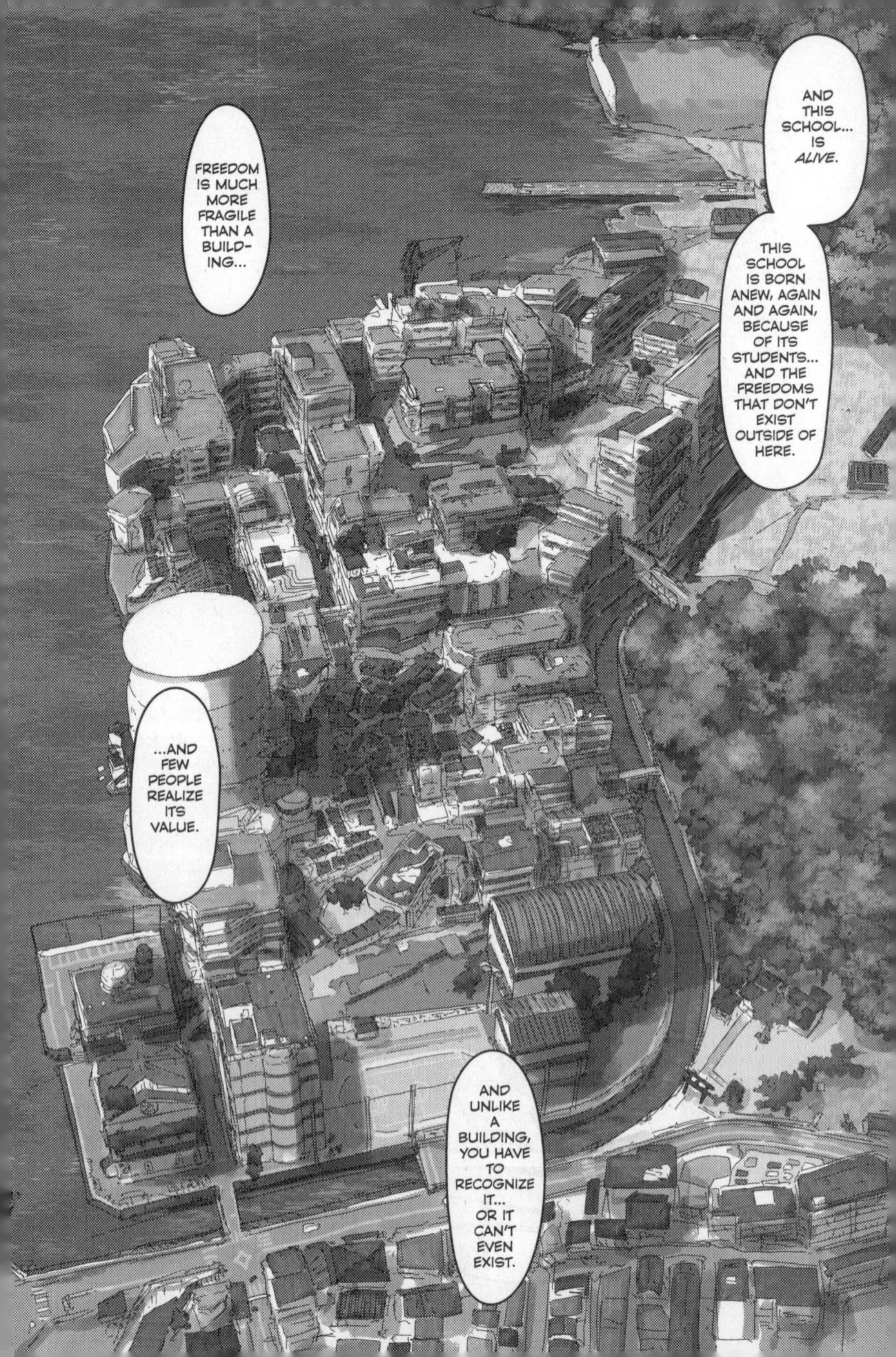
AND THIS SCHOOL... IS *ALIVE*.
THIS SCHOOL IS BORN ANEW, AGAIN AND AGAIN, BECAUSE OF ITS STUDENTS... AND THE FREEDOMS THAT DON'T EXIST OUTSIDE OF HERE.
FREEDOM IS MUCH MORE FRAGILE THAN A BUILDING...
...AND FEW PEOPLE REALIZE ITS VALUE.
AND UNLIKE A BUILDING, YOU HAVE TO RECOGNIZE IT... OR IT CAN'T EVEN EXIST.

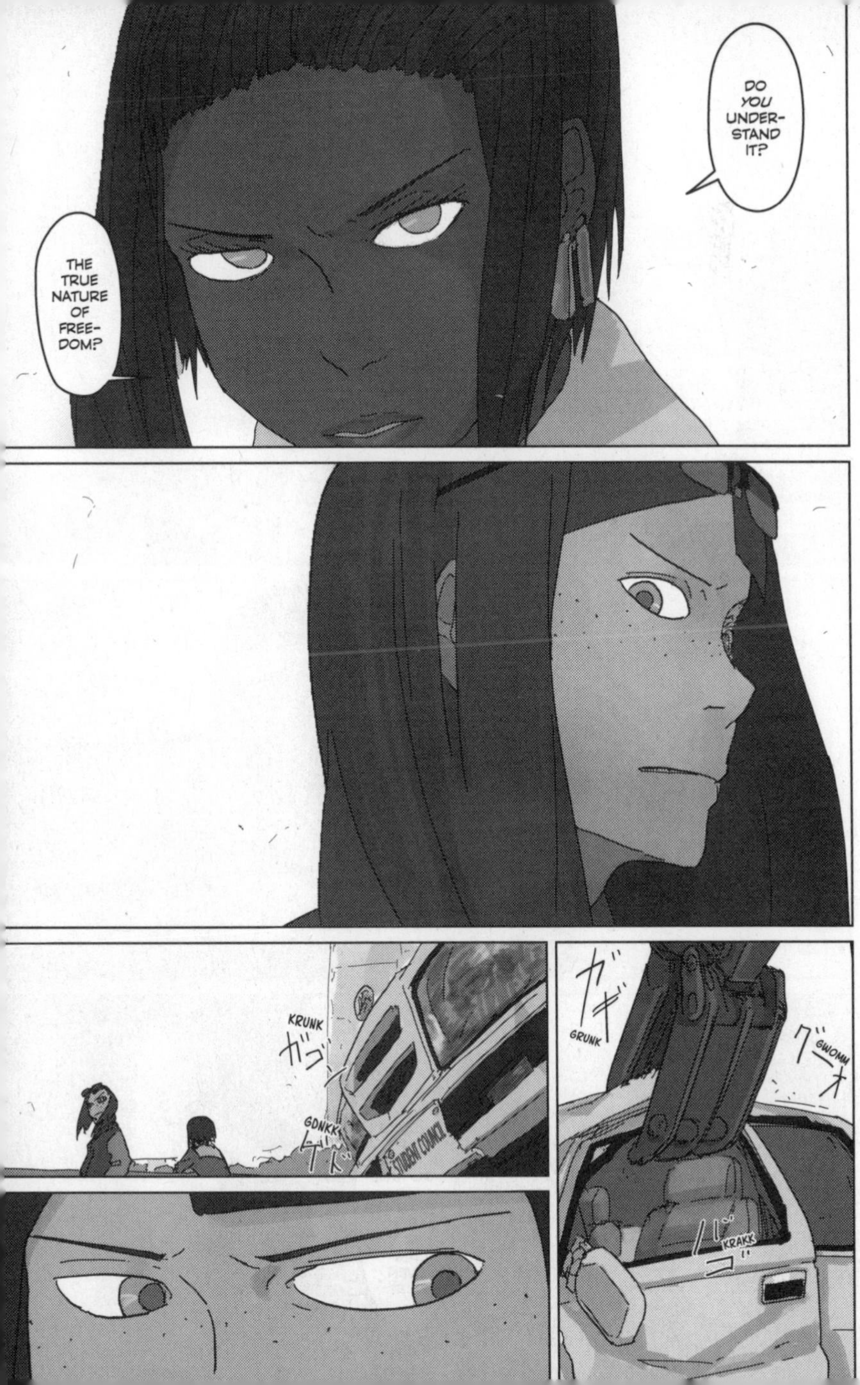
DO YOU UNDERSTAND IT?
THE TRUE NATURE OF FREEDOM?
ガギ
GRUNK
グオ
GWOMM
バゴ
KRAKK
ガゴン
KRUNK
ゲド
GDNKK
STUDENT COUNCIL

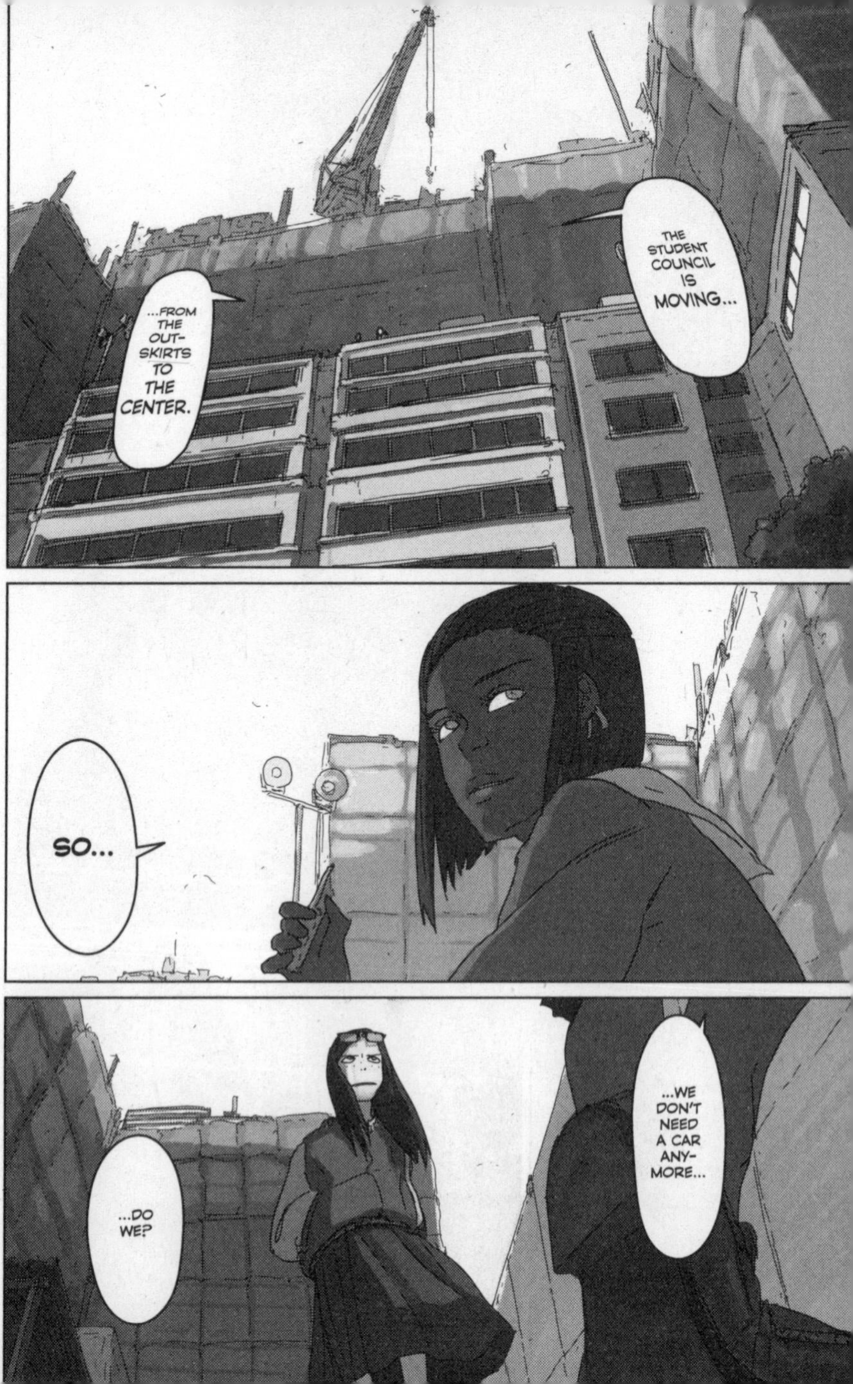
THE STUDENT COUNCIL IS MOVING...
...FROM THE OUT-SKIRTS TO THE CENTER.
SO...
...WE DON'T NEED A CAR ANY-MORE...
...DO WE?

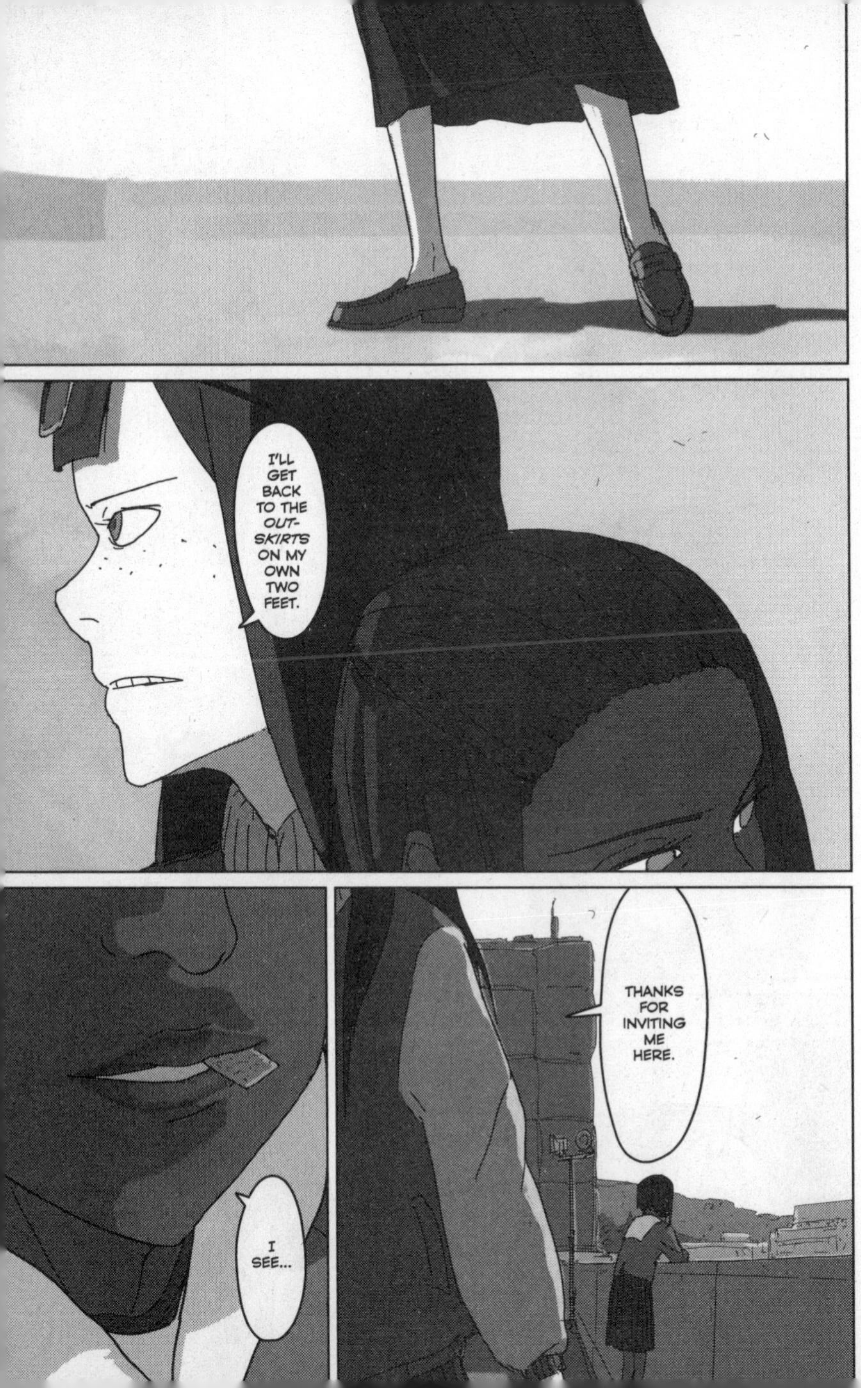
I'LL GET BACK TO THE OUT-SKIRTS ON MY OWN TWO FEET.
THANKS FOR INVITING ME HERE.
I SEE...

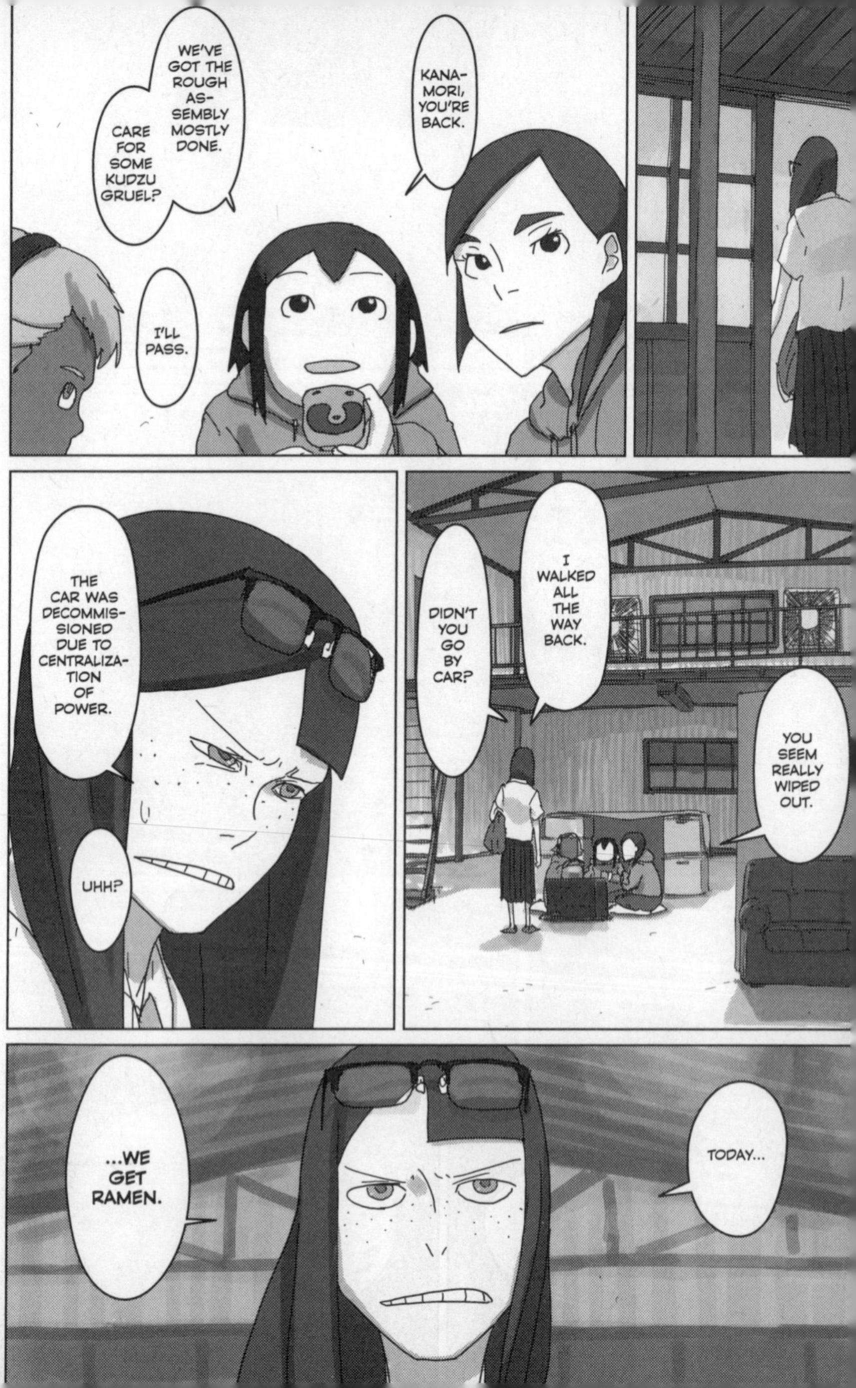
KANA-MORI, YOU'RE BACK.
WE'VE GOT THE ROUGH AS-SEMBLY MOSTLY DONE.
CARE FOR SOME KUDZU GRUEL?
I'LL PASS.
YOU SEEM REALLY WIPED OUT.
I WALKED ALL THE WAY BACK.
DIDN'T YOU GO BY CAR?
THE CAR WAS DECOMMIS-SIONED DUE TO CENTRALIZA-TION OF POWER.
UHH?
TODAY...
...WE GET RAMEN.

RA M EN
UFO
UFO

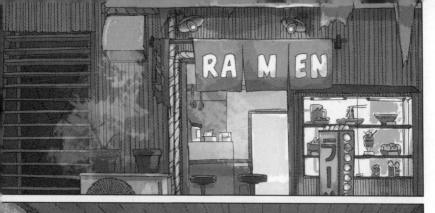

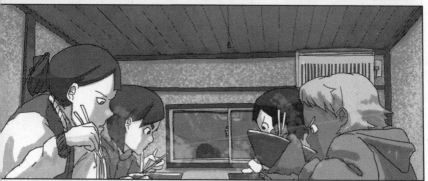

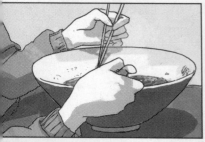

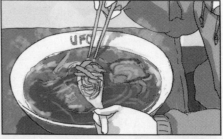

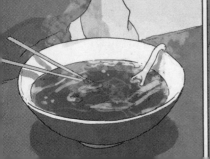

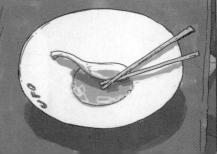

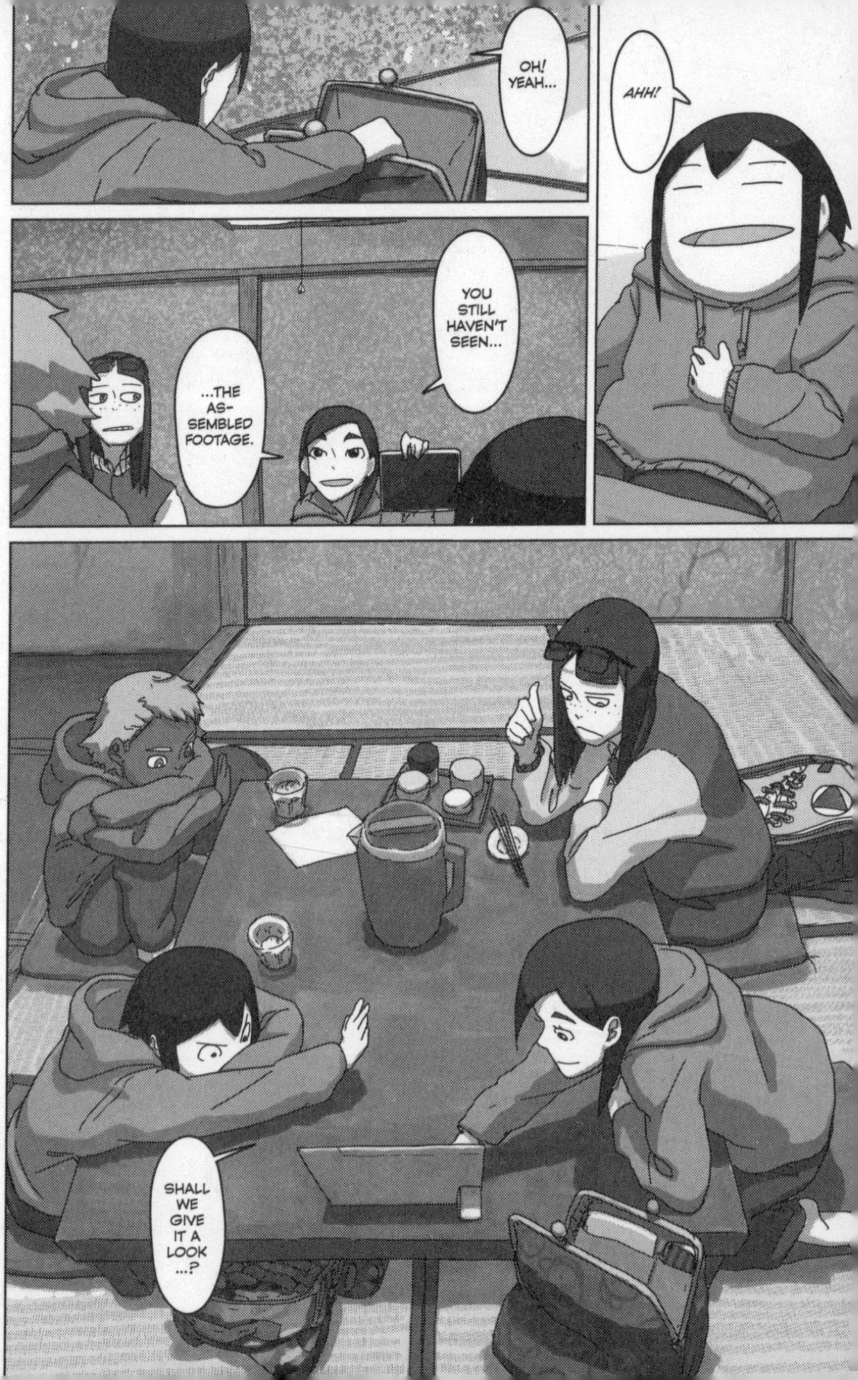
AHH!
OH! YEAH...
YOU STILL HAVEN'T SEEN...
...THE AS-SEMBLED FOOTAGE.
SHALL WE GIVE IT A LOOK ...?

KEEP YOUR HANDS OFF EIZOUKEN!

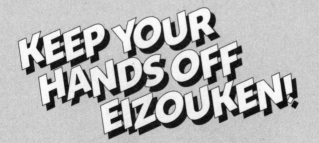

Memo from Mr. Oowara:

Sowande is driving a Debonair AMG. She calls it "pseudo-high-class," but it's a good car.

The plane that Kanamori looked up at was a Bugatti 100P, an aircraft that had a hapless destiny.

There's a glimpse of a DMC DeLorean as well, another with a famous story behind it.

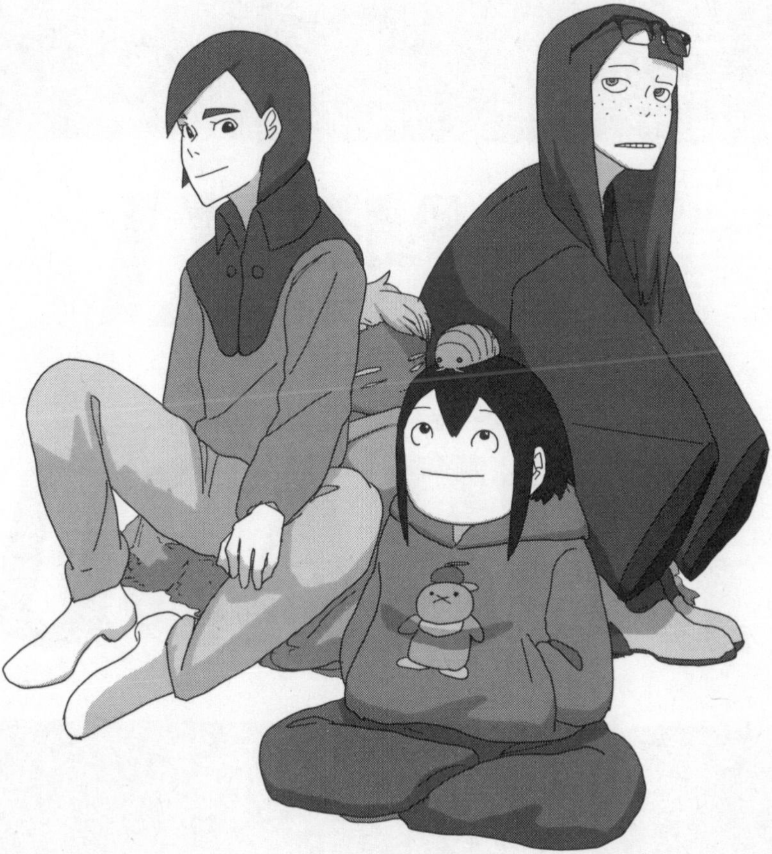

CHAPTER 29:
TANUKI EL DORADO

TANUKI EL DORADO

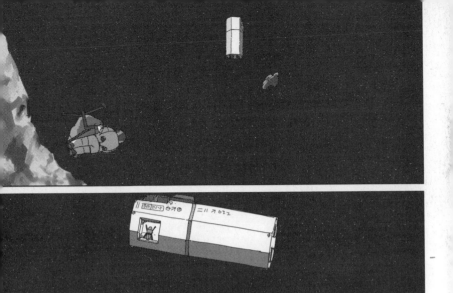

THERE'S A TINY BIT OF NBEOTOW ORE IN HERE. I'M NOT GONNA SELL THIS...

...I'LL KEEP IT FOR MY OWN USE.

OOh!

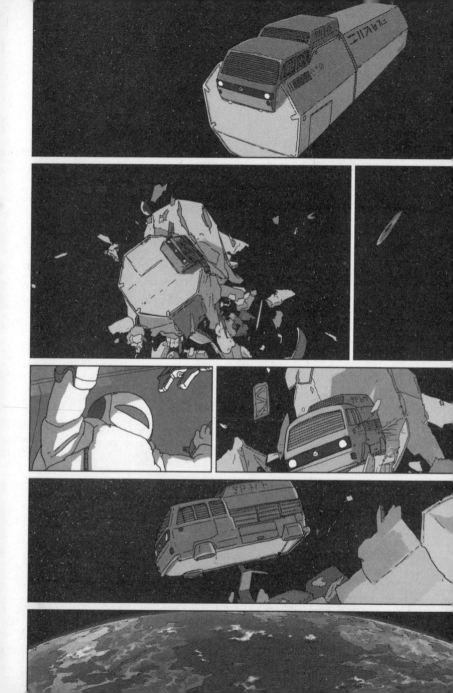

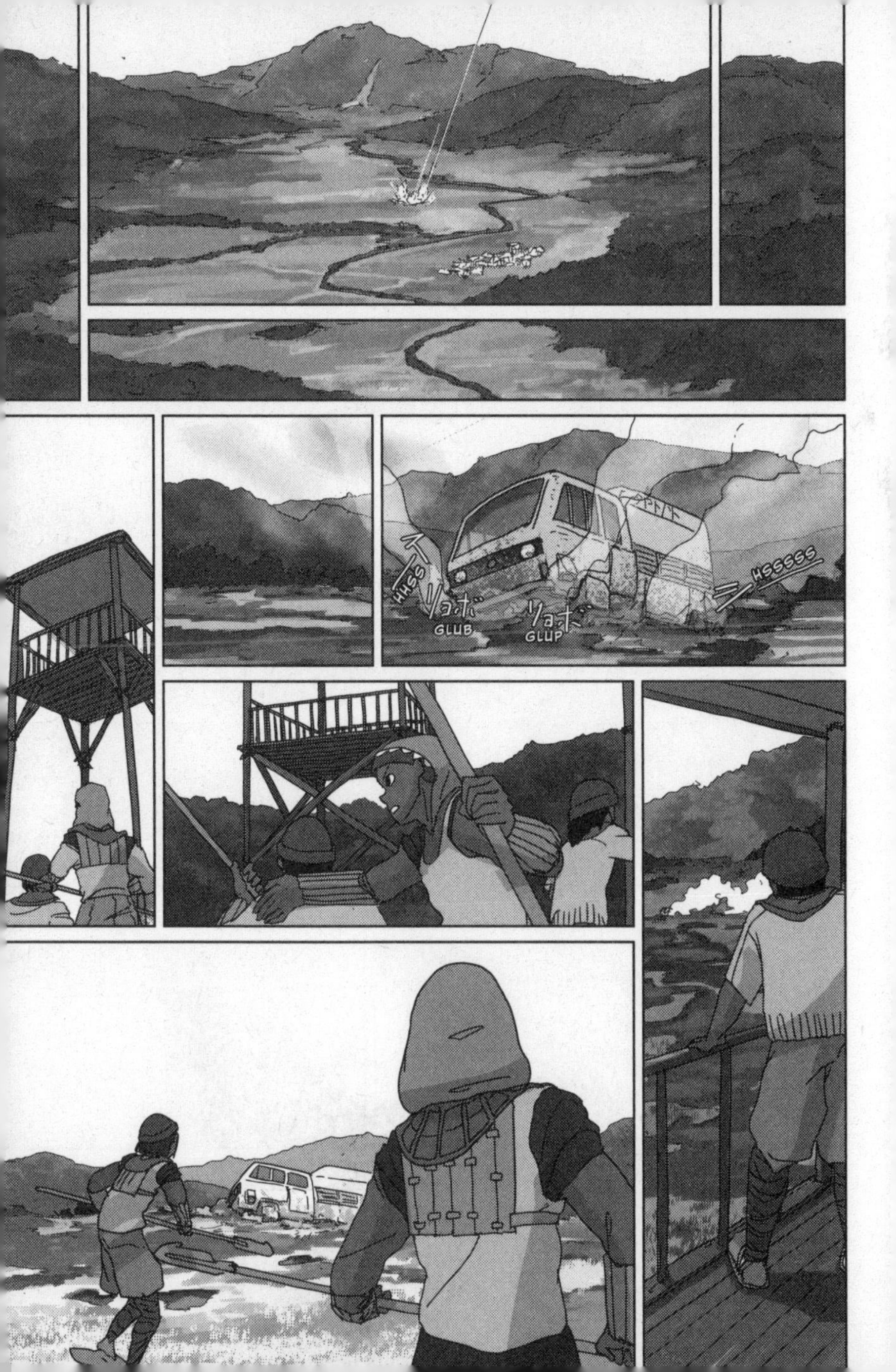
HSSSSS
GLUP
GLUB
HHSS

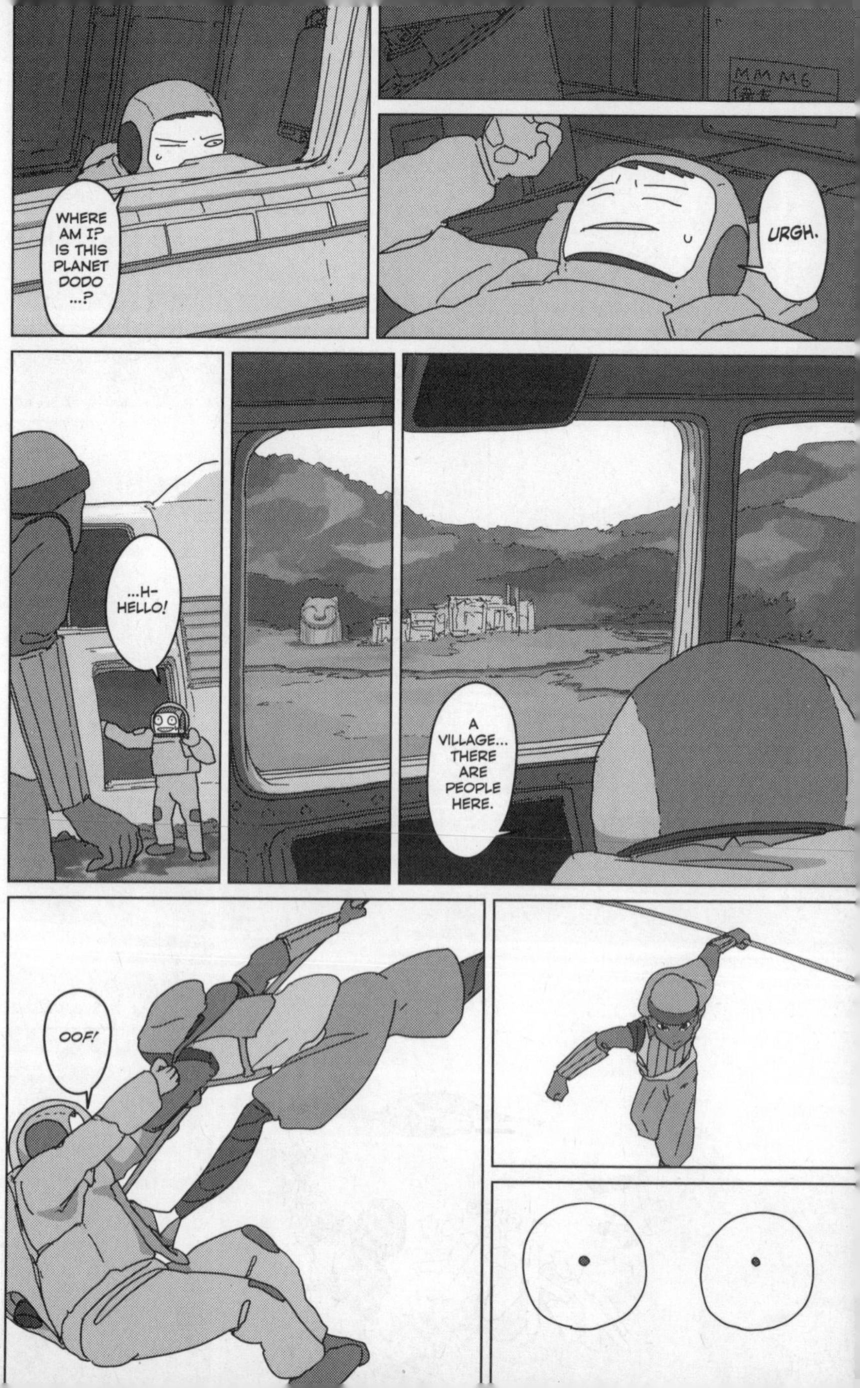

MMM6
URGH.
WHERE AM I? IS THIS PLANET DODO ...?
A VILLAGE... THERE ARE PEOPLE HERE.
...H- HELLO!
OOF!

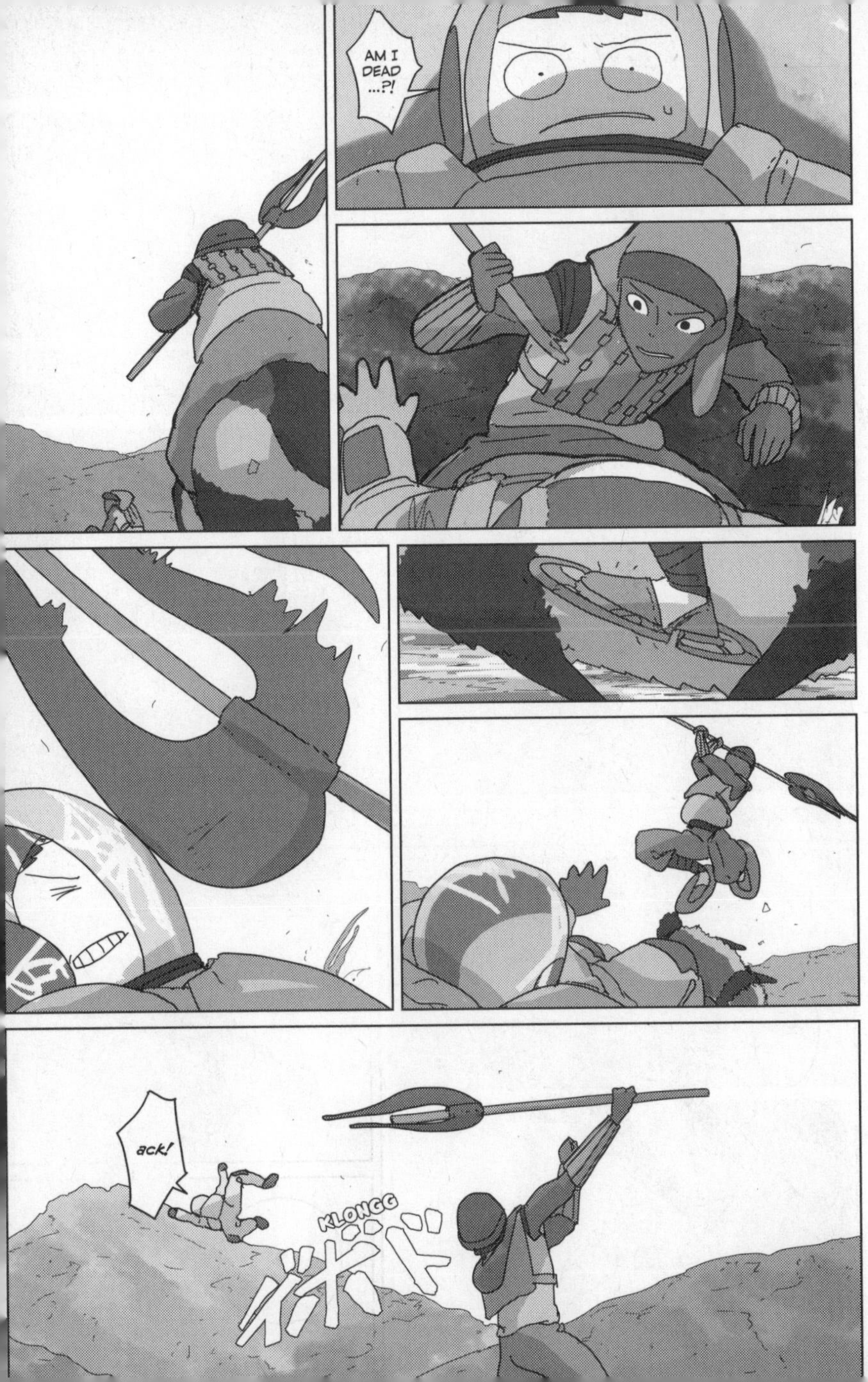
AM I DEAD ...?!
ack!
KLONGG

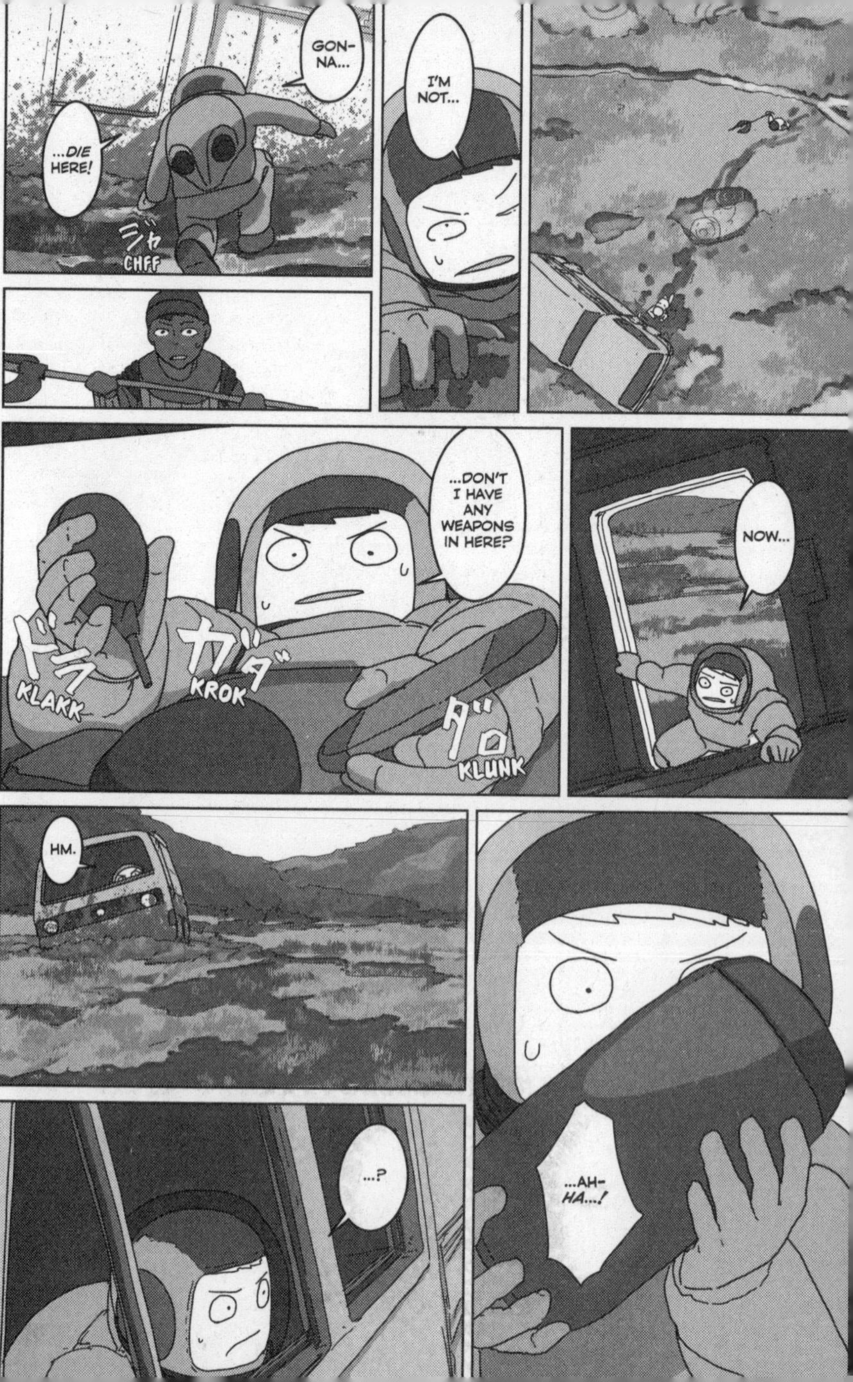
I'M NOT...
GON-NA...
...DIE HERE!
ジャ
CHFF
NOW...
...DON'T I HAVE ANY WEAPONS IN HERE?
ドラ
KLAKK
ガダ
KROK
ダロ
KLUNK
...AH-HA...!
HM.
...?

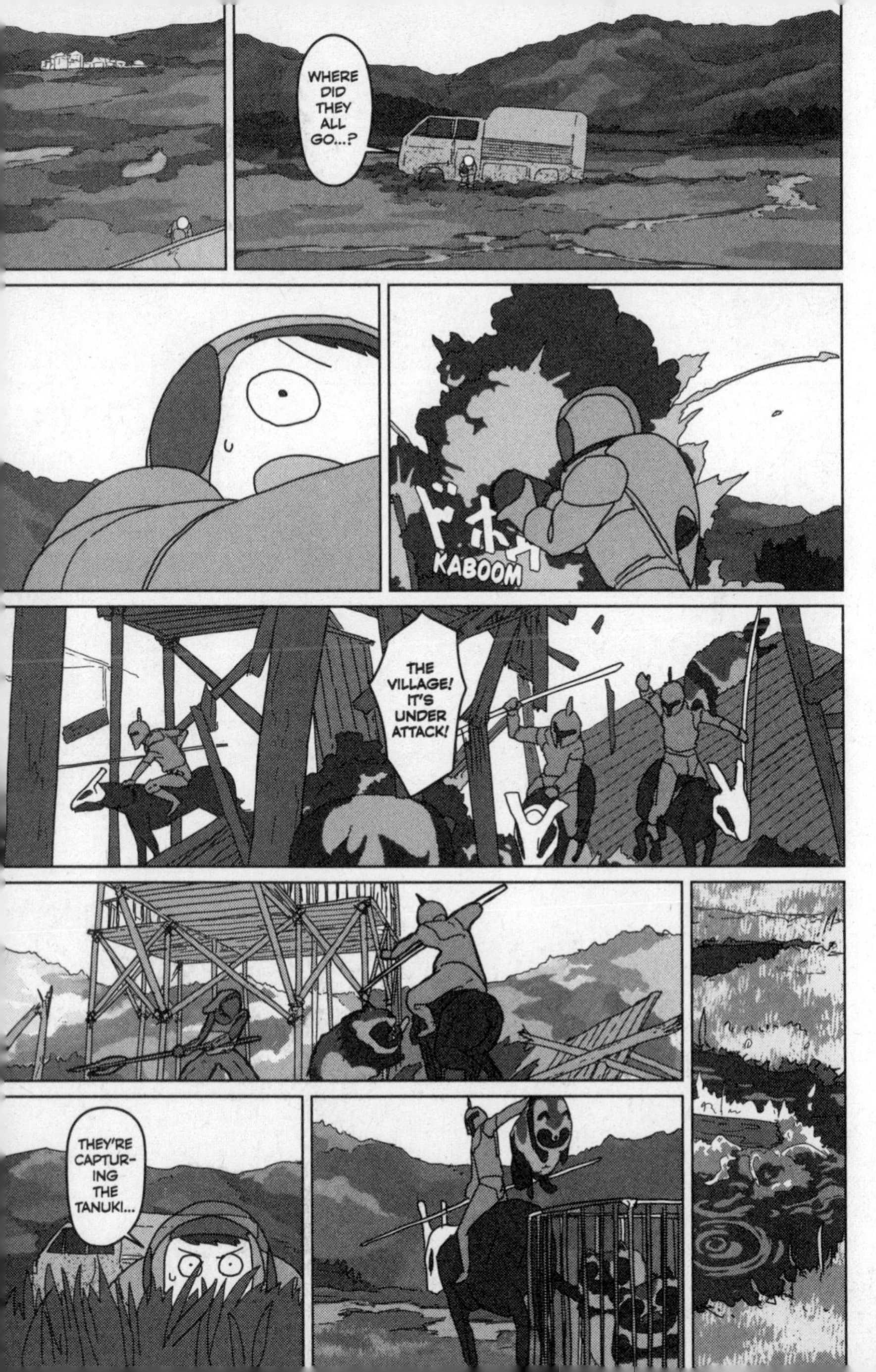
WHERE DID THEY ALL GO...?
KABOOM
THE VILLAGE! IT'S UNDER ATTACK!
THEY'RE CAPTUR-ING THE TANUKI...

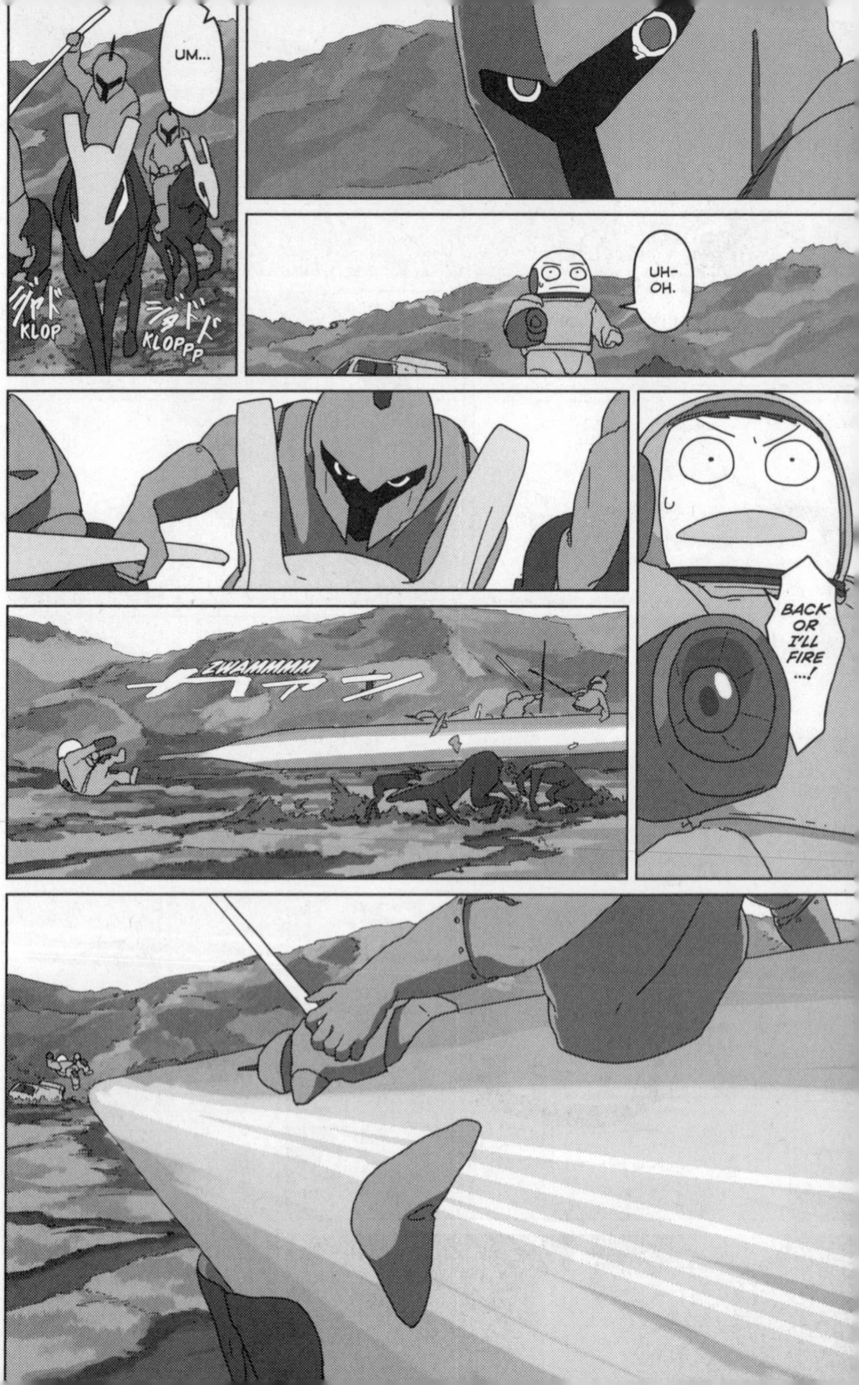
UH-OH.
UM...
KLOP
KLOPPP
BACK OR I'LL FIRE ...!
ZWAMMMM

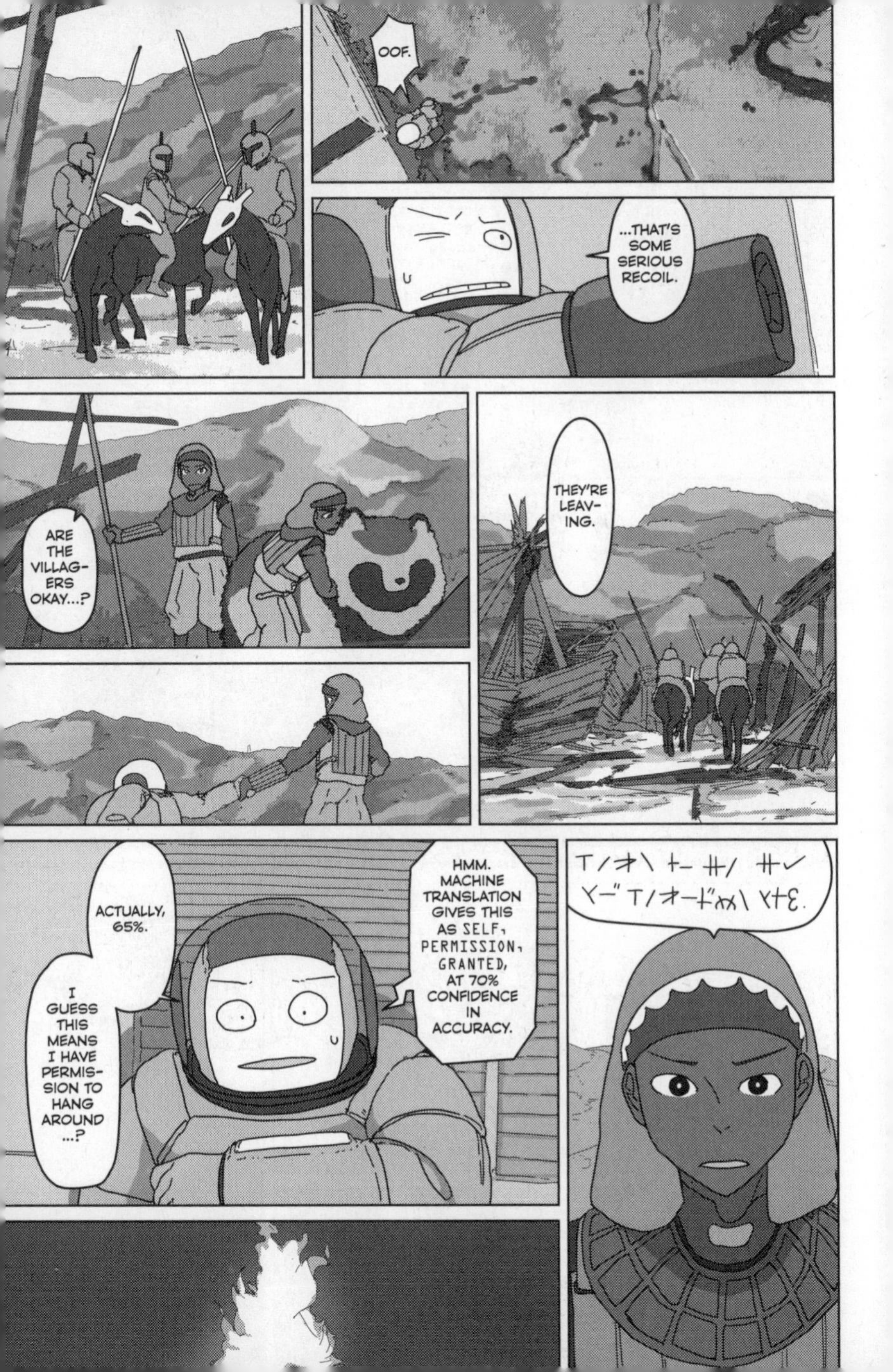
OOF.
...THAT'S SOME SERIOUS RECOIL.
THEY'RE LEAVING.
ARE THE VILLAGERS OKAY...?
HMM. MACHINE TRANSLATION GIVES THIS AS SELF, PERMISSION, GRANTED, AT 70% CONFIDENCE IN ACCURACY.
ACTUALLY, 65%.
I GUESS THIS MEANS I HAVE PERMISSION TO HANG AROUND...?

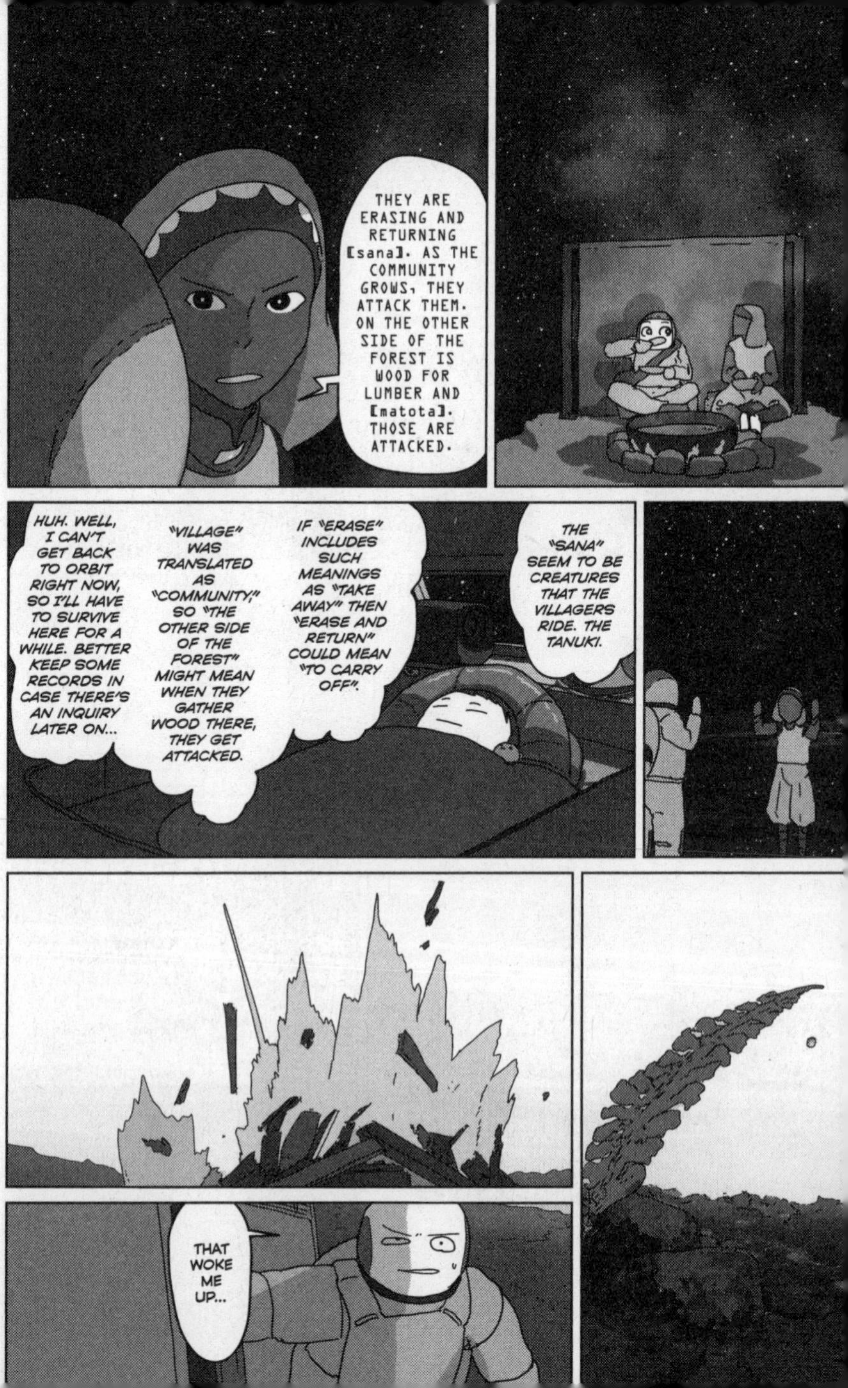
THEY ARE ERASING AND RETURNING [sana]. AS THE COMMUNITY GROWS, THEY ATTACK THEM. ON THE OTHER SIDE OF THE FOREST IS WOOD FOR LUMBER AND [matota]. THOSE ARE ATTACKED.
THE "SANA" SEEM TO BE CREATURES THAT THE VILLAGERS RIDE. THE TANUKI.
IF "ERASE" INCLUDES SUCH MEANINGS AS "TAKE AWAY" THEN "ERASE AND RETURN" COULD MEAN "TO CARRY OFF".
"VILLAGE" WAS TRANSLATED AS "COMMUNITY," SO "THE OTHER SIDE OF THE FOREST" MIGHT MEAN WHEN THEY GATHER WOOD THERE, THEY GET ATTACKED.
HUH. WELL, I CAN'T GET BACK TO ORBIT RIGHT NOW, SO I'LL HAVE TO SURVIVE HERE FOR A WHILE. BETTER KEEP SOME RECORDS IN CASE THERE'S AN INQUIRY LATER ON...
THAT WOKE ME UP...

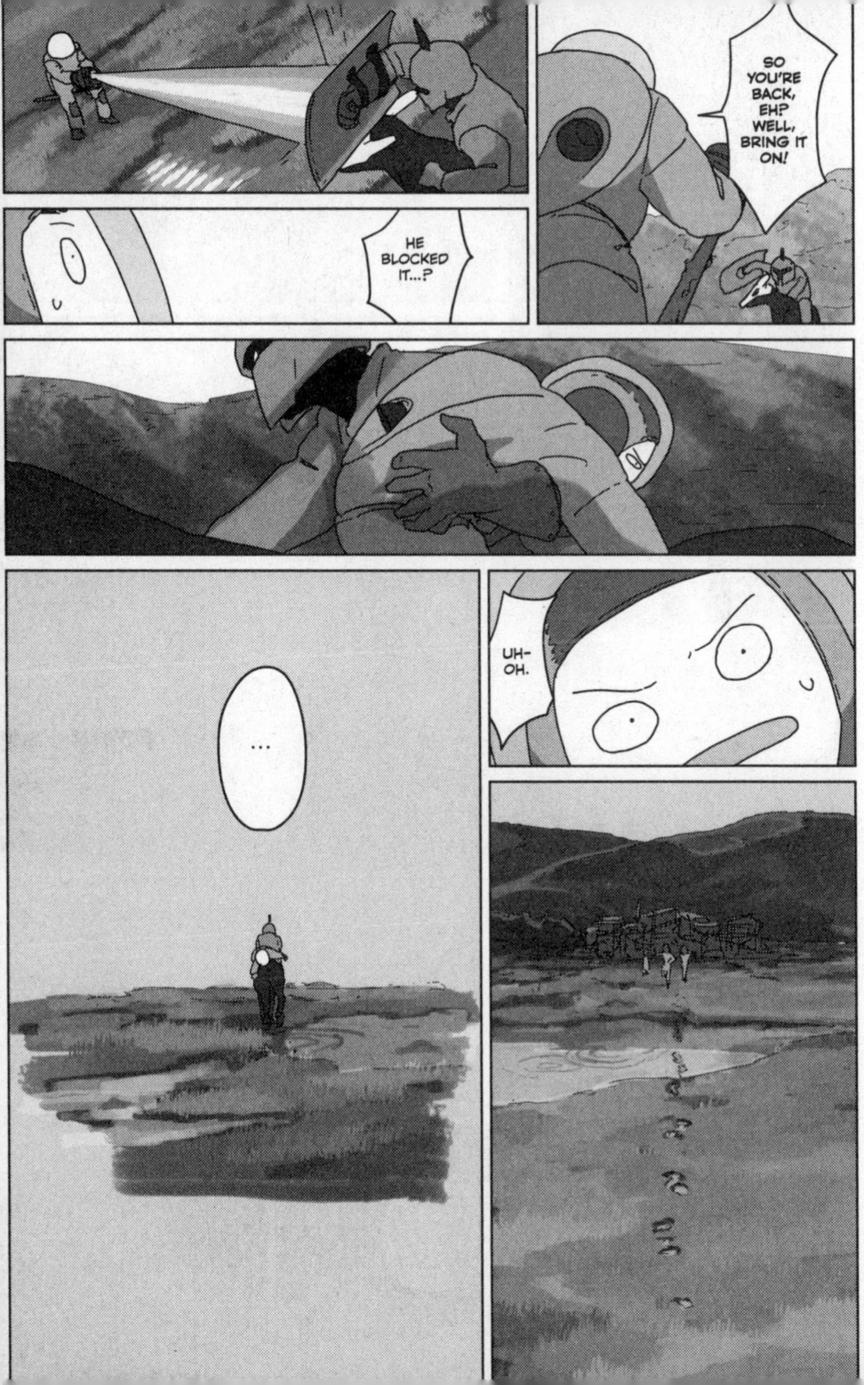
SO YOU'RE BACK, EH? WELL, BRING IT ON!
HE BLOCKED IT...?
UH-OH.
...

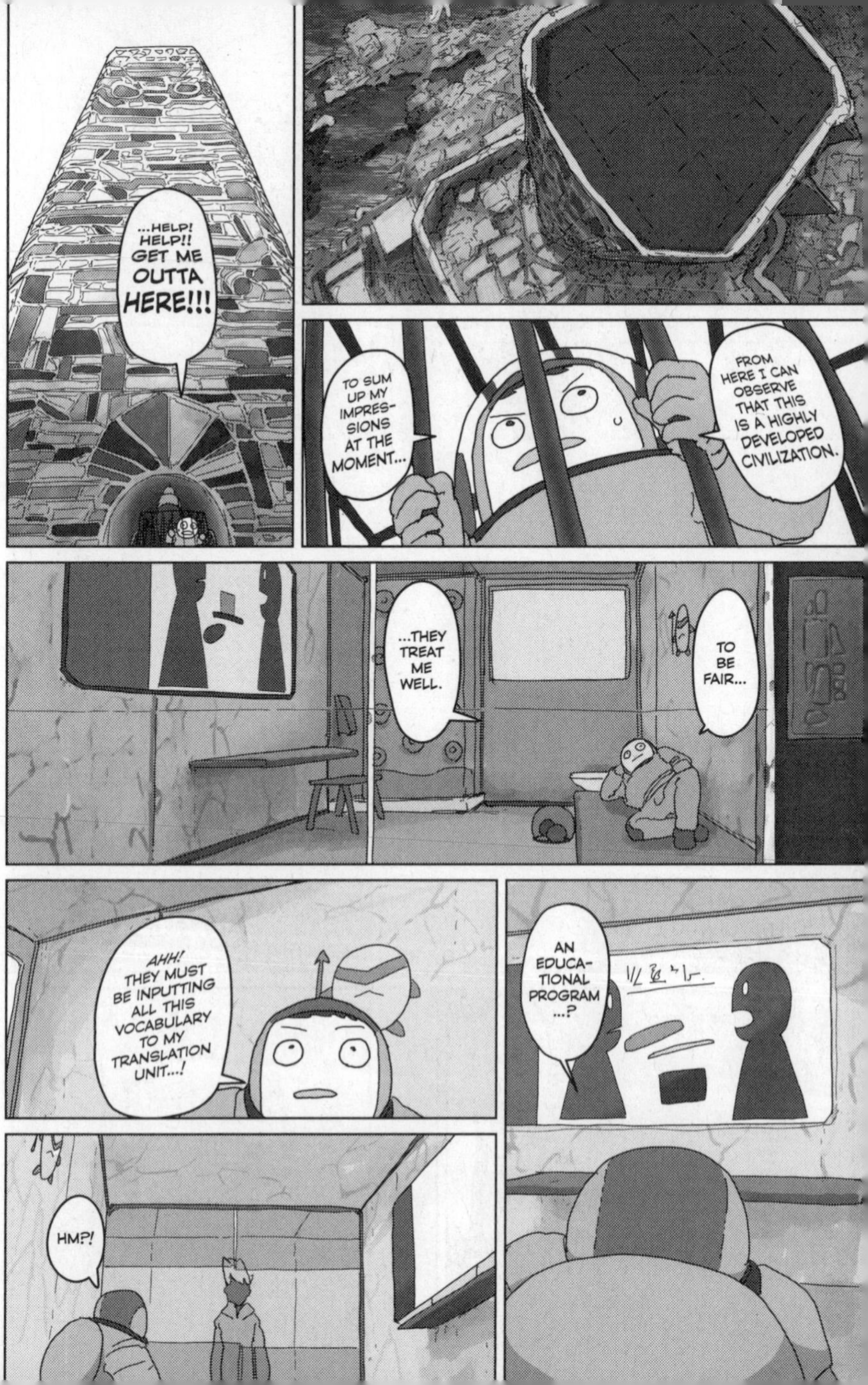
FROM HERE I CAN OBSERVE THAT THIS IS A HIGHLY DEVELOPED CIVILIZATION.
TO SUM UP MY IMPRESSIONS AT THE MOMENT...
...HELP! HELP!! GET ME OUTTA HERE!!!
TO BE FAIR...
...THEY TREAT ME WELL.
AN EDUCATIONAL PROGRAM ...?
AHH! THEY MUST BE INPUTTING ALL THIS VOCABULARY TO MY TRANSLATION UNIT...!
HM?!

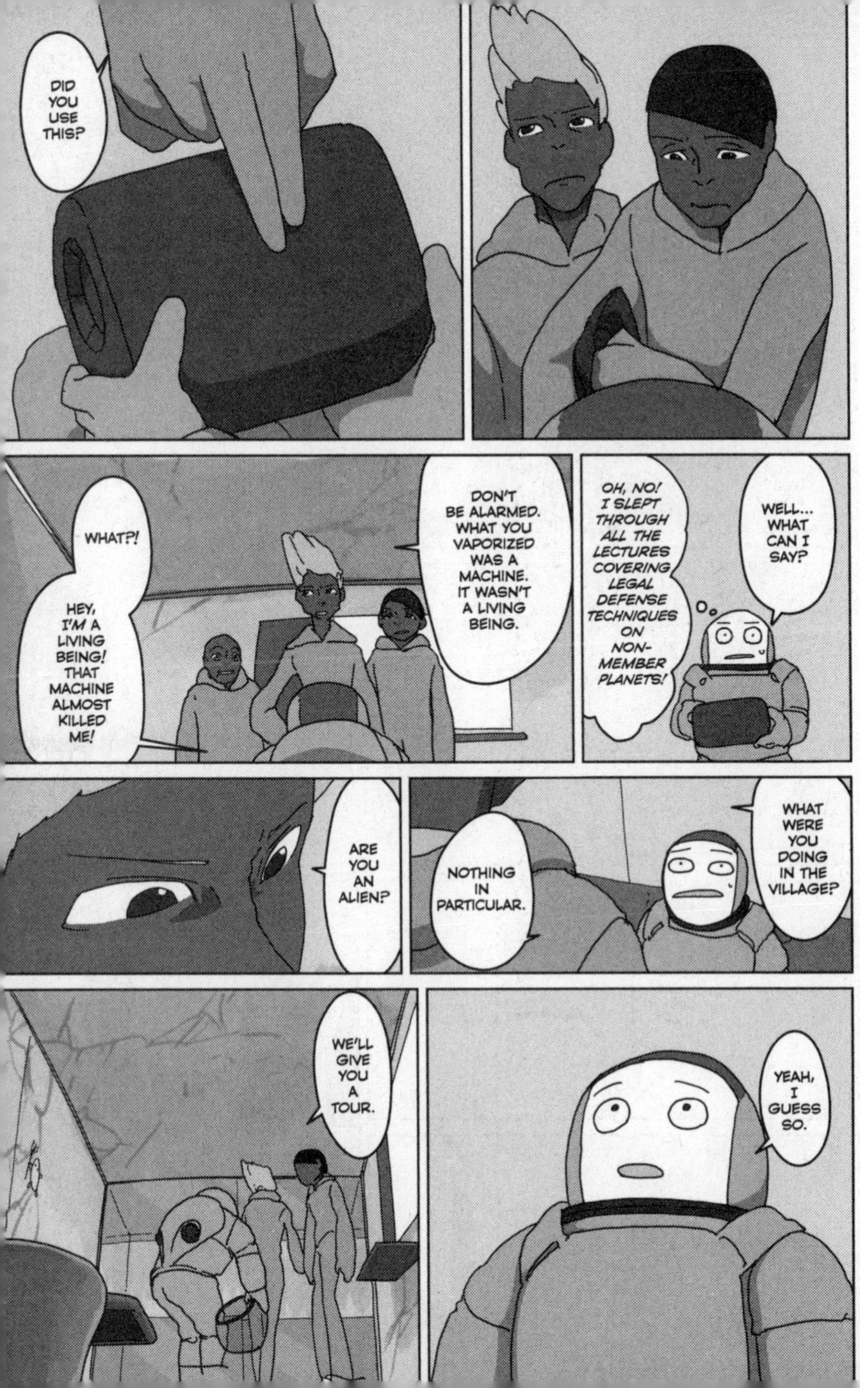
DID YOU USE THIS?
WELL... WHAT CAN I SAY?
OH, NO! I SLEPT THROUGH ALL THE LECTURES COVERING LEGAL DEFENSE TECHNIQUES ON NON-MEMBER PLANETS!
DON'T BE ALARMED. WHAT YOU VAPORIZED WAS A MACHINE. IT WASN'T A LIVING BEING.
WHAT?!
HEY, I'M A LIVING BEING! THAT MACHINE ALMOST KILLED ME!
WHAT WERE YOU DOING IN THE VILLAGE?
NOTHING IN PARTICULAR.
ARE YOU AN ALIEN?
YEAH, I GUESS SO.
WE'LL GIVE YOU A TOUR.

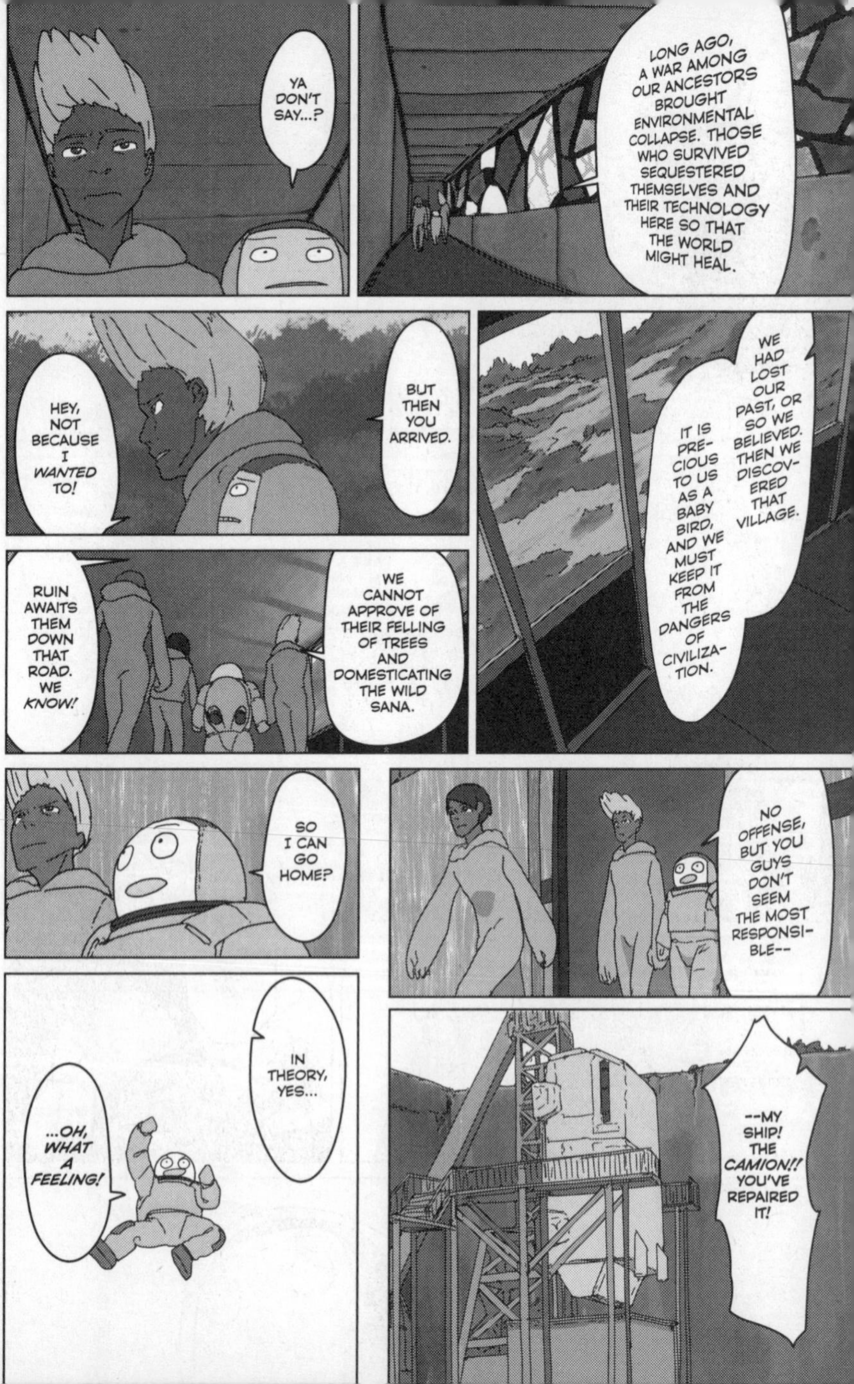
LONG AGO, A WAR AMONG OUR ANCESTORS BROUGHT ENVIRONMENTAL COLLAPSE. THOSE WHO SURVIVED SEQUESTERED THEMSELVES AND THEIR TECHNOLOGY HERE SO THAT THE WORLD MIGHT HEAL.
YA DON'T SAY...?
WE HAD LOST OUR PAST, OR SO WE BELIEVED. THEN WE DISCOVERED THAT VILLAGE.
IT IS PRECIOUS TO US AS A BABY BIRD, AND WE MUST KEEP IT FROM THE DANGERS OF CIVILIZATION.
BUT THEN YOU ARRIVED.
HEY, NOT BECAUSE I *WANTED* TO!
WE CANNOT APPROVE OF THEIR FELLING OF TREES AND DOMESTICATING THE WILD SANA.
RUIN AWAITS THEM DOWN THAT ROAD. WE *KNOW!*
NO OFFENSE, BUT YOU GUYS DON'T SEEM THE MOST RESPONSIBLE--
SO I CAN GO HOME?
--MY SHIP! THE *CAMION!!* YOU'VE REPAIRED IT!
IN THEORY, YES...
...OH, WHAT A FEELING!

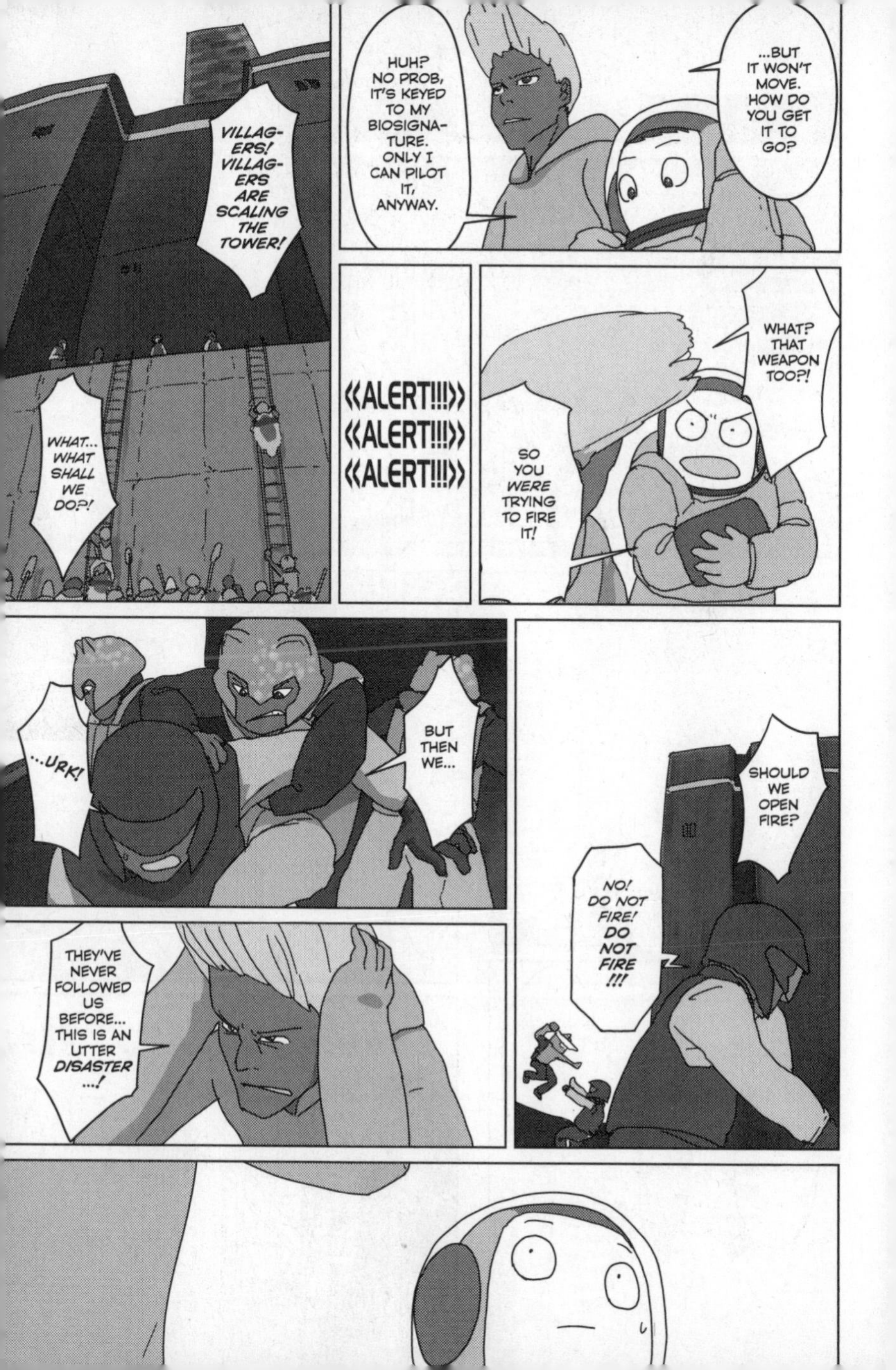
...BUT IT WON'T MOVE. HOW DO YOU GET IT TO GO?
HUH? NO PROB, IT'S KEYED TO MY BIOSIGNATURE. ONLY I CAN PILOT IT, ANYWAY.
WHAT? THAT WEAPON TOO?!
SO YOU *WERE* TRYING TO FIRE IT!
«ALERT!!!» «ALERT!!!» «ALERT!!!»
VILLAGERS! VILLAGERS ARE SCALING THE TOWER!
WHAT... WHAT SHALL WE DO?!
SHOULD WE OPEN FIRE?
NO! DO NOT FIRE! DO NOT FIRE!!!
BUT THEN WE...
...URK!
THEY'VE NEVER FOLLOWED US BEFORE... THIS IS AN UTTER *DISASTER*...!

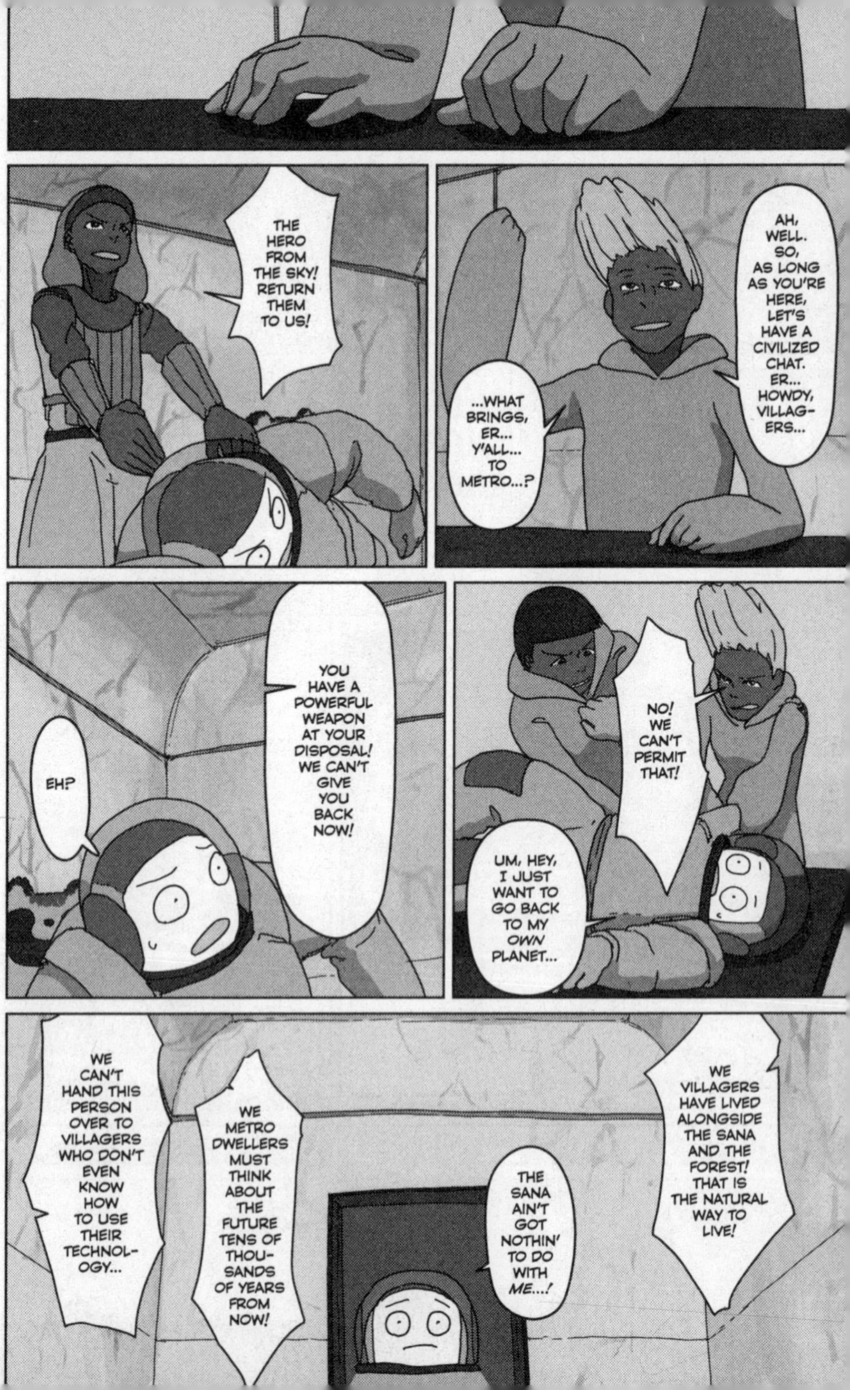
AH, WELL. SO, AS LONG AS YOU'RE HERE, LET'S HAVE A CIVILIZED CHAT. ER... HOWDY, VILLAGERS...
...WHAT BRINGS, ER... Y'ALL... TO METRO...?
THE HERO FROM THE SKY! RETURN THEM TO US!
NO! WE CAN'T PERMIT THAT!
UM, HEY, I JUST WANT TO GO BACK TO MY *OWN* PLANET...
YOU HAVE A POWERFUL WEAPON AT YOUR DISPOSAL! WE CAN'T GIVE YOU BACK NOW!
EH?
WE VILLAGERS HAVE LIVED ALONGSIDE THE SANA AND THE FOREST! THAT IS THE NATURAL WAY TO LIVE!
WE CAN'T HAND THIS PERSON OVER TO VILLAGERS WHO DON'T EVEN KNOW HOW TO USE THEIR TECHNOLOGY...
WE METRO DWELLERS MUST THINK ABOUT THE FUTURE TENS OF THOUSANDS OF YEARS FROM NOW!
THE SANA AIN'T GOT NOTHIN' TO DO WITH *ME*...!

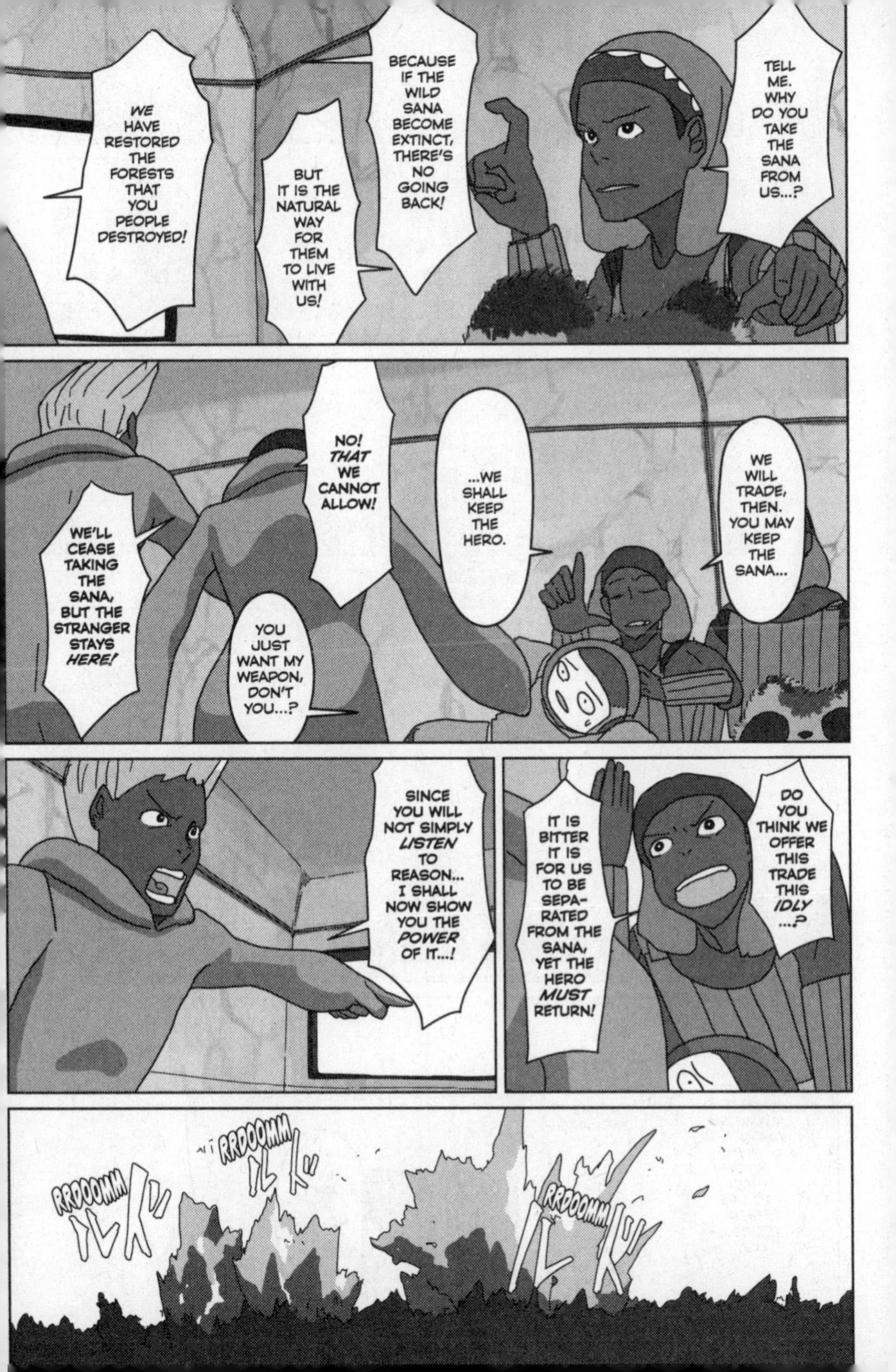
TELL ME. WHY DO YOU TAKE THE SANA FROM US...?
BECAUSE IF THE WILD SANA BECOME EXTINCT, THERE'S NO GOING BACK!
BUT IT IS THE NATURAL WAY FOR THEM TO LIVE WITH US!
WE HAVE RESTORED THE FORESTS THAT YOU PEOPLE DESTROYED!
WE WILL TRADE, THEN. YOU MAY KEEP THE SANA...
...WE SHALL KEEP THE HERO.
NO! *THAT* WE CANNOT ALLOW!
YOU JUST WANT MY WEAPON, DON'T YOU...?
WE'LL CEASE TAKING THE SANA, BUT THE STRANGER STAYS *HERE!*
DO YOU THINK WE OFFER THIS TRADE THIS *IDLY* ...?
IT IS BITTER IT IS FOR US TO BE SEPA-RATED FROM THE SANA, YET THE HERO *MUST* RETURN!
SINCE YOU WILL NOT SIMPLY *LISTEN* TO REASON... I SHALL NOW SHOW YOU THE *POWER* OF IT...!
RRDOOMM
RRDOOMM
RRDOOMM

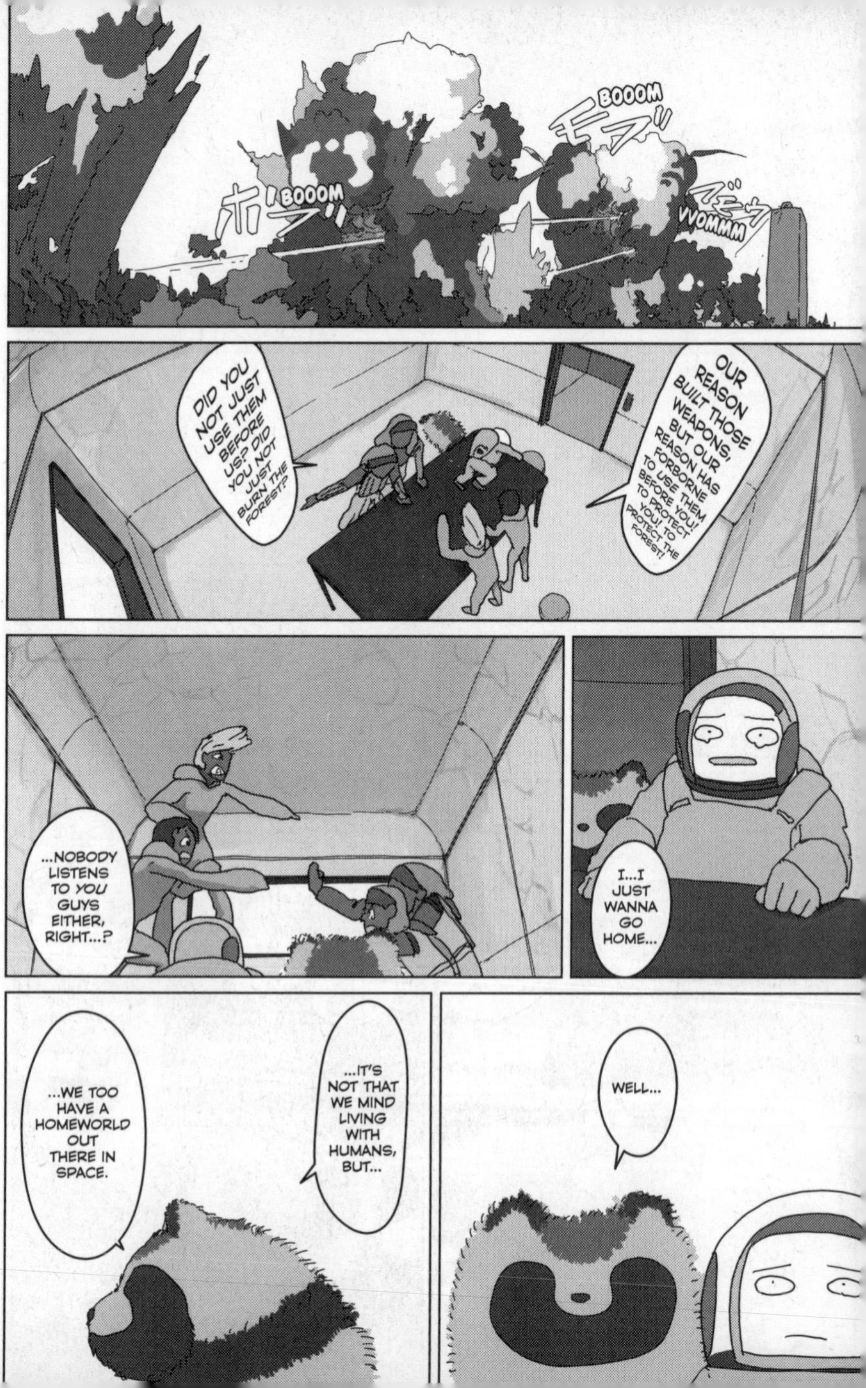
BOOOM
VVOMMM
BOOOM
OUR REASON BUILT THOSE WEAPONS, BUT OUR REASON HAS FORBORNE TO USE THEM BEFORE YOU! TO PROTECT YOU! TO PROTECT THE FOREST!
DID YOU NOT JUST USE THEM BEFORE US? DID YOU NOT JUST BURN THE FOREST?
I...I JUST WANNA GO HOME...
...NOBODY LISTENS TO *YOU* GUYS EITHER, RIGHT...?
WELL...
...IT'S NOT THAT WE MIND LIVING WITH HUMANS, BUT...
...WE TOO HAVE A HOMEWORLD OUT THERE IN SPACE.

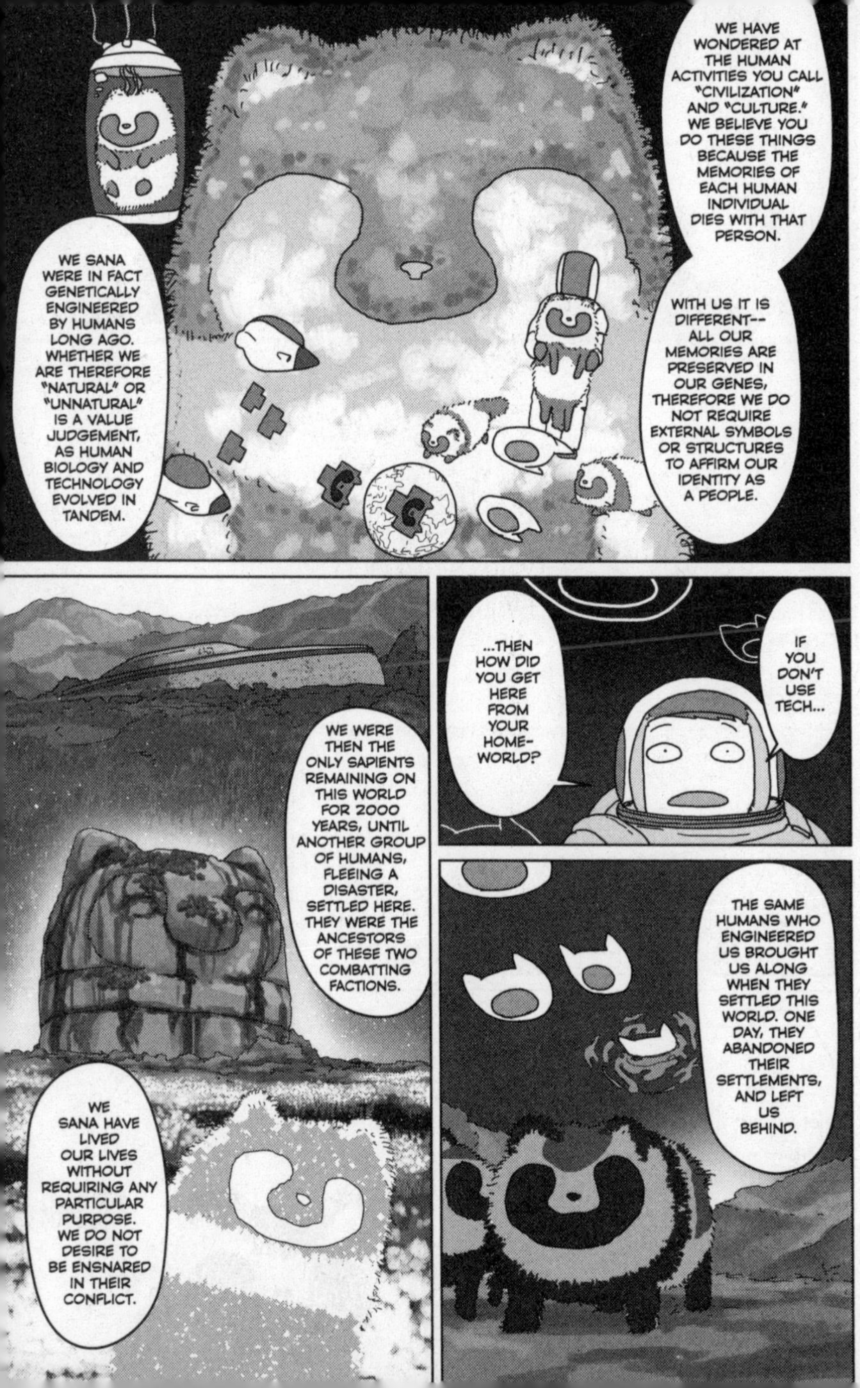
WE HAVE WONDERED AT THE HUMAN ACTIVITIES YOU CALL "CIVILIZATION" AND "CULTURE." WE BELIEVE YOU DO THESE THINGS BECAUSE THE MEMORIES OF EACH HUMAN INDIVIDUAL DIES WITH THAT PERSON.
WITH US IT IS DIFFERENT-- ALL OUR MEMORIES ARE PRESERVED IN OUR GENES, THEREFORE WE DO NOT REQUIRE EXTERNAL SYMBOLS OR STRUCTURES TO AFFIRM OUR IDENTITY AS A PEOPLE.
WE SANA WERE IN FACT GENETICALLY ENGINEERED BY HUMANS LONG AGO. WHETHER WE ARE THEREFORE "NATURAL" OR "UNNATURAL" IS A VALUE JUDGEMENT, AS HUMAN BIOLOGY AND TECHNOLOGY EVOLVED IN TANDEM.
IF YOU DON'T USE TECH...
...THEN HOW DID YOU GET HERE FROM YOUR HOME-WORLD?
THE SAME HUMANS WHO ENGINEERED US BROUGHT US ALONG WHEN THEY SETTLED THIS WORLD. ONE DAY, THEY ABANDONED THEIR SETTLEMENTS, AND LEFT US BEHIND.
WE WERE THEN THE ONLY SAPIENTS REMAINING ON THIS WORLD FOR 2000 YEARS, UNTIL ANOTHER GROUP OF HUMANS, FLEEING A DISASTER, SETTLED HERE. THEY WERE THE ANCESTORS OF THESE TWO COMBATTING FACTIONS.
WE SANA HAVE LIVED OUR LIVES WITHOUT REQUIRING ANY PARTICULAR PURPOSE. WE DO NOT DESIRE TO BE ENSNARED IN THEIR CONFLICT.

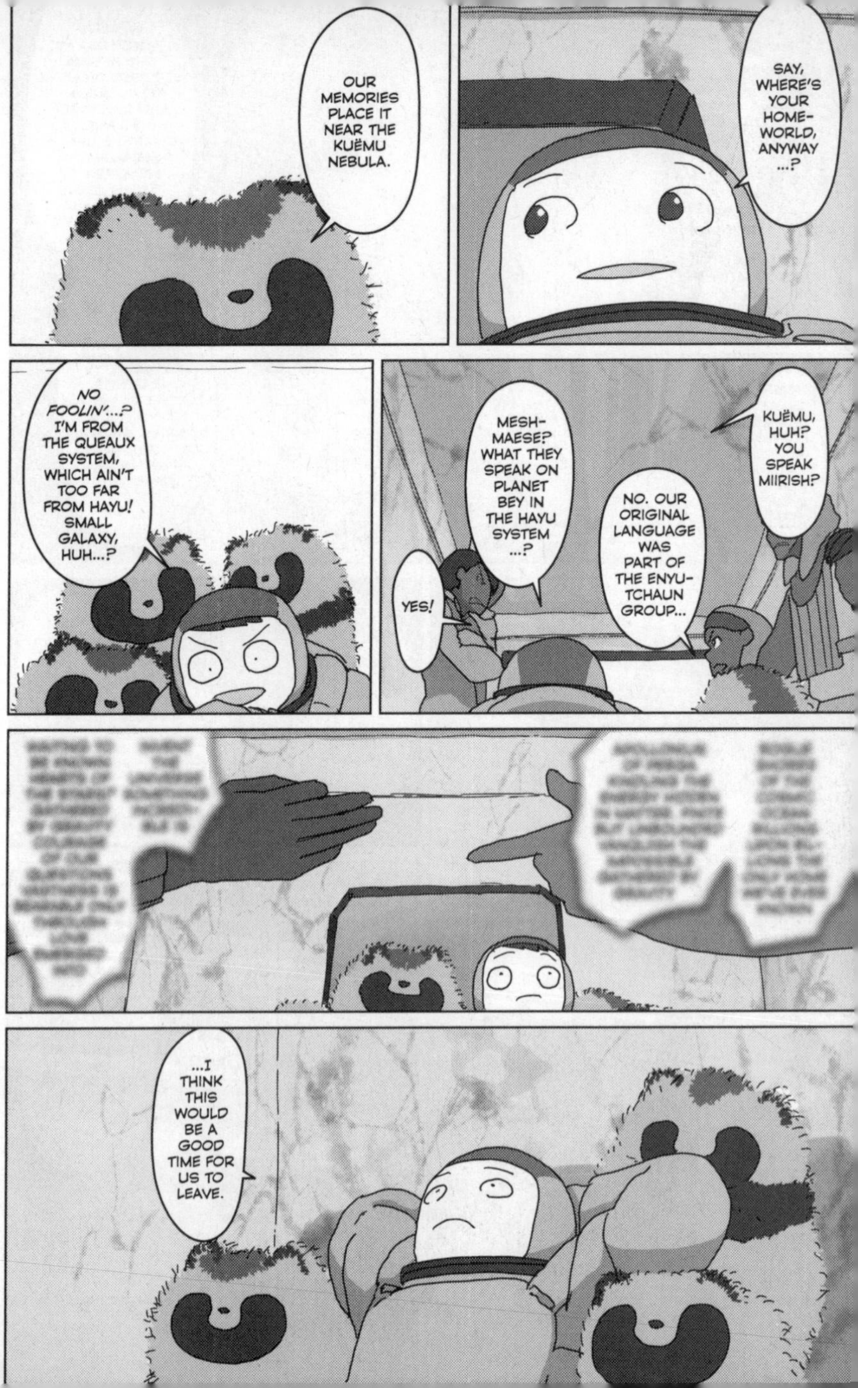
SAY, WHERE'S YOUR HOME-WORLD, ANYWAY ...?
OUR MEMORIES PLACE IT NEAR THE KUËMU NEBULA.
KUËMU, HUH? YOU SPEAK MIIRISH?
NO. OUR ORIGINAL LANGUAGE WAS PART OF THE ENYU-TCHAUN GROUP...
MESH-MAESE? WHAT THEY SPEAK ON PLANET BEY IN THE HAYU SYSTEM ...?
YES!
NO FOOLIN'...? I'M FROM THE QUEAUX SYSTEM, WHICH AIN'T TOO FAR FROM HAYU! SMALL GALAXY, HUH...?
...I THINK THIS WOULD BE A GOOD TIME FOR US TO LEAVE.

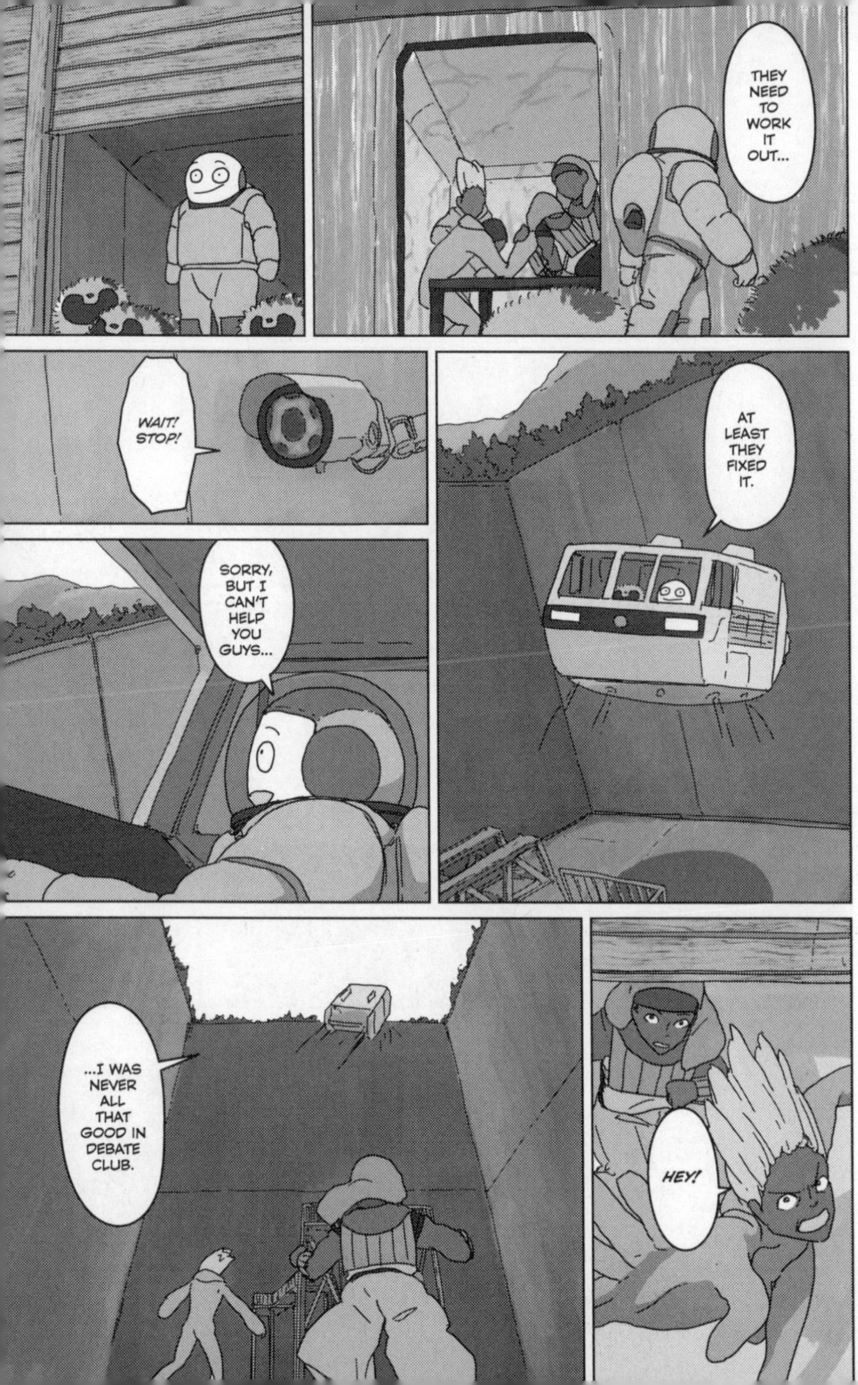
THEY NEED TO WORK IT OUT...
AT LEAST THEY FIXED IT.
WAIT! STOP!
SORRY, BUT I CAN'T HELP YOU GUYS...
HEY!
...I WAS NEVER ALL THAT GOOD IN DEBATE CLUB.

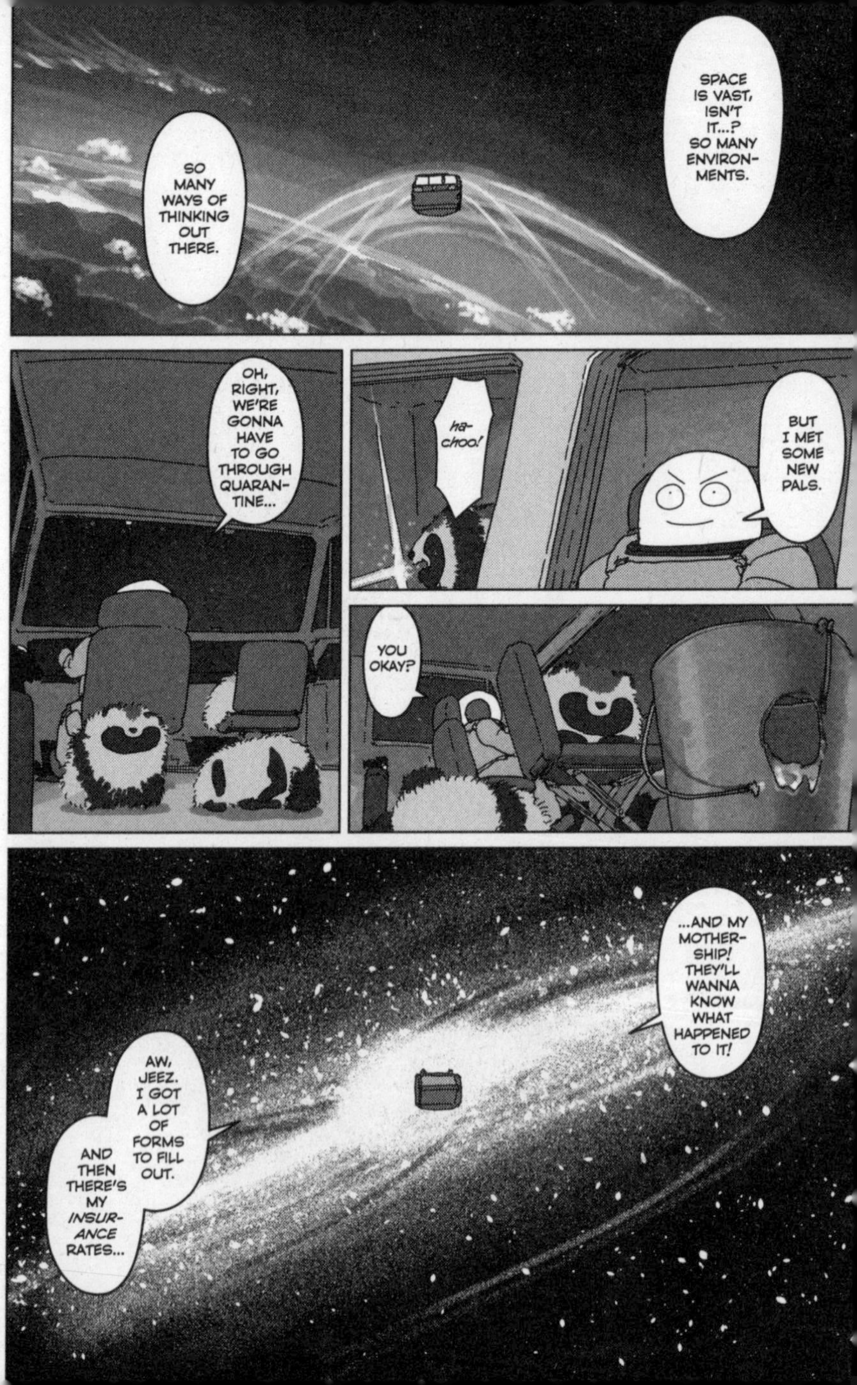
SPACE IS VAST, ISN'T IT...? SO MANY ENVIRONMENTS.
SO MANY WAYS OF THINKING OUT THERE.
BUT I MET SOME NEW PALS.
ha-choo!
YOU OKAY?
OH, RIGHT, WE'RE GONNA HAVE TO GO THROUGH QUARANTINE...
...AND MY MOTHERSHIP! THEY'LL WANNA KNOW WHAT HAPPENED TO IT!
AW, JEEZ. I GOT A LOT OF FORMS TO FILL OUT.
AND THEN THERE'S MY *INSURANCE* RATES...

CHAPTER 30: ASAKUSA'S CLEAR-HEADED WAY

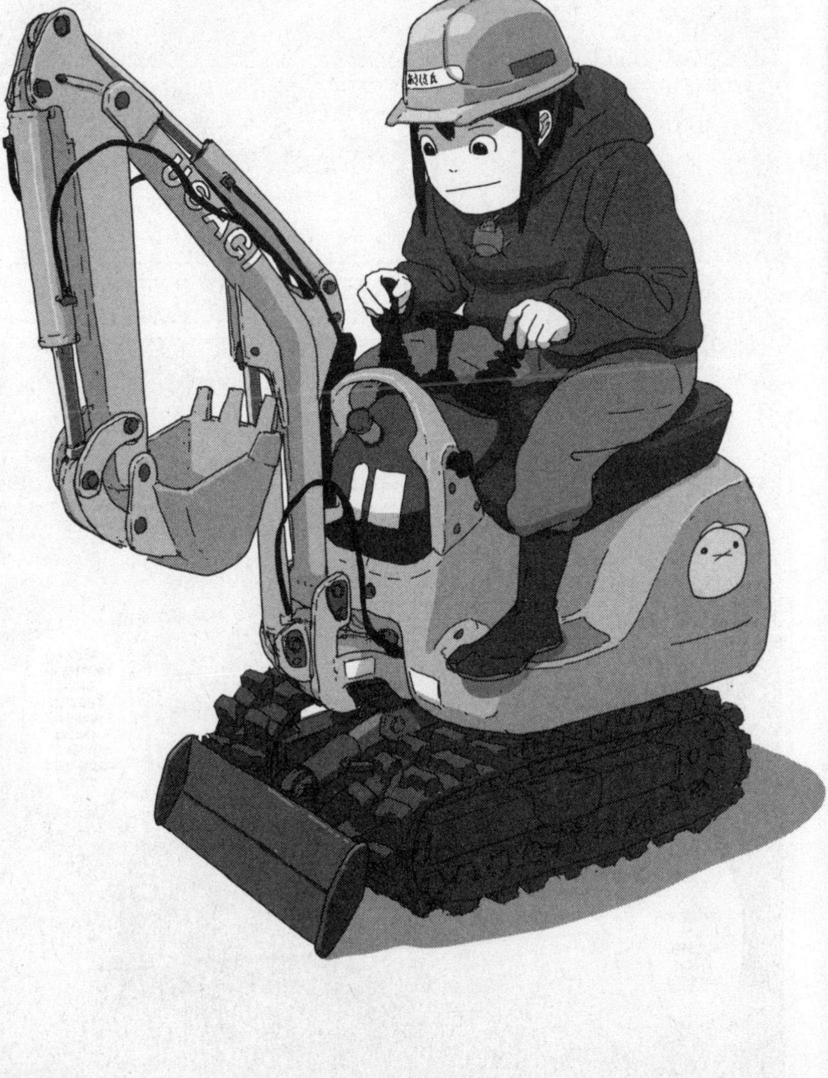

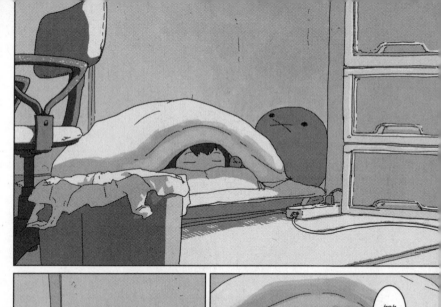

heh heh heh...

WE'VE GOT A COOL ANIME ...!

WE DID IT!

...AWE-SOME!

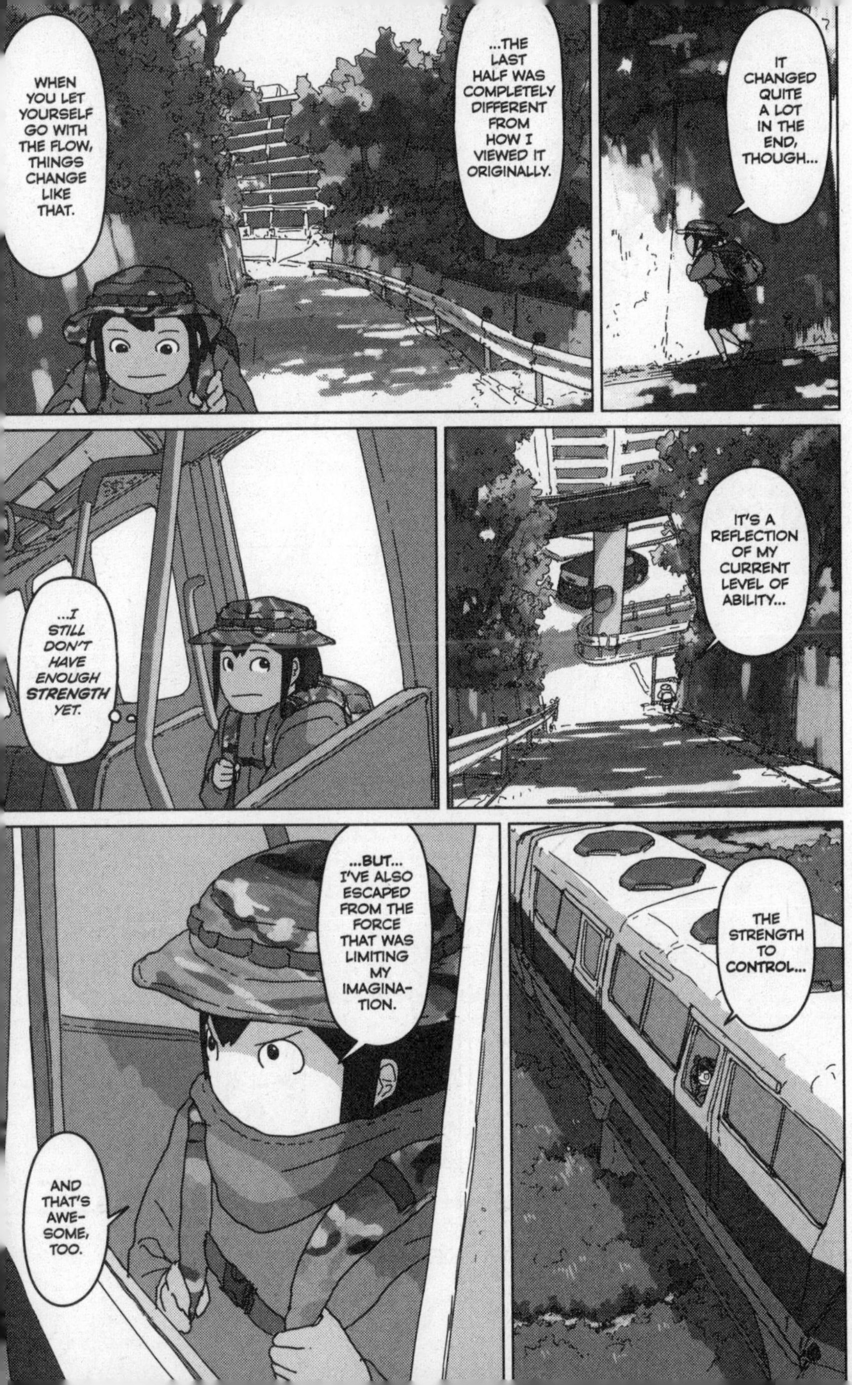
IT CHANGED QUITE A LOT IN THE END, THOUGH...
...THE LAST HALF WAS COMPLETELY DIFFERENT FROM HOW I VIEWED IT ORIGINALLY.
WHEN YOU LET YOURSELF GO WITH THE FLOW, THINGS CHANGE LIKE THAT.
IT'S A REFLECTION OF MY CURRENT LEVEL OF ABILITY...
...I STILL DON'T HAVE ENOUGH *STRENGTH* YET.
THE STRENGTH TO CONTROL...
...BUT... I'VE ALSO ESCAPED FROM THE FORCE THAT WAS LIMITING MY IMAGINA-TION.
AND THAT'S AWE-SOME, TOO.

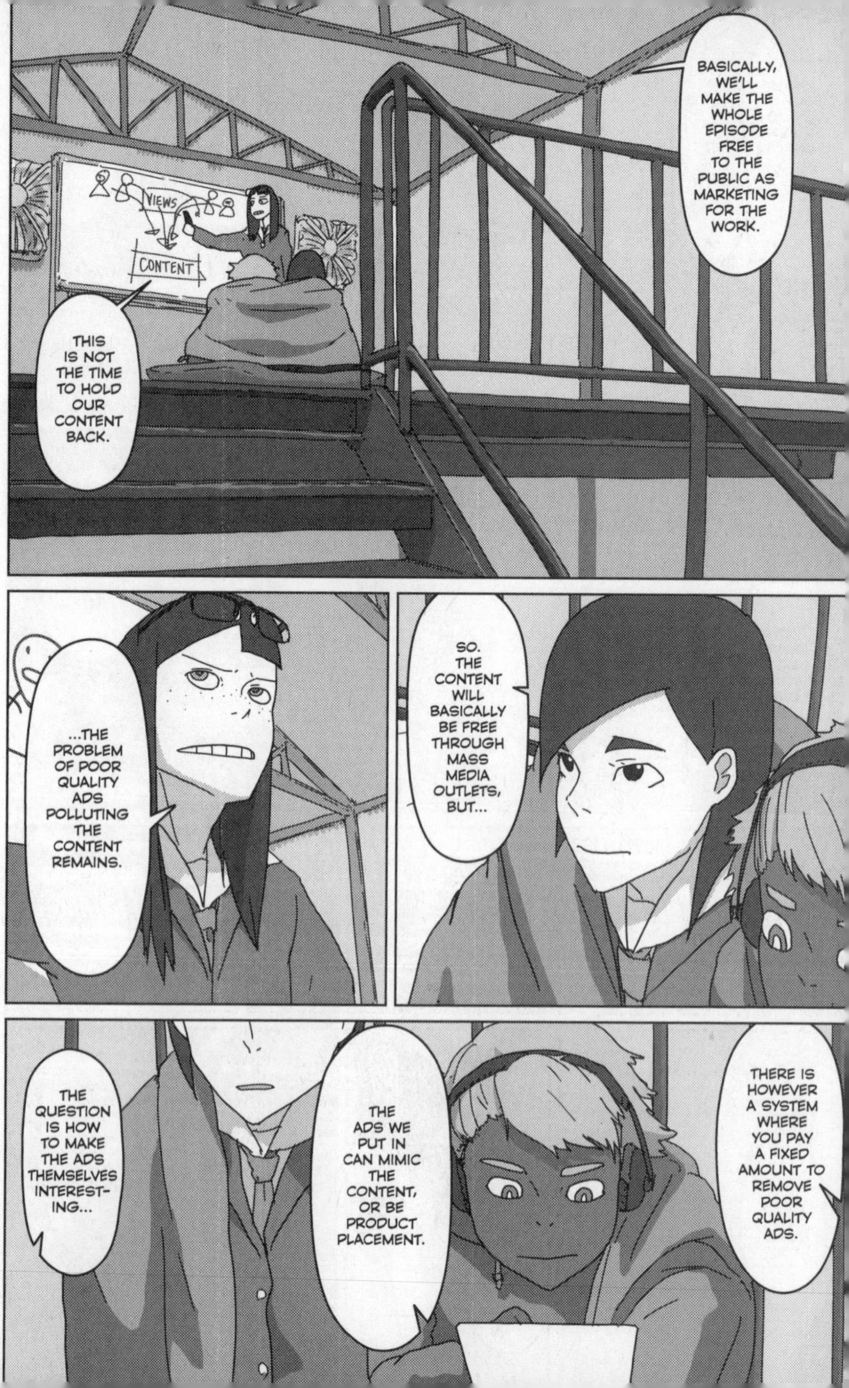
BASICALLY, WE'LL MAKE THE WHOLE EPISODE FREE TO THE PUBLIC AS MARKETING FOR THE WORK.
VIEWS
CONTENT
THIS IS NOT THE TIME TO HOLD OUR CONTENT BACK.
SO. THE CONTENT WILL BASICALLY BE FREE THROUGH MASS MEDIA OUTLETS, BUT...
...THE PROBLEM OF POOR QUALITY ADS POLLUTING THE CONTENT REMAINS.
THERE IS HOWEVER A SYSTEM WHERE YOU PAY A FIXED AMOUNT TO REMOVE POOR QUALITY ADS.
THE ADS WE PUT IN CAN MIMIC THE CONTENT, OR BE PRODUCT PLACEMENT.
THE QUESTION IS HOW TO MAKE THE ADS THEMSELVES INTEREST-ING...

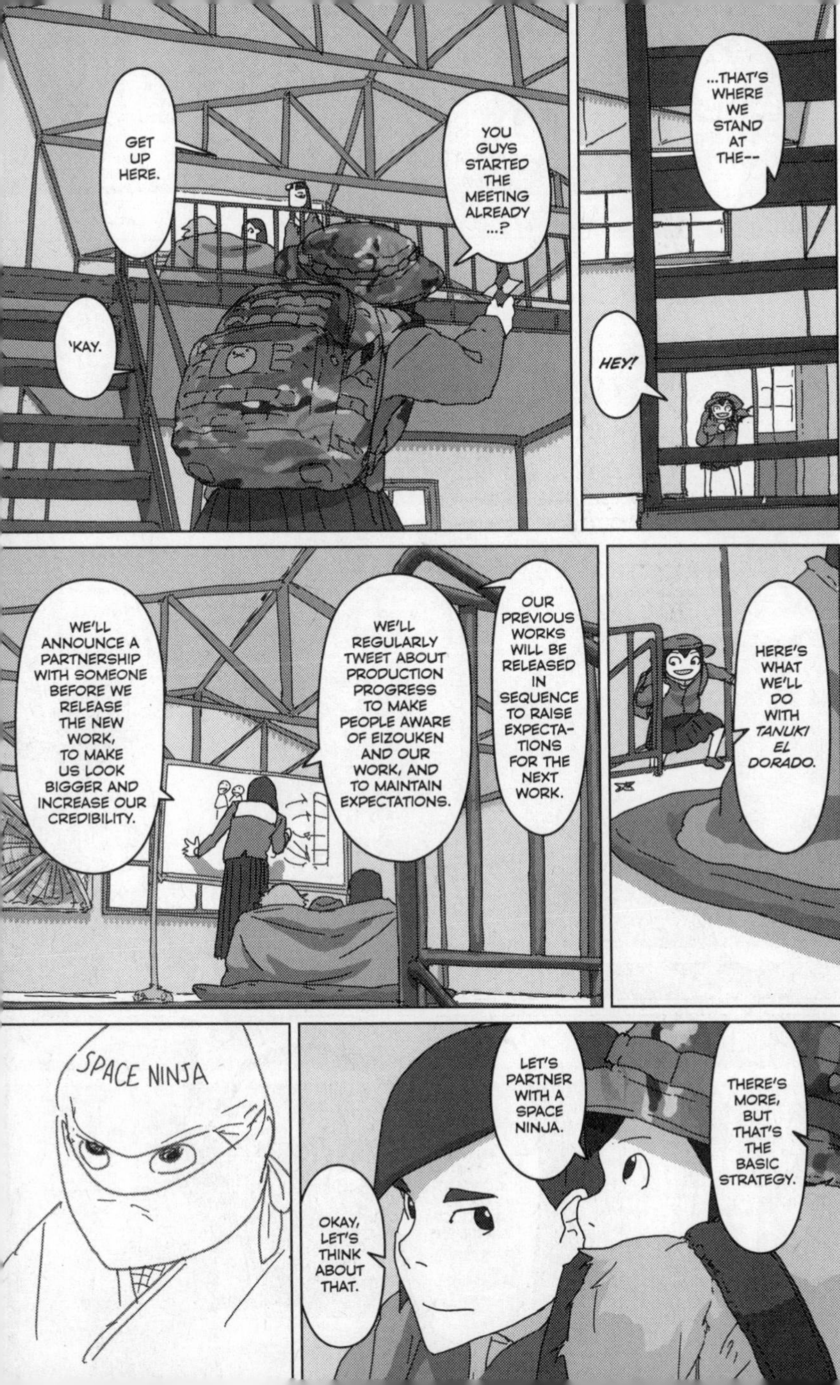
...THAT'S WHERE WE STAND AT THE--
HEY!
YOU GUYS STARTED THE MEETING ALREADY ...?
GET UP HERE.
'KAY.
HERE'S WHAT WE'LL DO WITH *TANUKI EL DORADO.*
OUR PREVIOUS WORKS WILL BE RELEASED IN SEQUENCE TO RAISE EXPECTA-TIONS FOR THE NEXT WORK.
WE'LL REGULARLY TWEET ABOUT PRODUCTION PROGRESS TO MAKE PEOPLE AWARE OF EIZOUKEN AND OUR WORK, AND TO MAINTAIN EXPECTATIONS.
WE'LL ANNOUNCE A PARTNERSHIP WITH SOMEONE BEFORE WE RELEASE THE NEW WORK, TO MAKE US LOOK BIGGER AND INCREASE OUR CREDIBILITY.
THERE'S MORE, BUT THAT'S THE BASIC STRATEGY.
LET'S PARTNER WITH A SPACE NINJA.
OKAY, LET'S THINK ABOUT THAT.
SPACE NINJA

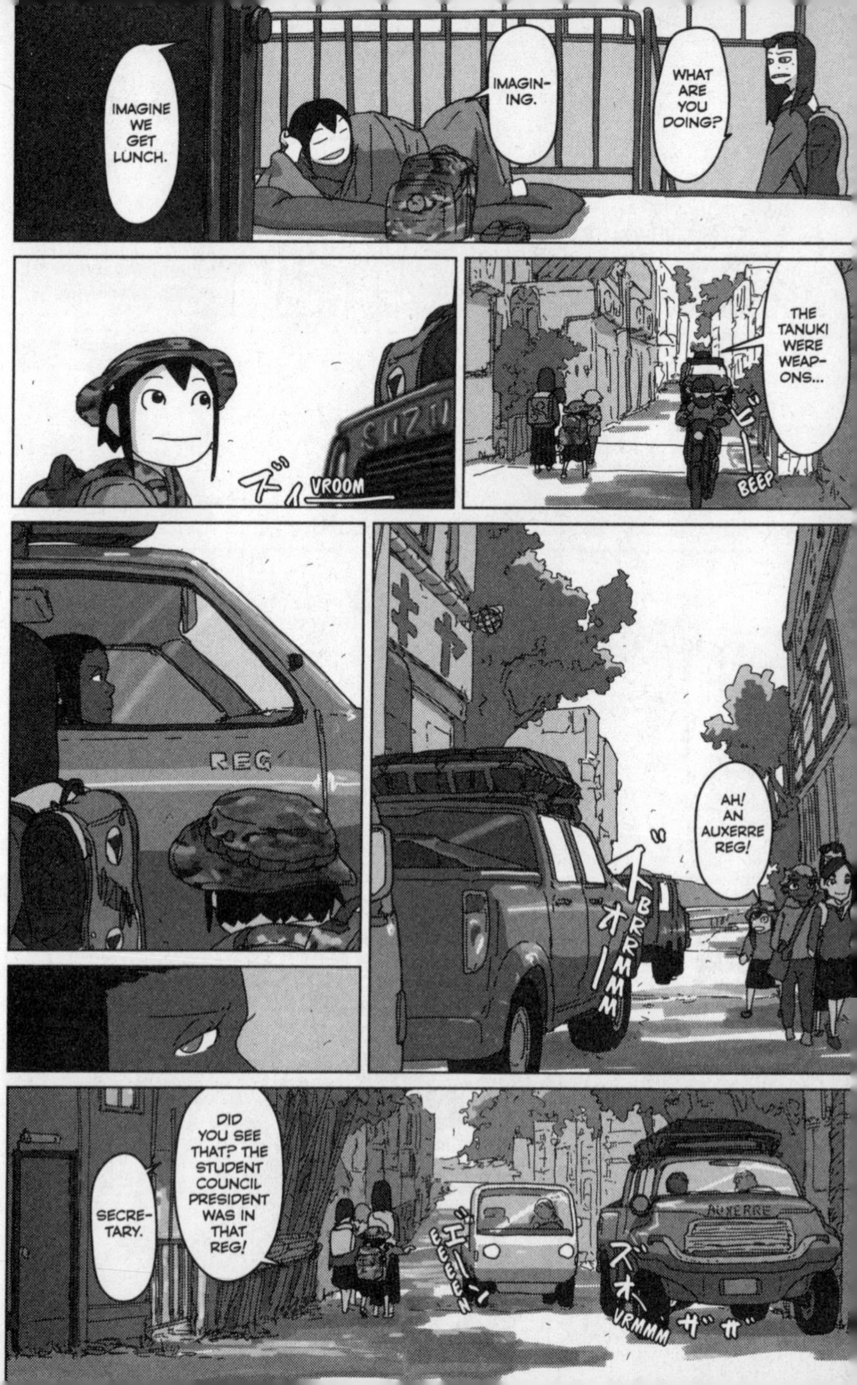
WHAT ARE YOU DOING?
IMAGINING.
IMAGINE WE GET LUNCH.
THE TANUKI WERE WEAPONS...
BEEP
VROOM
AH! AN AUXERRE REG!
BRRMMM
REG
DID YOU SEE THAT? THE STUDENT COUNCIL PRESIDENT WAS IN THAT REG!
SECRETARY.
AUXERRE
EEEEEN
VRMMM

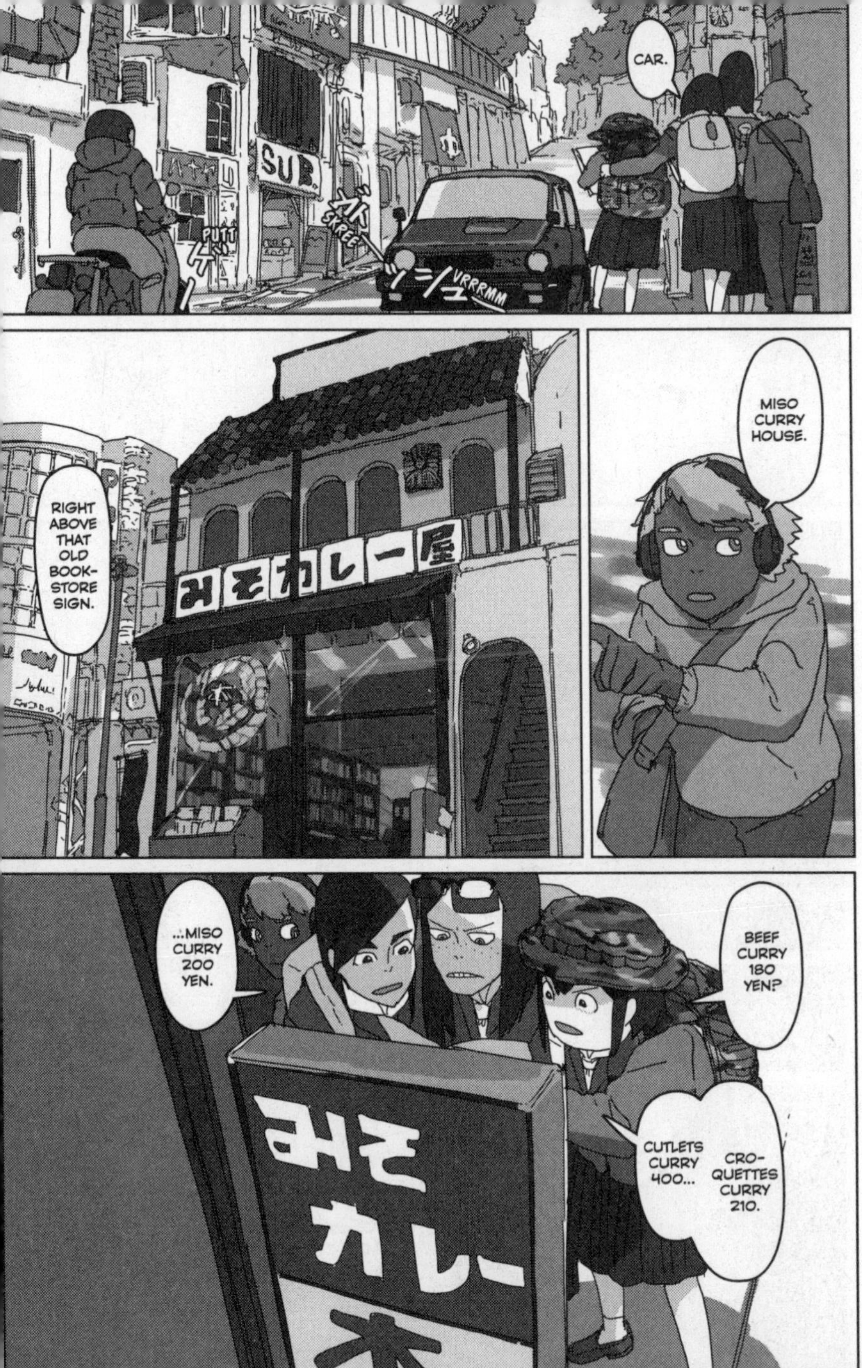
CAR.
SKREE
PUTT
VRRRMM
MISO CURRY HOUSE.
RIGHT ABOVE THAT OLD BOOK-STORE SIGN.
BEEF CURRY 180 YEN?
...MISO CURRY 200 YEN.
CRO-QUETTES CURRY 210.
CUTLETS CURRY 400...

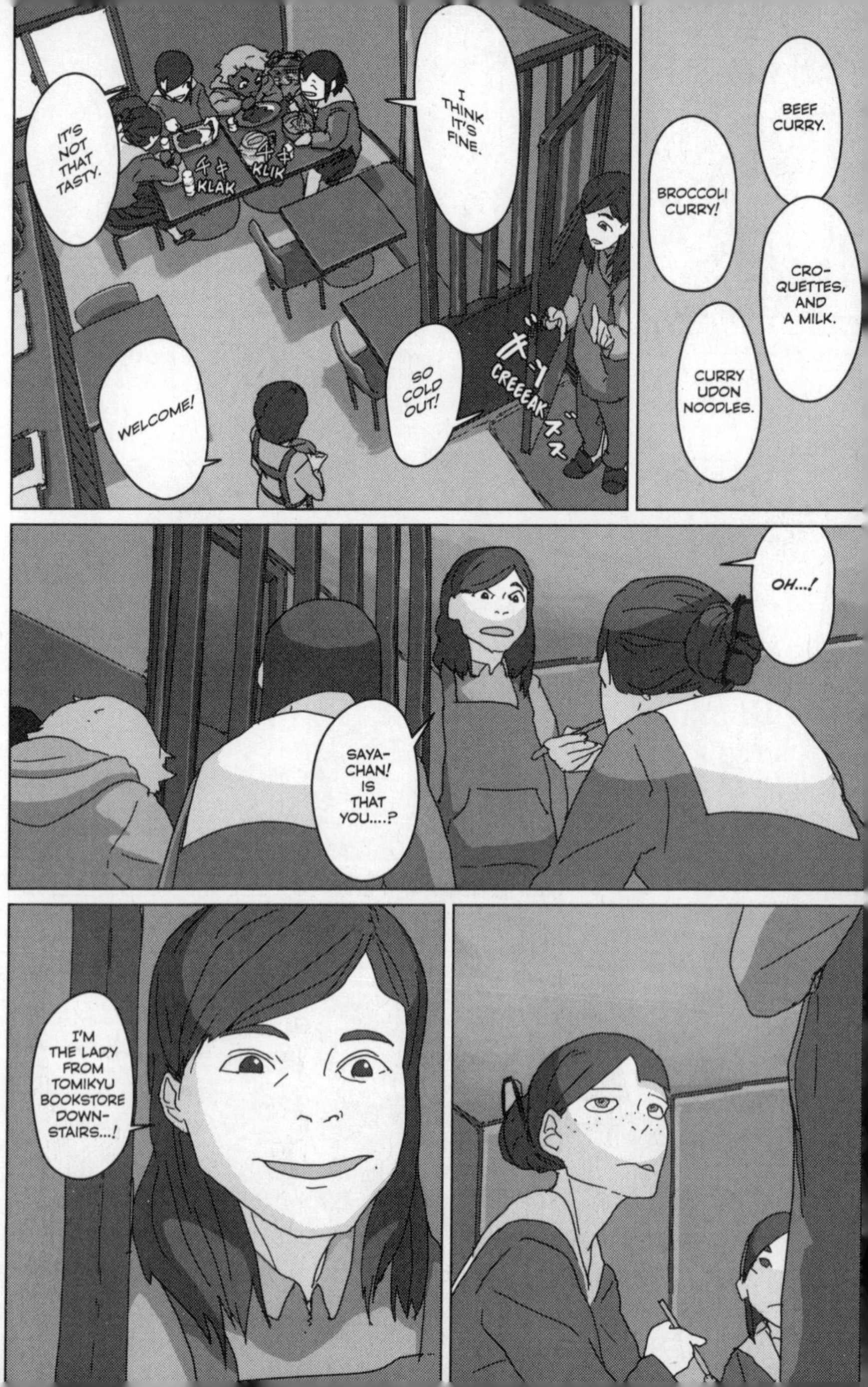
BEEF CURRY.
CRO-QUETTES, AND A MILK.
BROCCOLI CURRY!
CURRY UDON NOODLES.
I THINK IT'S FINE.
IT'S NOT THAT TASTY.
KLIK
KLAK
SO COLD OUT!
CREEEAK
WELCOME!
OH...!
SAYA-CHAN! IS THAT YOU....?
I'M THE LADY FROM TOMIKYU BOOKSTORE DOWN-STAIRS...!

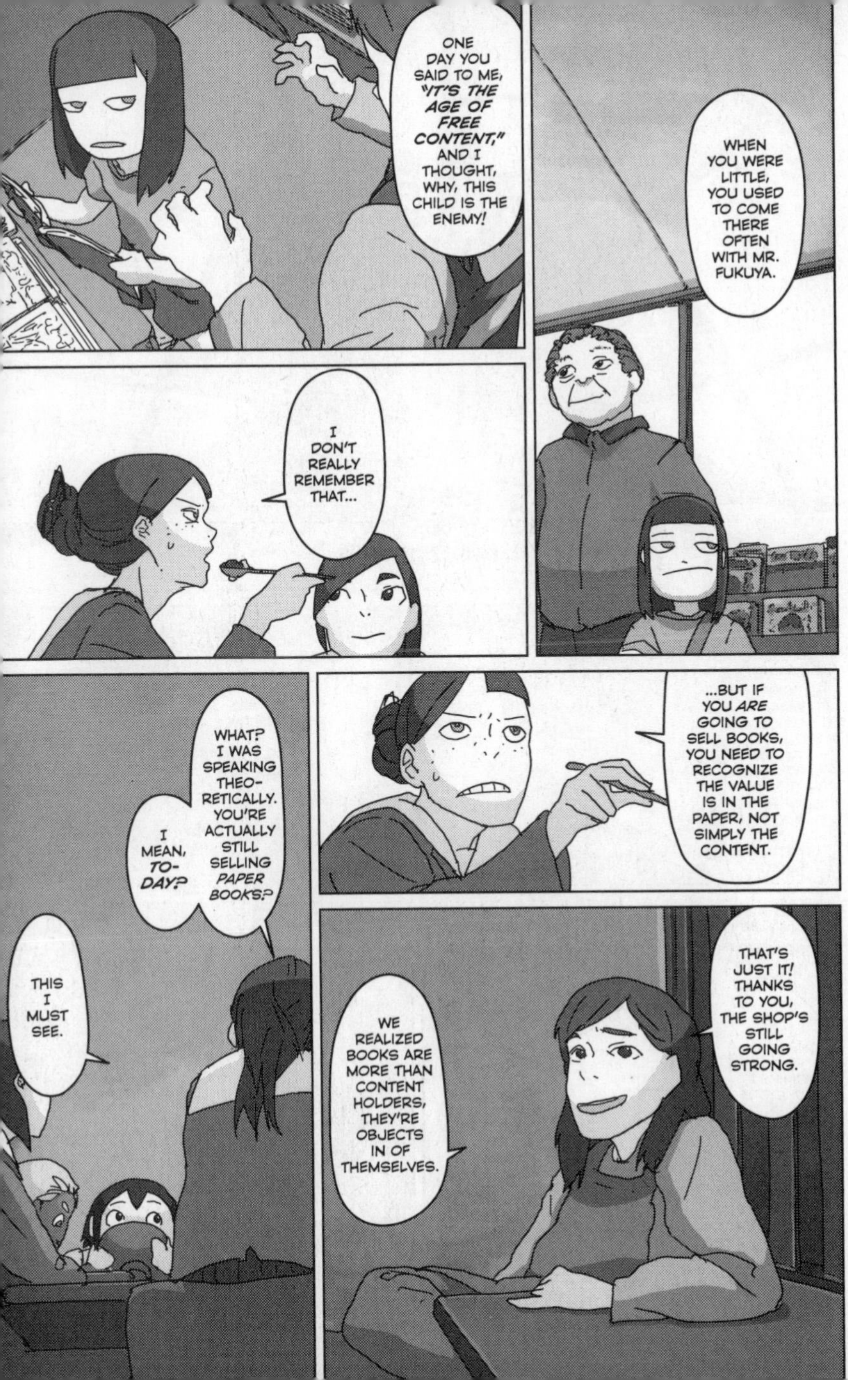
WHEN YOU WERE LITTLE, YOU USED TO COME THERE OFTEN WITH MR. FUKUYA.
ONE DAY YOU SAID TO ME, *"IT'S THE AGE OF FREE CONTENT,"* AND I THOUGHT, WHY, THIS CHILD IS THE ENEMY!
I DON'T REALLY REMEMBER THAT...
...BUT IF YOU *ARE* GOING TO SELL BOOKS, YOU NEED TO RECOGNIZE THE VALUE IS IN THE PAPER, NOT SIMPLY THE CONTENT.
THAT'S JUST IT! THANKS TO YOU, THE SHOP'S STILL GOING STRONG.
WE REALIZED BOOKS ARE MORE THAN CONTENT HOLDERS, THEY'RE OBJECTS IN OF THEMSELVES.
WHAT? I WAS SPEAKING THEO-RETICALLY. YOU'RE ACTUALLY STILL SELLING *PAPER BOOKS?*
I MEAN, *TO-DAY?*
THIS I MUST SEE.

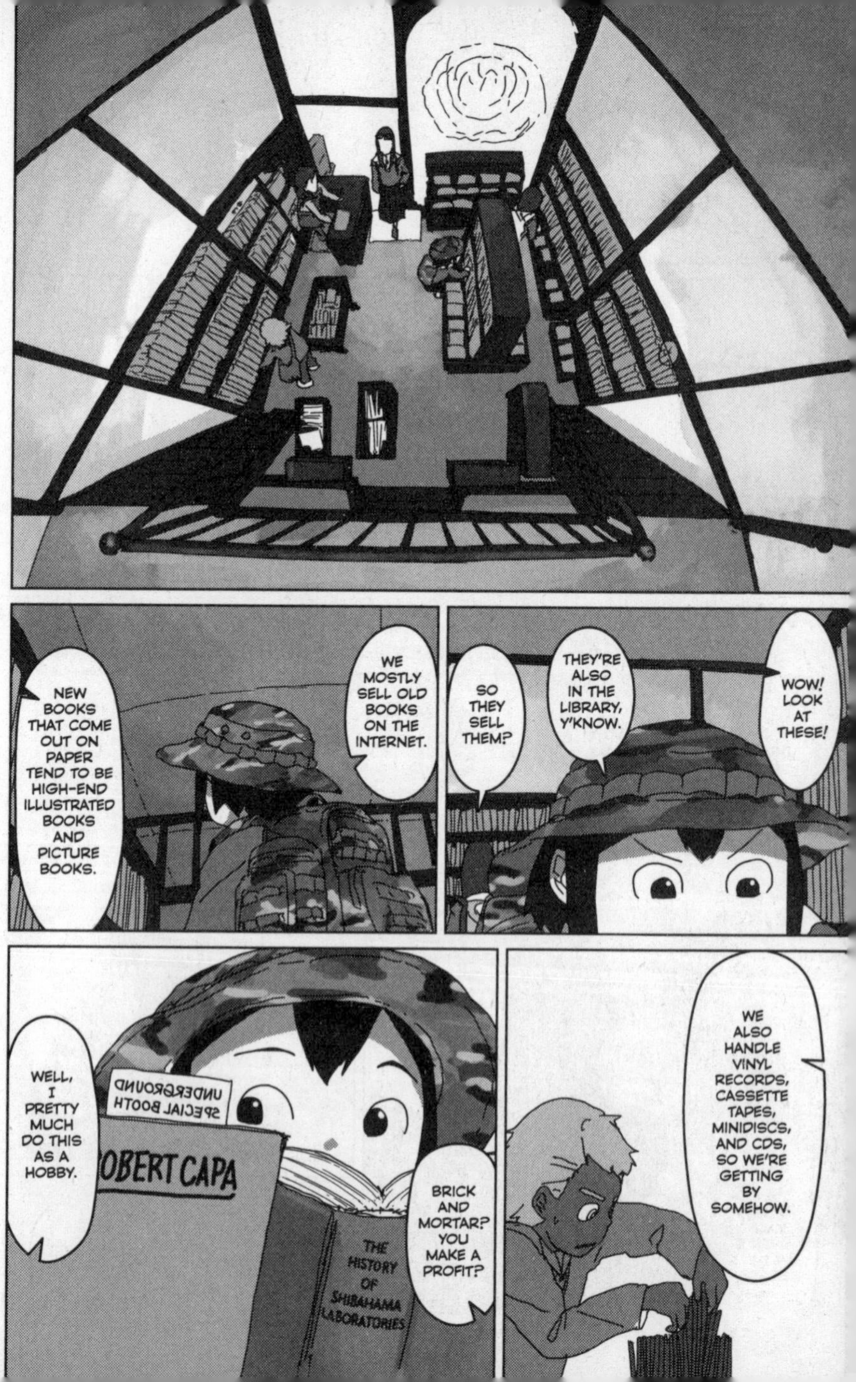
WOW! LOOK AT THESE!
THEY'RE ALSO IN THE LIBRARY, Y'KNOW.
SO THEY SELL THEM?
WE MOSTLY SELL OLD BOOKS ON THE INTERNET.
NEW BOOKS THAT COME OUT ON PAPER TEND TO BE HIGH-END ILLUSTRATED BOOKS AND PICTURE BOOKS.
WE ALSO HANDLE VINYL RECORDS, CASSETTE TAPES, MINIDISCS, AND CDS, SO WE'RE GETTING BY SOMEHOW.
UNDERGROUND SPECIAL BOOTH
ROBERT CAPA
THE HISTORY OF SHIBAHAMA LABORATORIES
BRICK AND MORTAR? YOU MAKE A PROFIT?
WELL, I PRETTY MUCH DO THIS AS A HOBBY.

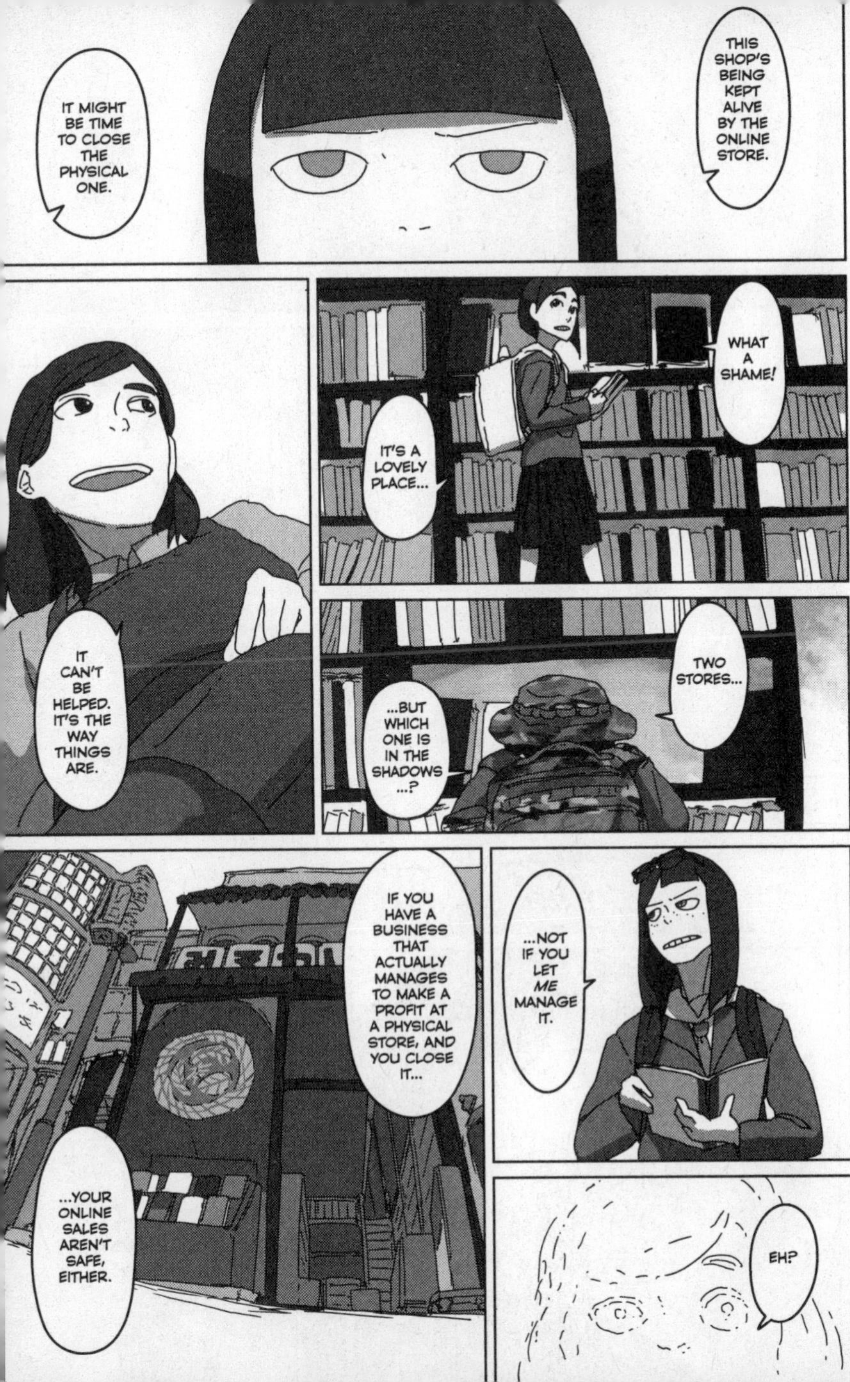
THIS SHOP'S BEING KEPT ALIVE BY THE ONLINE STORE.
IT MIGHT BE TIME TO CLOSE THE PHYSICAL ONE.
WHAT A SHAME!
IT'S A LOVELY PLACE...
TWO STORES...
...BUT WHICH ONE IS IN THE SHADOWS ...?
IT CAN'T BE HELPED. IT'S THE WAY THINGS ARE.
...NOT IF YOU LET *ME* MANAGE IT.
EH?
IF YOU HAVE A BUSINESS THAT ACTUALLY MANAGES TO MAKE A PROFIT AT A PHYSICAL STORE, AND YOU CLOSE IT...
...YOUR ONLINE SALES AREN'T SAFE, EITHER.

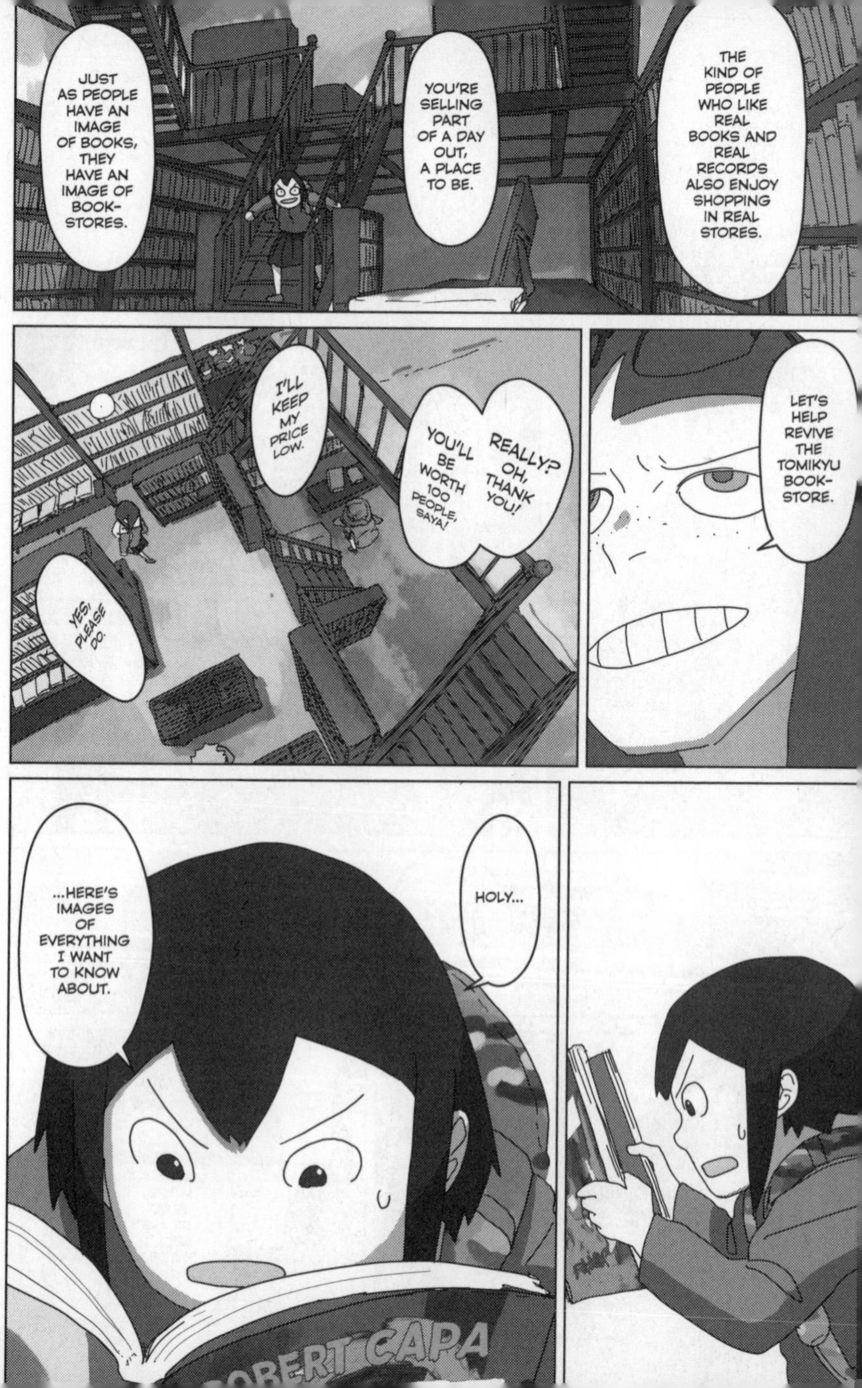
THE KIND OF PEOPLE WHO LIKE REAL BOOKS AND REAL RECORDS ALSO ENJOY SHOPPING IN REAL STORES.
YOU'RE SELLING PART OF A DAY OUT, A PLACE TO BE.
JUST AS PEOPLE HAVE AN IMAGE OF BOOKS, THEY HAVE AN IMAGE OF BOOK-STORES.
LET'S HELP REVIVE THE TOMIKYU BOOK-STORE.
REALLY? OH, THANK YOU!
YOU'LL BE WORTH 100 PEOPLE, SAYA!
I'LL KEEP MY PRICE LOW.
YES, PLEASE DO.
HOLY...
...HERE'S IMAGES OF EVERYTHING I WANT TO KNOW ABOUT.
ROBERT CAPA

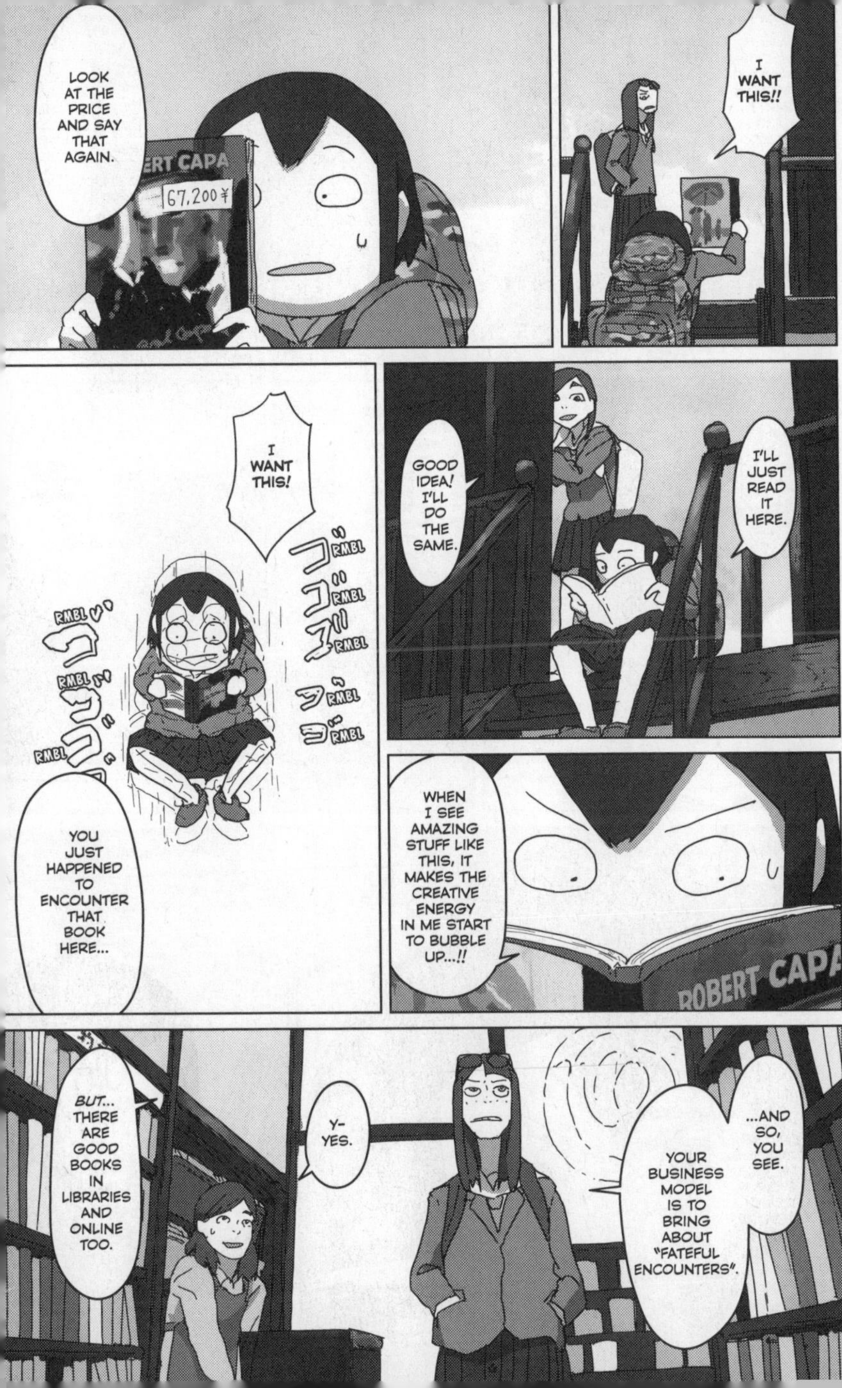
I WANT THIS!!
LOOK AT THE PRICE AND SAY THAT AGAIN.
ROBERT CAPA
67,200¥
I'LL JUST READ IT HERE.
GOOD IDEA! I'LL DO THE SAME.
WHEN I SEE AMAZING STUFF LIKE THIS, IT MAKES THE CREATIVE ENERGY IN ME START TO BUBBLE UP...!!
ROBERT CAPA
I WANT THIS!
RMBL RMBL RMBL RMBL RMBL RMBL RMBL RMBL RMBL
YOU JUST HAPPENED TO ENCOUNTER THAT BOOK HERE...
...AND SO, YOU SEE.
YOUR BUSINESS MODEL IS TO BRING ABOUT "FATEFUL ENCOUNTERS".
Y-YES.
BUT... THERE ARE GOOD BOOKS IN LIBRARIES AND ONLINE TOO.

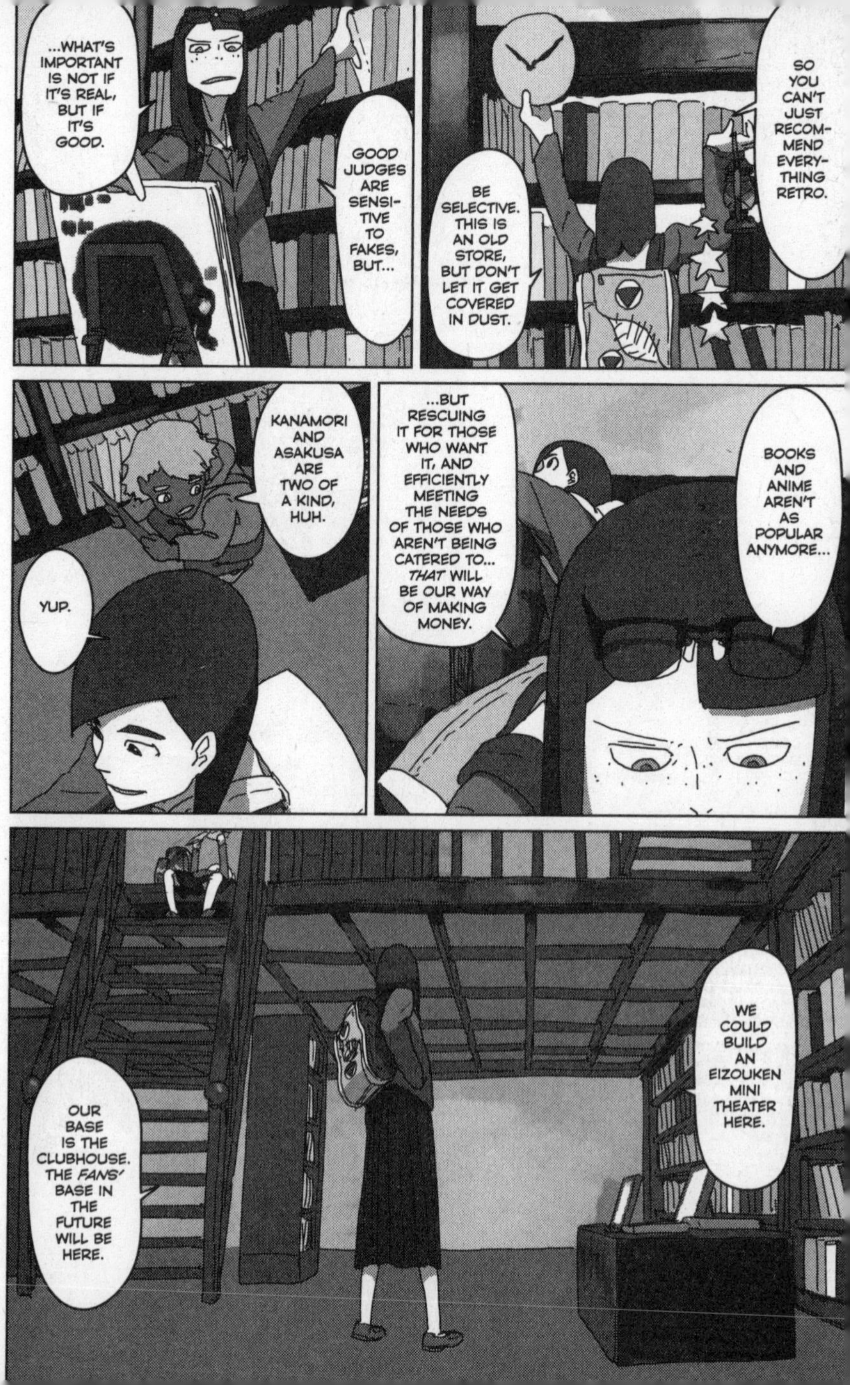
SO YOU CAN'T JUST RECOMMEND EVERYTHING RETRO.
BE SELECTIVE. THIS IS AN OLD STORE, BUT DON'T LET IT GET COVERED IN DUST.
GOOD JUDGES ARE SENSITIVE TO FAKES, BUT...
...WHAT'S IMPORTANT IS NOT IF IT'S REAL, BUT IF IT'S GOOD.
BOOKS AND ANIME AREN'T AS POPULAR ANYMORE...
...BUT RESCUING IT FOR THOSE WHO WANT IT, AND EFFICIENTLY MEETING THE NEEDS OF THOSE WHO AREN'T BEING CATERED TO... *THAT* WILL BE OUR WAY OF MAKING MONEY.
KANAMORI AND ASAKUSA ARE TWO OF A KIND, HUH.
YUP.
WE COULD BUILD AN EIZOUKEN MINI THEATER HERE.
OUR BASE IS THE CLUBHOUSE. THE *FANS'* BASE IN THE FUTURE WILL BE HERE.

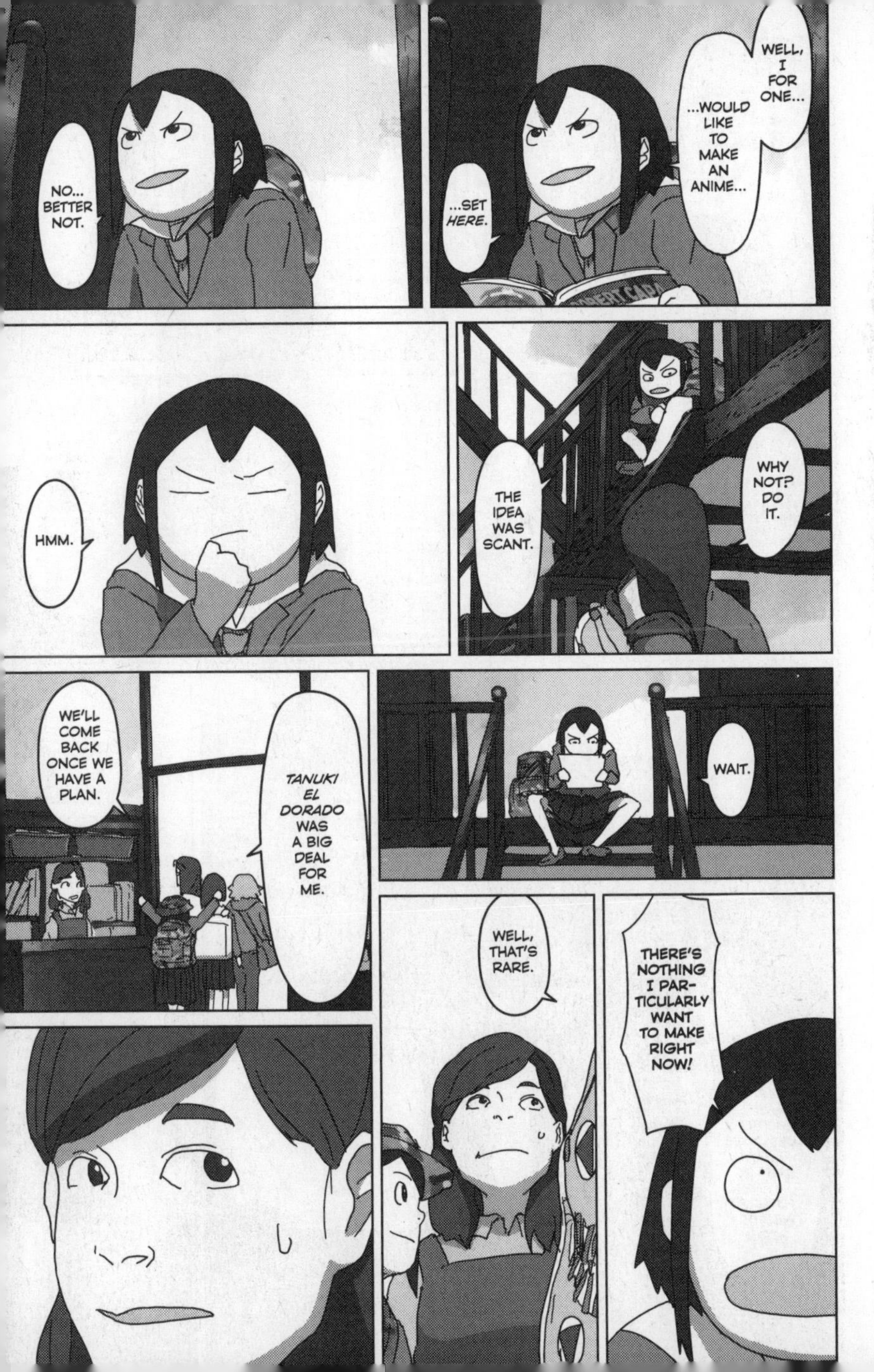
WELL, I FOR ONE...
...WOULD LIKE TO MAKE AN ANIME...
...SET *HERE*.
NO... BETTER NOT.
WHY NOT? DO IT.
THE IDEA WAS SCANT.
HMM.
WAIT.
TANUKI EL DORADO WAS A BIG DEAL FOR ME.
WE'LL COME BACK ONCE WE HAVE A PLAN.
THERE'S NOTHING I PARTICULARLY WANT TO MAKE RIGHT NOW!
WELL, THAT'S RARE.

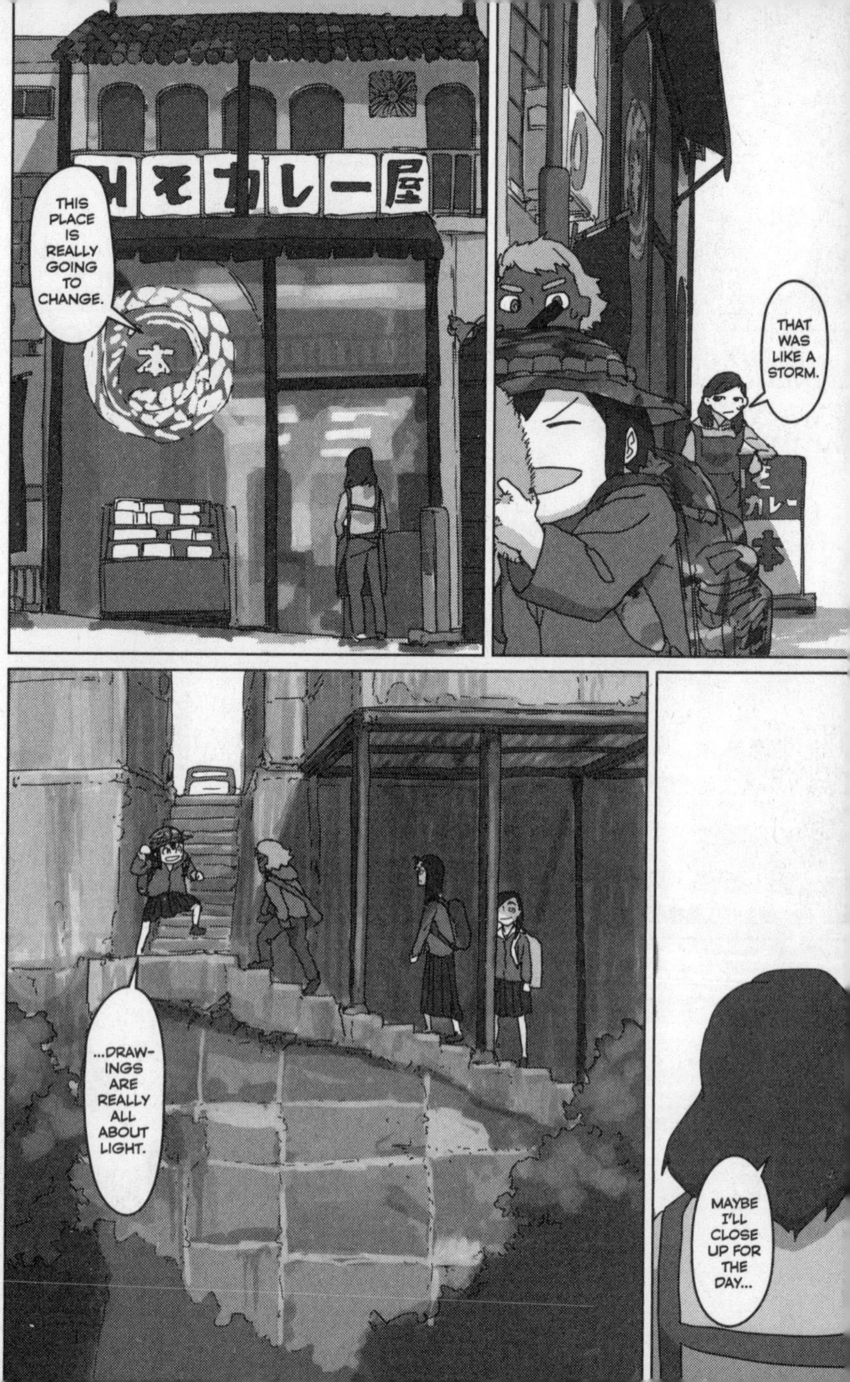
THAT WAS LIKE A STORM.
THIS PLACE IS REALLY GOING TO CHANGE.
MAYBE I'LL CLOSE UP FOR THE DAY...
...DRAW-INGS ARE REALLY ALL ABOUT LIGHT.

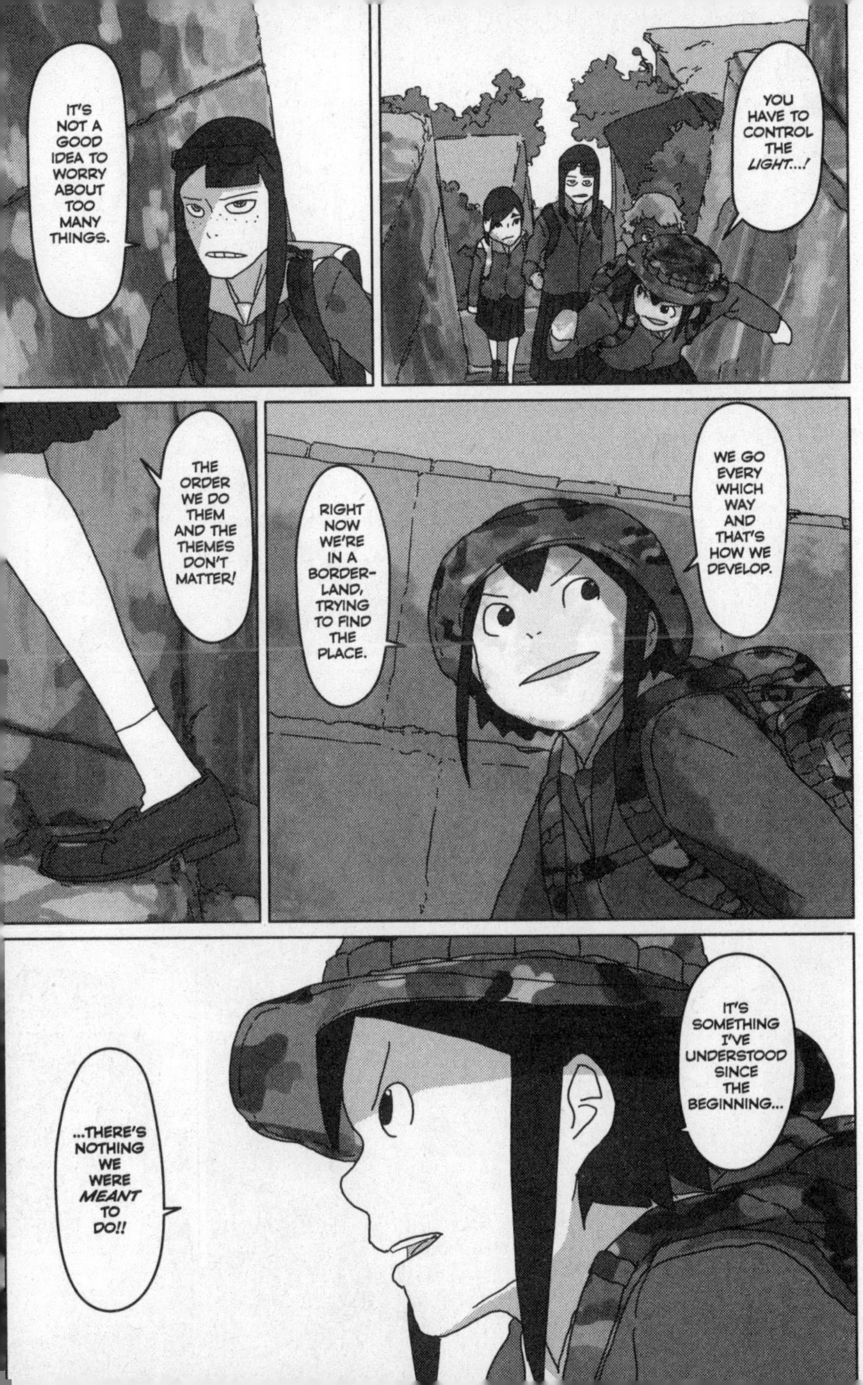
YOU HAVE TO CONTROL THE *LIGHT*...!
IT'S NOT A GOOD IDEA TO WORRY ABOUT TOO MANY THINGS.
WE GO EVERY WHICH WAY AND THAT'S HOW WE DEVELOP.
RIGHT NOW WE'RE IN A BORDER-LAND, TRYING TO FIND THE PLACE.
THE ORDER WE DO THEM AND THE THEMES DON'T MATTER!
IT'S SOMETHING I'VE UNDERSTOOD SINCE THE BEGINNING...
...THERE'S NOTHING WE WERE *MEANT* TO DO!!

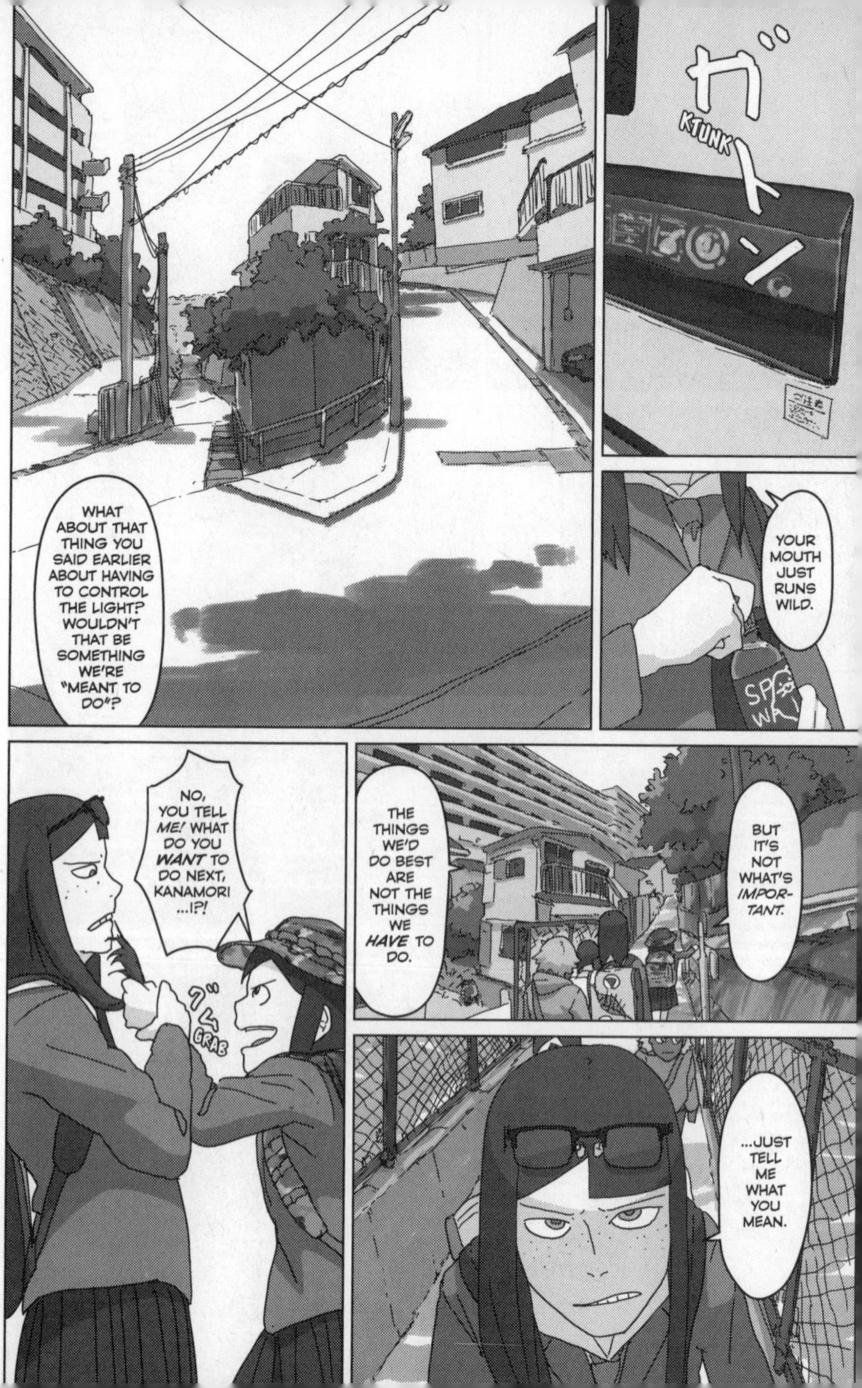
KTUNK
YOUR MOUTH JUST RUNS WILD.
WHAT ABOUT THAT THING YOU SAID EARLIER ABOUT HAVING TO CONTROL THE LIGHT? WOULDN'T THAT BE SOMETHING WE'RE "MEANT TO DO"?
BUT IT'S NOT WHAT'S *IMPORTANT.*
THE THINGS WE'D DO BEST ARE NOT THE THINGS WE ***HAVE*** TO DO.
...JUST TELL ME WHAT YOU MEAN.
NO, YOU TELL *ME!* WHAT DO YOU ***WANT*** TO DO NEXT, KANAMORI ...!?!
GRAB

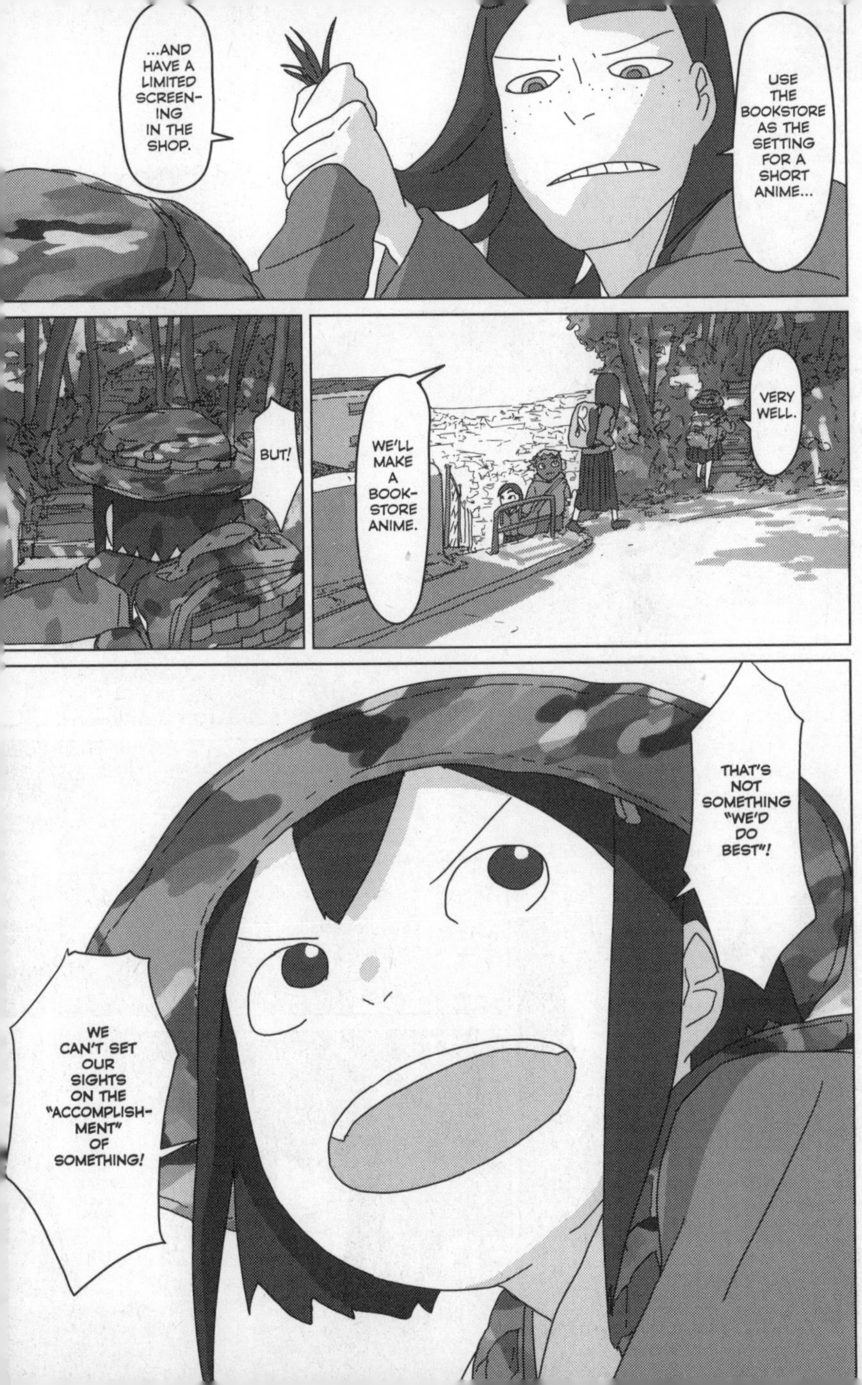
USE THE BOOKSTORE AS THE SETTING FOR A SHORT ANIME...
...AND HAVE A LIMITED SCREENING IN THE SHOP.
VERY WELL.
WE'LL MAKE A BOOKSTORE ANIME.
BUT!
THAT'S NOT SOMETHING "WE'D DO BEST"!
WE CAN'T SET OUR SIGHTS ON THE "ACCOMPLISHMENT" OF SOMETHING!

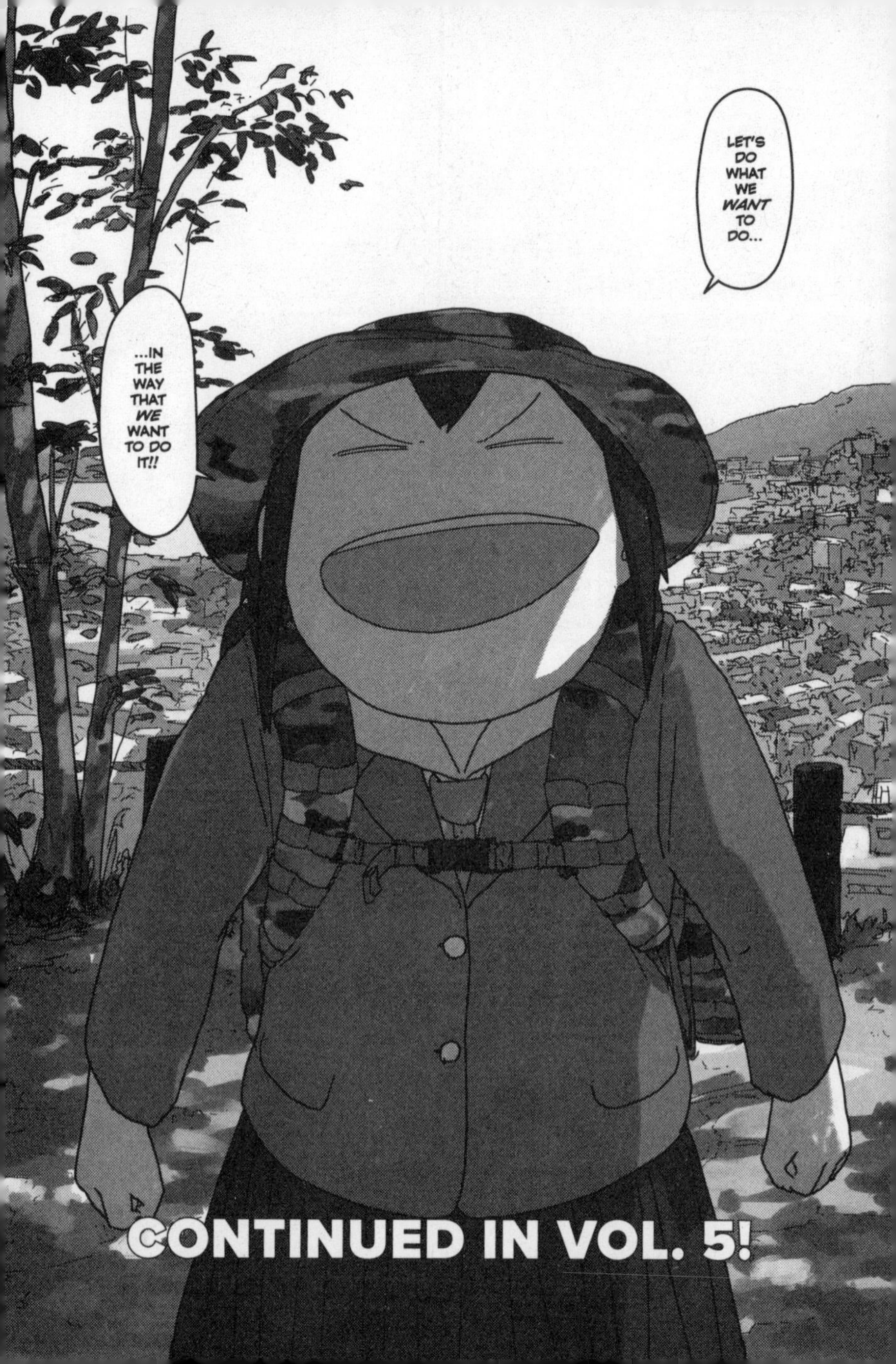
LET'S DO WHAT WE *WANT* TO DO...
...IN THE WAY THAT *WE* WANT TO DO IT!!
CONTINUED IN VOL. 5!

President and Publisher
MIKE RICHARDSON

Editor
CARL GUSTAV HORN

Designer
SKYLER WEISSENFLUH

Digital Art Technician
CHRIS HORN

English-language version produced by Dark Horse Comics

KEEP YOUR HANDS OFF EIZOUKEN!

Published by
Dark Horse Manga
A division of Dark Horse Comics LLC
10956 SE Main Street
Milwaukie, OR 97222

DarkHorse.com

To find a comics shop in your area, visit comicshoplocator.com.

First edition: November 2022
ISBN 978-1-50673-149-0

1 3 5 7 9 10 8 6 4 2

Printed in the United States of America

Neil Hankerson Executive Vice President • Tom Weddle Chief Financial Officer • Dale LaFountain Chief Information Officer • Tim Wiesch Vice President of Licensing • Matt Parkinson Vice President of Marketing Vanessa Todd-Holmes Vice President of Production and Scheduling • Mark Bernardi Vice President of Book Trade and Digital Sales • Randy Lahrman Vice President of Product Development and Sales • Ken Lizzi General Counsel • Dave Marshall Editor in Chief • Davey Estrada Editorial Director • Chris Warner Senior Books Editor Cary Grazzini Director of Specialty Projects • Lia Ribacchi Art Director • Matt Dryer Director of Digital Art and Prepress • Michael Gombos Senior Director of Licensed Publications • Kari Yadro Director of Custom Programs Kari Torson Director of International Licensing

NOTES ON VOL. 4 BY THE TRANSLATOR AND EDITOR

Welcome back...and welcome to brand new territory for *Keep Your Hands Off Eizouken!*, as volume 4 takes us into a storyline beyond the anime series. I think the artistic ambition of both *Eizouken* the club and Eizouken the manga is continuing to grow, as is its character development. Last time, I mentioned that we planned to continue the *Eizouken* manga into volumes 4 and 5; I can now say that our plan is to do vol. 6 as well. Since the 2020 anime TV series was an adaptation of the first three volumes, vols. 4-6 will be like getting a second season of story!

I realized that with all my discussion of the doujinshi event Comitia last volume, I neglected to mention the kinda relevant point ^_^ that *Keep Your Hands off Eizouken!* itself has its origins in a doujinshi Sumito Oowara-sensei sold at Comitia, as the creator related in an interview with the Japanese site Comicspace in 2018. Oowara had made live-action films in his own high school club, and later wanted to make his own anime, but found that in two years he had only managed to make two minutes' worth of animation footage. He decided to reformat all the storyboards he had drawn up for the anime as manga panels for an original doujinshi (as you'll recall, the focus at Comitia is on doujinshi that are original works rather than fan art or fan fiction), and it was at that same event he was scouted by a manga editor from Shogakukan. Oowara relates that over the next year, he developed *Eizouken* through feedback from his editor, until it made its professional debut in *Monthly Comics Sprits* magazine in September 2016, where *Eizouken* is still serialized.

Looking into the details of vol. 4, on page 4, panel 5, Kanamori appears to be wearing a t-shirt with the visage of Thomas Edison. He would seem to be a good role model for her, as Edison was not only famous for combining inventive talent with business skill, he established what is generally considered to be the world's first dedicated film production studio in 1893. *Zunda mochi*, referenced on page 9, panel 5, is a variety of chewy rice cake with a salty-sweet (or sweet-salty) green soybean paste on top. On page 11, panel 4, the translator notes that instead of the traditional *koma-inu* (stone guardian dog figures) that would usually flank the gate of a Shinto shrine, Asakusa observers that this shrine uses *koma-tanuki*.

Kanamori, who seems to be an expert in currency both current and not-so-current, remarked on page 18, panel 7 that *mon*, the commonest Japanese coin in use during the samurai era, were copper, although they were also made in bronze and iron. Some readers will have also picked up on how on page 26, the names of Hattori Hanzo and Tokugawa Ieyasu are given in the traditional Japanese order (i.e., family names first), yet when a contemporary character in *Eizouken*'s name is given, the order is as it would be in English (i.e., family names last), as in Tsubame Mizusaki or Sowande Sakaki. This is admittedly a debatable choice in the translation, as in the original Japanese, all the names were given family name first, but it felt natural to leave Hattori and Tokugawa's names that way, as they are known to history (and pop culture). The English version of the manga, however, preserves the way characters tend to refer to each other (and be referred to) by their last names. This would seem affected or formal in much of the English-speaking world, but many readers will also be aware that even friends and associates who socialize regularly in Japan may still use last names with each other.

In the original Japanese, the "swank suburb" Asakusa refers to on page 37, panel 5, was Den-en-chofu, a neighborhood in Ota, one of the outermost wards of Tokyo. It's about 14 kilometers from Tokyo Station, and indeed had a more suburban character when it was originally constructed in the early 1900s. Developer Eiichi Shibusawa deliberately patterned it on the "garden cities" advocated by the British urban planner Ebenezer Howard. Den-en is used to refer to the "garden" element in the Japanese term for "garden city," den-en toshi, although den-en is also used to convey the same sense as the English term "pastoral," which has more of a rural than a suburban shading to it. Or perhaps it's a word that suggests an urban person's romantic view of rural existence, which is arguably where the notion of suburbs—many of which are after all (as was Den-en-chofu) built on redeveloped farmlands—began their concept. Anyway ^_^ Den-en-chofu would not be considered suburban in today's Tokyo, yet it's still an expensive neighborhood, featuring some large homes by Tokyo standards.

But how could Asakusa afford to live there, if she only found copper coins? Well, of course, old copper coins are collectible, but from the look of the partially-melted pieces she discovered, maybe the treasure was gold after all. Copper mon were round and generally had a square hole in their center (it was common to then string the mon together to make a larger unit of money, something like a roll of coins). But these coins, with their rounded rectangle shape and brushstroke writing, resemble the oban, the largest size gold coin of the Tokugawa period, weighing 165 grams—almost six ounces of gold each, not even considering their collector's value (like most gold coins, they weren't pure, however— the early Tokugawa coins were about 20 karat gold, but by the end of the era they had relatively little gold left in them). I suppose Kanamori would have been even more upset on pages 41 and 42 if she knew the treasure really had been gold, but it also shows she is, as she told Sakaki in vol. 3, not so much interested in money as in activity that generates returns; she accepted the idea that the creative inspiration Asakusa took from her treasure hunt would be worth more than the treasure itself. Of course, we would all like to find buried treasure (or win the lottery), but Kanamori intends to earn wealth for Eizouken through everyone's intelligent efforts, including her own.

Asakusa's mention of the Ship of Theseus in panel 2 of page 50 references a question that arose in ancient Greek philosophy—namely, are Theseus and Pirithous the OTP? Sorry; that was nothing but the otaku in me. Actually, the question concerned the sailing ship that had belonged to Theseus, the king who, according to legend, founded the city of Athens. The Athenians were said to have maintained the ship as a relic for centuries, gradually replacing parts of the vessel as they decayed or wore away with new parts. However, if eventually all the original parts were replaced with new parts, could you then truly say it was still the Ship of Theseus? Some would say no; others would argue that it was the original concept and plan that defined the identity of the ship, and even if you added new parts while restoring it, if the intent was to preserve the original design and purpose, then it was still the Ship of Theseus. The philosophical question applies elsewhere as well (we humans are ourselves examples, as in the course of our lives, most of the cells in our body die and are replaced by newly generated ones several times—some, like skin and blood cells, many times) and helps to illustrate that the things people build or create are not just material objects that happen to exist, but that come into existence because there was a certain thought and conception behind them.

In the original manga, the slogan to the right of Asakusa's protest sign on page 62, panel 1 was written out in katakana, which, as you probably already know ^_^ is a phonetic syllabary used for various purposes in Japanese, a major one being writing foreign words and phrases; in this case it was: 「ネ イチャー　イズ　ナンバーワン　ファックオ フ　ヒューマン」, *neichaa izu nambaawan fakkuofu hyuuman*. In other words, it was an English slogan in the original as well, but written out in a Japanese script. This raises the question of how it should be rendered in this English version of the manga. It could be argued that the proper translation would tone it down a little, on the grounds that using swear words from a secondary language lessens their impact in the context of your primary language, and almost all of the original dialogue in *Eizouken* is in Japanese. On the other hand, it's been established (as seen at the end of vol. 2, when everyone's

rushing to buy the *UFO Wars* anime), that at least five different languages are cursed in at Shibahama High School, including English. And, of course, the original manga *did* spell out the English phrase, "Nature is Number One! Fuck Off, Human(s)!" here. So I think the answer will actually require you, as an English-language reader, to work on the next stage of the interpretation, and consider, based on the context, how that English phrase might have had a different impact or impression within a.) the fictional world of *Eizouken*'s story, and b.) among the real Japanese readers of *Eizouken*.

If you stop to think about it, this raises a good point about translation. If there were actually a single correct, straightforward, and unambiguous meaning to words and phrases in English, English literature classes and English language exams would be much simpler, right? Even people who have earned PhDs in English still argue and debate all the time over how to "interpret" the uses of... English. The same thing, of course, applies just as much to Japanese and to people whose primary language is Japanese—being born and raised in a language, and using it to interact with one's society every day, doesn't mean you will understand it the exact same way as every other native speaker. It's not necessarily a matter of your education or proficiency level; it's also a matter of the simple fact two people can read the exact same book, watch the exact same movie, or listen to the exact same song, and come away from it with different impressions. And before we completely overthink this, and even scheme to get some class credit out of it, reflect that there is a lot of comedy in this manga, and this is a scene that asks us to imagine Asakusa in a protest rally, with a tanuki in the background atop a heap of human bodies. Whew—who knew swearing could be so educational?

On page 89, the title of Chapter 28, "Sowande's Freedom," perhaps raises the question of what the Secretary's last name actually is. The only time we've seen her full name written out in the original Japanese version of the manga is on page 140 of vol. 1, when she was introduced alongside the other officers of the student council, as "Sakaki Sowande" 「さかき・ソワンデ」. Since in the original Japanese the other officers were introduced last names first, and since "Sakaki" is generally encountered as a last name in Japan, the assumption was that it was in fact her last name. We might have been able to get a clue by seeing how the other characters in *Eizouken* address her, but as far as I can see, no one in the story thus far has actually addressed her by either name—she's only been referred to formally, by her title on the student council—*shoki*, "Secretary." You'll notice in the last chapter of vol. 4 that a running joke has developed that began in vol. 3 (and which will continue) where Asakusa refers to her instead as *kaichoo*, "President," and gets corrected; possibly Asakusa simply assumes Sowande leads the student council, since she seems to, well, lead the student council.

"Sowande" has its origins as a last name from the Yoruba cultural region of West Africa that today includes portions of the modern nations of Nigeria, Benin, and Togo. Azizi Powell notes that the famous Nigerian musician and scholar, Fela (Olufela) Sowande, wrote in his 1966 book *The Mind Of A Nation—The Yoruba Child* that "Sowande" is derived from the phrase *Oso wa mi de*, meaning "'Oso has sought and found me.'...Oso...refers to Orisanla; it is the Yoruba word for 'wizard,' understood in its original sense of 'one who is wise in the knowledge of spiritual things,' and not in the distorted and superimposed incorrect sense of 'sorcerer.'" However, at least in the United States, "Sowande" can also be found as a first name, as with Washington University historian Sowande Mustakeem. What prompted my curiosity, as you might guess, is the fact Chapter 30 is called "Asakusa's Clear-Headed Way"—Asakusa is the character's last name (her first name is Midori, but thus far we've only seen her mother use it, just as Mizusaki's parents address her by her own first name of Tsubame, and the proprietor of Tomikyu Bookstore, who knew Kanamori as a child, greets her as "Saya-chan" [from Sayaka, her first name]).

So is Sowande in fact the Secretary's last name? The question is perhaps further complicated by the way her name was written in Japanese when she was introduced, 「さかき・ソワンデ」. The use of a *nakaten* 「•」 between the first and last names is common when writing foreign names, but Sowande's is the only character's name introduced thus far to be written this way. Incidentally, in the case of both Fela Sowande and Sowande Mustakeem, the first syllable of "Sowande" is pronounced *sho*, which makes me wonder if the name of the *Eizouken* character could be written 「ショワンデ」 rather than 「ソワンデ」. In case you were wondering, in the original Japanese, Doumeki's name is written with the kanji 「百目鬼」. We didn't get to see too much of Doumeki in this volume—but she is a major player in the events of vol. 5, so don't worry.

In the original manga, Sowande spoke to Kanamori in panel 3 of page 98 with 「ファッキンルーフじゃない。車内の席さ。」, a phrase that was a mixture of English ("*Fakkin ruufu...*) and Japanese ("*. . . ja nai. Shanai no seki sa.*"). Anyone familiar with the development of modern Japanese will be aware that Japanese as it is actually used every day in Japan employs many words and expressions that derive from other languages. This, of course, is common for languages in general—after all, before the 1980s, *manga* was a completely foreign word to English speakers, but in 2022 it is found in many English dictionaries, meaning it has now become an English word of foreign derivation, just as words such as *president*, *kindergarten*, and *amen* are.

The car Sowande is driving, as Oowara-sensei references, is a Mitsubishi Debonair V3000 Royal AMG. AMG was an independent German automotive engineering firm mainly associated with customized Mercedes vehicles (it was fully acquired by Mercedes in 1999), but in 1987 it was approached by Mitsubishi to modify their Debonair sedan to create an prestige variant, the result being the Debonair V3000 Royal AMG. The car was reportedly priced at 4,516,000 yen when it first hit the market, so a 100 million yen value in the future would be quite an appreciation. At current exchange rates, that's $767,000 US dollars. It's a tradition in manga and anime to have prideful student councils that flaunt their wealth and power (the only power my high school's student council possessed was to design the homecoming floats), but you can't help but wonder how Kanamori felt about seeing such an valued asset junked by the very organization that requires the Shibahama clubs to submit to stringent oversight of their modest budgets. Sowande, of course, is asserting a philosophy to someone she seems to acknowledge as a leader like herself, and perhaps a peer, but still . . .

The kudzu gruel Kanamori's clubmates are consuming on page 108, panel 2 is called *kuzuyu*, and is also known as "arrowroot tea"; the term gruel is sometimes applied to it instead, as it is a thick beverage whose recipe involves stirring flour made from starchy kudzu roots into hot water. The early 1980s DeLorean referenced on page 112 can be spotted on page 99, panel 2, in the lower left corner. The vehicle, paneled in stainless steel with gull-wing doors, was in retrospect an exemplar of period style, but was also associated with scandal in the real world; just a few years later, the car became a pop cultural icon when a DeLorean was converted into a time machine in the *Back to the Future* films. The Bugatti 100P was a sleek, custom-made aircraft with contra-rotating propellers, designed by Vicomte Louis-Pierre-Benoît de Monge de Franeau to be the fastest plane in the world, and constructed just before World War II by the firm of eccentric automotive engineer Ettore Bugatti (if I say that all of this would have fit right into a Miyazaki film, you'll understand). When the outbreak of the war cancelled the race that the 100P had been built to enter, it was placed into storage; the original plane today is in the EAA Museum in Wisconsin. An experimental replica of the 100P, the *Rêve Bleu/Blue Dream*, whose construction was partially funded on Kickstarter, unfortunately crashed on its third flight in 2016, an incident that took the life of its pilot, Scotty Wilson.

Camion「カミオン」, the name of truck-like spacecraft flown by *Tanuki El Dorado*'s astronaut protagonist (is "hero" in fact too strong a word...? ^_^), is very possibly a reference to the Japanese magazine of the same name published by Geibunsha that covers the world of decorated trucks (dekotora), also known as art trucks. Note the appearance of the dialogue in the argument between the villagers and Metro on page 134, panel 5; although the *Eizouken* manga is known for its stylized treatment of dialogue text, including Asakusa's "out-of-focus" dialogue on page 102 of volume 2, this time in the original Japanese the dialogue was blurred completely out of readability (i.e., what was being said couldn't be made out at all, even in the Japanese edition), so the English lettering is done the same way. In case you're wondering how we knew what English dialogue to insert here before we blurred it (if we couldn't make out the original blurred Japanese in the first place), the answer is that as it was impossible to tell what they were supposed to be saying in the original Japanese, I asked the letterer, Susie Lee, to just create some English dialogue and then blur it. That's right—even I don't know what Susie wrote there in English unblurred, but an editor's life is not without mystery.

On that note, the meaning of Asakusa's remark on page 142, panel 2, that "the tanuki were weapons" is unclear; whether it is to be taken metaphorically (in the struggle between the villagers and Metro, or as a weapon of inspiration Asakusa wielded to create the anime) or literally (perhaps as a science fiction aspect of their genetic engineering). Finally, on the same page, panel 4, Sowande rolls past the footbound

Eizouken in a truck (of course, she had earlier told Kanamori "we don't need a car anymore," but perhaps this is her way of technically sticking to that assertion) that Asakusa identifies as an "Auxerre Reg." Here, Oowara-sensei, after previously giving us glimpses of genuine vintage vehicles, throws us a curve, as there is no such truck as an "Auxerre Reg;" the creator has remarked that he spent an hour or so trying to come up with a good name for a non-existent vehicle make and model. Finally, the book Asakusa is so taken by is about the legendary wartime photographer Robert Capa (1913-1954), who is famed in Japan to the extent that the Takarazuka Revue performed a musical based on his life in 2012 and 2014.

Well, as was said at the beginning, vol. 4 of *Keep Your Hands off Eizouken!* picks up where the anime left off, and I think it shows the continuing strength of Oowara's original manga story. As I'm sure you do, I hope there is more *Eizouken* anime made in the future, and if so, this and the upcoming volumes of the manga will provide a solid foundation. I'm also hoping we can see an English dub of the 2020 anime TV show soon (fans in Latin America already have official dubs in Spanish and Portuguese). Until then, thank you for reading *Eizouken*, and we'll look forward to seeing you again in vol. 5!

—CGH

Ms. Koizumi loves ramen noodles.

The original manga that inspired the anime series from Crunchyroll!

$10.99 EACH!

Ms. Koizumi loves ramen noodles . . . and Yu likes Ms. Koizumi! But she soon discovers that the only way to get closer to this cool, mysterious transfer student is to become her pupil on the path of ramen!

Translated by Japanese chef Ayumi Kato Blystone, *Ms. Koizumi Loves Ramen Noodles* is a fun food manga that shows you all around the authentic ramen culture of everyday Japan, from crazy home-cooked versions to famous restaurants reached by bullet train! Do you know about sauce vs. broth? How to pair sushi with ramen? Or even sweet ramen dishes like chocolate, pineapple, and ice cream? You soon will—and with bonus notes on real ramen shops to visit, this manga will leave you hungry for more!

VOL. 1 | ISBN 978-1-50671-327-4 | 136 pages ♥ **VOL. 2** | ISBN 978-1-50671-328-1 | 136 pages
VOL. 3 | ISBN 978-1-50671-329-8 | 136 pages

EMANON

FROM KENJI TSURUTA, THE ARTIST OF THE EISNER-NOMINATED *WANDERING ISLAND*, AND THE AWARD-WINNING JAPANESE SCIENCE FICTION AUTHOR SHINJI KAJIO!

Emanon is the eternal stranger who belongs here more than any of us— a woman possessing a mind that evolved over the entire history of life on earth, and who carries within her over three billion years of memories. Set in 1960s and 70s Japan, *Emanon* tells of her encounters with the lives of people who can no more forget her, than she can forget any person. Drawn in both Tsuruta's elegant black-and-white linework and his signature painted color, *Emanon* is a literary SF manga at the intersection of life, memory, family, and existence.

VOL. 1 : MEMORIES OF EMANON
ISBN 978-1-50670-981-9 - 192 pages

VOL. 2 : EMANON WANDERER PART ONE
ISBN 978-1-50670-982-6 - 216 pages

VOL. 3 : EMANON WANDERER PART TWO
ISBN 978-1-50670-983-3 - 240 pages

$14.99 EACH!

FOR MORE INFORMATION OR TO ORDER DIRECT, VISIT DARKHORSE.COM.
*PRICES AND AVAILABILITY SUBJECT TO CHANGE WITHOUT NOTICE.

DARK HORSE MANGA

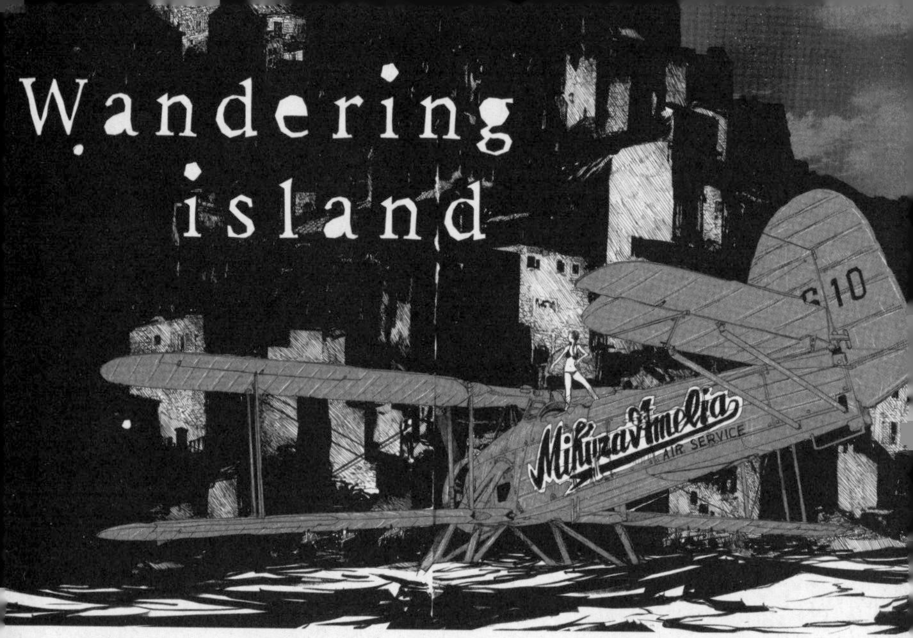
Wandering island
MikuraAmelia
AIR SERVICE
610

FROM THE ARTIST OF *EMANON*—

AN EISNER-NOMINATED TALE OF EXPLORATION AND ADVENTURE

Mikura Amelia is a free-spirited young woman who operates an air delivery service. When her beloved grandfather passes away suddenly, Mikura discovers he had been obsessed with the legend of an island that seems to appear and disappear in the Pacific. Soon the obsession becomes her own, and Mikura turns explorer . . . but what is she truly searching for?

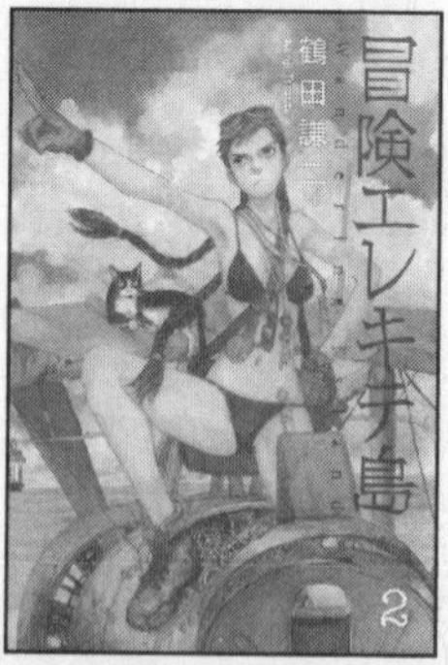
冒険エレキテ島
鶴田謙二
2

WANDERING ISLAND

Story and art by Kenji Tsuruta

Vol. 1: ISBN 978-1-50670-079-3 | $14.99

Vol. 2: ISBN 978-1-50671-021-1 | $14.99

DARK HORSE MANGA

AVAILABLE AT YOUR LOCAL COMICS SHOP OR BOOKSTORE

To find a comics shop near you, visit comicshoplocator.com. For more information or to order direct visit DarkHorse.com or call 1-800-862-0052 Mon.– Fri. 9 a.m. to 5 p.m. Pacific Time.